MY TRIALS

Inside America's
Deportation Factories

Judge Paul Grussendorf

MY TRIALS: Inside America's Deportation Factories
Copyright 2011. Judge Paul Grussendorf
All Rights Reserved

No part of this book may be used or reproduced in any manner whatsoever without written permission of the author except in the case of brief quotations embodied in critical articles and reviews

ISBN: 978-1-7359536-0-1 (paperback)
978-1-7359536-1-8 (ebook)

Cover photo by Paul Grussendorf
Cover design by Hyang Suk OH

Dedication

This book is dedicated to
Immigration Judge Dana Marks,
tireless fighter for Justice and the Rule of Law,
and my former colleague in San Francisco

"Injustice anywhere is a threat
to justice everywhere."

Dr. Martin Luther King

Forword

IN 2016, AFTER A LEGAL career of 30 years in refugee and asylum protection, including eight years as a federal refugee officer and seven years as an immigration judge, I accepted a position in the Arlington, Virginia asylum office as a Supervisory Asylum Officer. I had tremendous respect for the U.S. asylum program and I knew from experience that most asylum officers choose the job as a humanitarian calling; their ranks include many attorneys and individuals with graduate degrees, with experience in the Peace Corps and other humanitarian backgrounds. And I can affirm that Asylum Officers have the hardest job of any immigration officers in USCIS-United States Citizenship and Immigration Services, due to the complex and ever-changing asylum law, and the nature of the intensive interviews.

The law enforcement side of our immigration system is exercised by ICE – Immigration and Customs Enforcement, a sub-agency of DHS that was created, along with Department of Homeland Security, in 2003 after the tragedy of 9/11. ICE officers are hired from a completely different profile of applicants and receive much less training in the humanitarian aspect of immigration law. The equivalent at the border is CBP – Customs and Border Protection.

The Netflix Series Immigrant Nation, airing in August 2020, exposes how, soon after Trump's ascendancy to the presidency, he and his nativist cronies put into place a series of executive measures designed to practically eliminate refugee admissions; to curtail and eventually eliminate access to our asylum system; and even to severely reduce lawful migration to the United States. Virtually all of these executive measures are unlawful, in conflict with our nation's immigration statute and in violation of our international treaty obligations, and even demonstrably harmful to the economic well-being of the U.S. They have all been challenged in court and practically every such executive measure has been deemed unlawful by federal district and appellate courts, yet the anti-immigrant juggernaut sails on. Recently the GAO – Government Accounting Office, an independent body, declared that, according to the Federal Vacancies Reform Act the current Acting Directors of both DHS, Chad Wolf, and USCIS, Ken Cuccinelli, were unlawfully appointed, and presumably every edict that they have issued since their appointments this past year will also be deemed unlawful.

One of the first ignoble acts of the administration's new appointee to head U.S. Citizen and Immigration Services, Director Lee Cissna, was the removal of this truism from the agency's mission statement: "America is a Nation of Immigrants." Why would the head of the agency that receives all applications for visas, both temporary and permanent, and for asylum and refugee protection choose to redact such seemingly innocuous and self-evident verbiage from the agency's mission statement?

In the same time frame the Department of Housing and Urban Development, headed by Trump's appointee Ben Carson, removed the words "inclusion" and "free from discrimination" from its mission statement. We've seen in history how totalitarian regimes try to control the dialogue within their populace by changing and sanitizing language, including the use of language within federal institutions.

When this White House requested a study to map the net costs of refugees, conducted by the Department of Health and Human Services, and the results showed a net benefit to the economy over a period of ten years of $63 billion, the White House buried the study. https://www.nytimes.com/2017/09/18/us/politics/refugees-revenue-cost-report-trump.htm

Simultaneously the administration was implementing the so-called Muslim ban against citizens and residents of seven mostly-Muslim countries out of supposedly national security reasons. No one has ever explained why Saudi Arabia, the home of 15 of the 19 9/11 bombers, was not included in the list. (Saudi Arabia is also the home of the Al Qaeda sympathizer who shot up the Naval Air Station at Pensacola,Florida Air Base in December, 2019, killing three sailors and wounding eight.)

In the early days of this administration there was much hype over the "migrant caravans" composed mostly of Central Americans from the "northern triangle" countries, El Salvador, Honduras and Guatemala, that were "invading" our country – the old "barbarian hordes" trope that is a favorite of every totalitarian regime. In fact the numbers of each such "caravan" for the most part would easily fit inside a typical college stadium. (Current demographics demonstrate that even if we admitted all of them as potential workers and residents, the U.S. would still experience labor shortfalls in the near future and they would not supplant the decline of our native-born population.)

In the final months of 2016, I traveled with a group of asylum and refugee officers to San Salvador where we interviewed and vetted minors who were requesting refugee protection because of threats to themselves and their families by the ruthless MS-13 and 18th Street gangs. The children we spoke with or their parents had all received such threats as, "Either you work for us or you and your parents will be dead next week," or "Give me your daughter or you have two days to leave the country." And they all knew neighbors or close relatives who had died when such threats were ignored. We felt gratified knowing that we were granting these kids a lifeline of resettlement to the U.S.. I would only hope that any American father or mother, if ever faced with such a choice by a credible threat, would have the courage and means to flee across borders in order to protect their children, just as those parents joining the caravans with their children have chosen to do.

The new administration ordered a halt to such in-country interviews and even the resettlement of the cases we had already approved for travel. Its spokesmen have continuously and falsely characterized such asylum applicants as fraudsters who are gaming the system. The administration's first morally challenged Attorney General, Jeff Sessions, claimed there was a conspiracy of corrupt attorneys who are manufacturing all of their stories. Believe me, they are not manufactured. All credible international reporters, including our own State Department, rebut the claim that such migrants are merely seeking jobs in the U.S. International reports affirm that some gangs in El Salvador are able to maintain such power and territorial control that they exercise the functioning equivalent of State authority, making it impossible for potential victims to resist their demands.

Sessions even admonished the assembled group of immigration judges at a conference, telling them they must not let their humanitarian impulses interfere with some fictitious mandate to deport as many applicants as possible. (Stephen Miller, the self-hating white nationalist who has dictated this administration's immigration policy from the beginning, was once a staffer for then-Senator Jeff Sessions. Miller subscribes to the "white replacement" or "white genocide" theory that the brown-skinned migrant hordes will replace the superior descendants of Western civilization if not stopped.)

Jeff Sessions also chose to meddle in the administration of the immigration courts, in such a bungling manner that his mandated reforms achieved the opposite of his goal to reduce backlogs. By restricting the ways in which immigration judges can control their own docket, such as eliminating a judge's ability to place a case on hold or "administratively close" a case while collateral legal action is ongoing in the migrant's case, and by taking away ICE trial attorneys' discretion to agree to grants of compelling cases, backlogs blossomed by the tens of thousands – within the two and a half years of this administration from approximately 500,000 to currently one and a half million.

The Netflix film crew obtained unprecedented access to ICE and CBP operations in the making of their series. I have trained asylum officers at the Federal Law Enforcement Training Center at Glencoe, Georgia, featured in the first episode of the Netflix series, and I have supervised asylum officers at the ICE family detention centers in Texas featured in the first episode. And I experienced, along with my colleagues, the devastating effects of the administration's continuing attempts to deter refugees from coming to our southern border through abuse and cruelty, the so-called family separation policy. It is telling to see how many ICE and CBP officers and supervisors conceded, on camera, that the deterrence of ripping children from their parents' arms upon arrival at the border is cruel and inhumane and un-American, but they felt compelled to follow the orders because "it's the law."

The so-called Zero Tolerance policy that was advanced by retired

Marine General Kelly, first DHS Secretary and later White House Chief of Staff, and AG Sessions was a sham from the get-go. An impossible task, launched for public consumption and to create the impression that only by locking up all unlawful border crossers could any order be returned to the enforcement of our laws. The sham is that no law enforcement body in the country, federal or state, has a zero tolerance policy, simply because no one has the resources to detain, charge, prosecute, adjudicate and jail all offenders. (This stark reality is in fact the reason for the plea bargaining system in criminal court). In my career I observed how the U.S. Attorney's Offices in Washington, D.C., and in San Diego, would, within their discretion, "no-paper" cases they considered too minor or insignificant to prosecute, saving their powder for bigger game. This was also the policy that the Obama Administration, under guidance of then DHS Secretary Janet Napolitano, established as ICE policy, when ICE agents and prosecuting attorneys were advised to let the low-hanging fruit go, such as hard-working but undocumented laborers, and concentrate instead on serious felons for apprehension and removal. The admitted consequences of this administration's Zero Tolerance policy was to require all migrants be detained and prosecuted. Since children cannot be detained in an adult facility, they were to be separated from their parents, in order to achieve the maximum of trauma and pain upon the children and their parents. The trauma itself was to be a deterrent to future unlawful crossers, by "sending a message" not to come to the U.S. The notorious photos of kids in cages have tarnished our international reputation and provided talking points for terrorists.

Netflix film crews accompanied agents on raids in multiple locations, when the Zero Tolerance policy initially led to mass inland roundups. The cameras recorded agents blatantly lying to targets about who they are and their authority to enter private dwellings and arrest suspects without criminal arrest warrants, clear violations of the Fourth Amendment. We see numerous ICE veterans, and even FODs-Field Office Directors – lamenting the new 'catch everyone' policy, knowing from experience that such tactics are inhumane and bound to fail in the long run.

We see a gung-ho ICE public affairs officer trying to convince the Field Office Director of the Charlotte, North Carolina office to lie in a press briefing and indicate that 90% of the migrants detained in a community-wide sweep have criminal records; the FOD twice corrects him that the correct figure is 30-35%, meaning the remaining 70% are harmless field workers, hotel employees, construction workers or single mothers with U.S. citizen children.

Even though political appointees such as DHS Secretary Kirsjten Nielsen and AG Sessions were willing to blatantly lie to Congress about the motivation and consequences of such cruel policies, they were still tossed out by the president when the reality on the ground impaired their ability to achieve deportation numbers sufficient to satisfy the Nativist in Chief. Ultimately it took an even more barbaric policy, the Migrant Protection Protocol (MPP), another unlawful executive order, to force legitimate asylum seekers to remain on the Mexican side of the border while their cases were piling up in the bureaucracy. MPP is Orwellian double-speak, because the migrants, rather than being protected, are being sent into circumstances where they are easy prey for cartels targeting them and are notoriously subject to kidnappings, rapes, robberies and murders. No migrant being forced to wait for months in tents or temporary shelters along the border is safe.

Most disappointing to me as a Supervisory Asylum Officer was how management at the Arlington Asylum office, as soon as the MPP operating instructions came down in early 2019, was so willing to coerce asylum officers into violating their oaths to uphold the Constitution and the laws of the U.S. At an internal meeting with management and the asylum officers, supposedly to hash out the ground rules of this new MPP program, one of my officers complained that he felt both ethically and morally conflicted for the first time in his career, knowing that forcing asylum seekers to wait in Ciudad Juarez, one of the most dangerous cities in the world, was a violation of his oath and his training to offer protection to asylum seekers.

I wondered how our managers could justify to themselves the cruel and unlawful policies they were insisting that their subordinates carry out. Were they hoping that the federal courts would soon overturn the blatantly illegal policy and they would thus be off the hook? Were they thinking that at least they, as a federal officer with some limited power, were better than whoever might replace them if they were to resign? I'm sure that is how many attorneys and jurists, working within totalitarian regimes, justify their collaboration and acceptance of policies that are dehumanizing and deadly. When they were asked by their subordinates for justification they threw up a disingenuous wall of semantics, and when asked what procedures Customs and Border Protection were following in the context of MPP, they were told, "We believe CBP knows how to do their jobs." Basically, just shut up and do what we tell you to do.

I was one of the first supervisors sent to oversee our officers conducting the new MPP screening interviews at the San Ysidro border crossing south of San Diego. Under the new guidelines the migrant must demonstrate to the asylum officer that it is "more likely than not" that they would meet serious harm if forced to wait for many months in Mexico until returning for an audience in front of an immigration judge, in order to be exempted from the requirement of waiting in Mexico. One of my very conscientious officers decided to refer for protection a young Guatemalan woman who had been held captive in an apartment in Tijuana by her domestic partner and brutalized and assaulted, and then viciously stalked when she fled from the dwelling. She should be allowed to remain in the U.S. pending her court date because it was clearly too dangerous for her to return to where her tormentor could easily locate her. I reviewed the interview notes and consulted with my officer and I agreed that it was a good case for protection. We informed CBP and our chain of command of the decision. The next day I received a call from the Deputy Director of the Arlington Asylum office., Jennifer Rellis. I was told that we had to be very careful with our assessments of the MPP cases because the "front office" had eyes on these cases. I was instructed to overturn our decision and to deny the young woman protection. And I was instructed that, going forward, any time I was inclined to approve any of my officers' decisions to grant protection, I must first have one of my managers also review and sign off on it. There was no such requirement if we decided to deny protection to an applicant. Thus a presumption was created that we should deny protection in our MPP adjudications, a reversal of all of our training as asylum and refugee officers, and a blatant violation of our own statute and of U.N. refugee guidelines. In the following months this presumption against protection has continued to be enforced.

    I wondered how Ms. Rellis could live with herself in so callously stripping me of my discretion to afford protection to legitimate refugees, given her training as a humanitarian lawyer. I'm sure if asked, she would argue we have no choice but to comply, and we can still protect asylum seekers within the limits of this new program. But there was no articulable reason why she would order me to enact an unlawful presumption of 'not qualified' where none exists in our asylum statute, regulation, case law, or international refugee law. The fact that such managers, whom we had always believed were motivated by their own humanitarian commitments, would so enthusiastically fall in line with a blatantly unlawful program caused great distress among the ranks of asylum officers. Many of my colleagues sought reassignment to other divisions within USCIS or even left the agency altogether. When I received that phone call I also began making arrangements to leave what had become a compromised agency.

Only months after I departed in June, the much-beloved Director of the Asylum Division was reassigned by the unlawfully appointed Acting USCIS Director Ken Cuccinelli to a management position in an uncontroversial department of USCIS. It was conceded that he had lamented to his asylum officers in an internal e-mail that it was unfortunate that the troops were being asked to adjust to these new policies with no forewarning or opportunity to adequately train.

It is remarkable that American Federation of Government Employees Union Local 1924, the union that represents asylum officers, has submitted "friend-of-the-court" briefs in numerous lawsuits against the administration's attempts to implement the MPP program and otherwise curtail and dismantle the asylum program; and that Union Local 1924 President Michael Knowles has testified before Congress in opposition to such policies.

Jeff Session's replacement AG William Barr has shown himself willing to continue the dismantling of our asylum program. He issued an edict that immigration judges would no longer have the discretion to grant bonds to asylum seekers in custody – clearly another attempt to discourage applicants from seeking shelter in the U.S. through the use of cruelty. This is an issue that is especially dear to my heart, as it has always been my principle that no asylum applicant should remain detained a day longer than necessary for routine administrative procedures. In fact, I testified before the Senate Judiciary Committee in 2013, at a time that comprehensive immigration reform was optimistically expected to be passed, in favor of granting immigration judges **additional** authority to issue bonds. My proposal wound up in the Senate's draft legislation, which regretfully was never even taken up by the House. (In a meeting with Senator Marco Rubio's immigration staffer I was assured that "the Senator is behind your proposals 100%." During his subsequent presidential campaign in 2016 Rubio claimed he had never been in favor of comprehensive immigration reform). Again, several weeks after Barr's edict against bond, a federal court blocked Barr's draconian and heartless ban on conditional release from custody of asylum seekers from taking effect.

From the earliest campaign rallies in 2016, Trump has used fear and hatred of others to divide Americans and energize his base. The forefathers of most European Americans gained entry to the U.S. in exactly the same fashion as all those "illegal aliens" at our southern border; by showing up and asking for admission, at Ellis Island, at a time when there were no immigration controls in place other than routine screening for communicable diseases. Today the vast majority of Americans would not qualify for admission if measured against the standards this administration is trying to implement.

I was a refugee officer in the field at the time of the current President's election. My colleagues and I were already conducting "extreme vetting" on Syrian, Iraqi, Somali, and numerous other populations, in conjunction with security resources of the CIA, FBI, Defense Intelligence Agency and Pentagon, years before this President decided to use fear as a means of control. My last assignment at the Refugee Affairs Division in 2015, before transferring to the asylum program, was to assist in the heightened vetting of all Syrian applicants at headquarters. Ironically, it is demonstrable that, on average, Syrian and Iraqi migrants to the U.S. are among the highest educated migrants in sciences and technology.

Refugee Admissions Decimated

During the last year of the Obama administration, in the context of the worst international refugee crisis since the end of the 2nd World War, the Obama administration asked that the Refugee Affairs Division increase refugee admissions from the already admirable number of 90,000 in fiscal year 2016 to 110,000 for 2017. However, on the heels of the Muslim ban came the new administration's pronouncement that rather than 110,000, in fiscal year 2017 the program would be suspended for the rest of the year, thus grounding all refugee officers. . In 2018 the admissions was capped at 45,000 refugees, and it was determined that a ceiling of 30,000 admissions would be set for 2019. At a time when the U.S. should have been manning the bulwarks of refugee protection (Germany received a million refugees in 2015, comparable to the U.S. taking in 4 million) the U.S. effectively withdrew from the field, sending the signal that the U.S. no longer considers itself a leader in the world for refugee protection. A ceiling of 18,000 was set for fiscal year 2020, and this amount was only agreed to after push back from the Pentagon in reference to promises we had made to allies and interpreters working with our troops in the field in Irag, Afghanistan and Syria.

In 2018 Director Cissna also made the shocking announcement that USCIS would close all of its overseas offices, passing numerous tasks onto the State Department and domestic offices. The offices, established over a period of decades in such countries as Kenya, Ghana, South Africa, China, South Korea, Thailand, Mexico and Peru, primarily function as facilitators for family unity and refugee operations. Perhaps the first time that a federal bureaucracy has voluntarily given up turf, but in line with the administration's seeming loathing for family unity.

The Myth of Skilled Migration

When then Chief of Staff General Kelly, formally DHS Secretary, disparagingly pronounced that most Central American migrants are "rural" migrants, as though of less value than presumably better educated "urban" migrants from white European countries, I took personal offense. My grandfather Grussendorf migrated with his family from a rural village in Lower Saxony, Germany at the end of the 19th Century at a time when there were no immigration controls at Ellis Island. He settled in the farming community of Grand Rapids, Minnesota, where he ran a farm and begat five children, one of whom became a high school math teacher; one became a state judge, one opened a nursery in Duluth, and one, my father, became a highly decorated Marine colonel, former company commander at the WWII landings at Saipan, Iwo Jima, and Okinawa. (I was born at Camp Pendleton). The state judge's children included Cousin Benny Grussendorf who became Speaker of the House in the Alaskan Legislature. My father's children included a Navy Captain and minister, a Navy enlisted man and transportation professional; a political activist, and an immigration judge. My brother the Navy Captain's children include an Air Force flight surgeon and base hospital director; a veterinary, and a multi-lingual translator with her own business in France. All of these offspring were imbued with strong "rural" family values. That's how migration works.

The idea of skilled-based migration, to be administered by a point system involving education, employment background, and language skills, isn't all that bad in and of itself. Our close alleys Canada, the U.K., Australia and New Zealand all administer a version of this skills-based migration. The problem is the suggestion to eliminate family-based migration, when clearly the vast majority of our nation's people, including the President's own family, have benefited from it. The better idea is to double the current admissions level of permanent residents, half to be drawn from a skills-based system. It is the unnaturally low numbers of annual permanent resident admissions that is partly responsible for the log-jam of our immigration system, in today's world where there is such an interest in immigration to the U.S., and given that our otherwise native-born population is in decline.

We must recognize that the recent surge at our southern border is not some kind of existential challenge to the nation's existence, as seen in a vacuum, but rather only one component of the world-wide refugee crisis, a symptom of wars and world-wide insecurity. The long-term solution to any refugee crisis is always peace and prosperity in the country/region that is generating the refugees. Only peace and stability in Syria and northern Africa can allay the human waves of refugees into Europe. Only a Marshal-type program for the northern triangle countries, coupled with short term humanitarian protection for those fleeing eminent death, can resolve the crisis at our southern border.

And finally, regarding the present state of the U.S. Immigration Court system under this white nationalist administration, I'd like to quote my friend and colleague, Judge Paul Schmidt:

Once upon a time, there was a court system with a vision: Through teamwork and innovation, one of the world's best administrative tribunals guaranteeing fairness and due process for all. Two decades later, that vision has become a nightmare. (…)

Today, the U.S. Immigration Court betrays due process, mocks competent administration, and slaps a false veneer of "justice" on a "deportation railroad" designed to evade our solemn Constitutional responsibilities to guarantee due process and equal protection. It seeks to snuff out every existing legal right of migrants. Indeed, it is designed specifically to demean, dehumanize, and mistreat the very individuals whose rights and lives it is charged with protecting.

It cruelly betrays everything our country claims to stand for and baldly perverts our international obligations to protect refugees. In plain terms, the Immigration Court has become an intentionally "hostile environment" for migrants and their attorneys.

https://immigrationcourtside.com/ tag: Good Litigating in a Bad System

Forword to the 2nd Edition (2012)

THIS BOOK WAS PUBLISHED IN June 2011 to coincide with the annual conference of the American Immigration Lawyers' Association which took place in San Diego. I self-financed a West Coast press tour, commencing in San Diego, my birthplace, and moving up the coast to San Francisco, Eugene, Oregon, Portland, and Seattle. The debate about immigration reform was stalled in Washington, or at least any progress had been stalled for some time and I felt it was important for me to jump into the fray and make whatever contribution I could at that crucial time. And I was delighted to be able to reconnect with many colleagues at the conference in San Diego.

I enjoyed press coverage in the order of 6 TV interviews, five on the West Coast and one in Arlington, Virginia, and a dozen radio interviews. I had to learn to conform to the dictates of modern TV journalism – how to be able to hammer home a couple of sound bites in a short period of time. In my first TV interview in San Diego, when the camera's red light went on, I was quite astonished and moved to see my book cover displayed on the studio monitor, while the show host read from his teleprompter phrases from the introduction of my book about the crisis in the immigration courts. In that first show, when I was emoting about migrant workers and what a shame it is that ICE continues to focus on detaining such easy targets rather than prioritizing the hardened criminals and absconders in our community, I was searching for the time-worn phrase "salt of the earth" to describe the migrants in America. I couldn't exactly put my tongue on it —one of those brain freeze moments. But I had just been to the historic used record store, Cow Records in Ocean Beach the day before, where I had purchased a copy of the Neil Young album Harvest, and had been listening to it on the rental car's CD player. When my brain glitched-out on "salt of the earth," the Neil Young phrase "I've been searching for a heart of gold" volunteered to fill the gap, and I said on air, "These people are the heart of gold of America!" And it felt so right that I used it in every subsequent interview.

One of my repeated demands in the interviews was that the Obama administration should rethink the priorities of the types of migrants put into deportation hearings, because if the money isn't there to double the number of immigration judges, which is what it would take to bring any order to an impossible backlog, then we have to cut down on the quantity of removal hearings. I demanded repeatedly that we stop deporting migrant workers, students and single undocumented mothers of U.S. citizens, in order to concentrate our resources instead on the bad guys. I opined that the masses of low-priority common workers who were being funneled into the courts were "clogging the courts" making the system untenable. And I repeatedly threw in the zinger that the prior George W. Bush administration had actually been more progressive on immigration issues than the current one.

On August 18th 2011 the Obama administration declared that it was revamping its priorities in immigration enforcement and taking the focus off of migrant workers and students, essentially encouraging ICE prosecutors to put those types of cases on the back burner in order to focus on criminal elements and absconders, and DHS

Secretary Janet Napolitano used my exact words, that "it makes no sense to expend our resources on low priority cases" and that we had to stop "clogging the courts" with the low-priority cases. Coincidence?

Of course I am not taking full credit for the ray of sunshine that fell on the Capitol City, but I do have it on good information that my remarks, that had been broadcast just weeks before, had found their way into policy circles at the White House. I am therefore comfortable in the thought that my decision to take several costly weeks in order to push my agenda of policy reform did not fall on deaf ears. I also credit the efforts of the American Bar Association and their Commission on Immigration. A representative had testified before Congress that very spring, making the same plea for prioritization of enforcement that I had made.

This book is in many ways an angry and polemical book. Anger at a system that purports to represent the rule of law, but in which upwards of 80% of detained respondents in immigration court find it impossible to find an attorney. They often relinquish their rights to a hearing when faced with the the obstacles of trying to communicate with family and lawyers while detained thousands of miles from their families, being misled by prison staff and ICE officials about their prospects of fighting deportation. Anger when I still hear from colleagues and read in appellate decisions about judges who abuse immigrants in their courtrooms.

I had a very well-connected agent in Washington, DC, himself a lawyer, who begged me to cut out the political content and guaranteed me he could get the book published with a traditional publisher, if I would just reduce the book to more of a scholarly treatise. But that's not the book I wanted to publish.

The response from readers, especially immigrants' rights attorneys and law students, has been so positive that I feel vindicated in choosing the course of publication I did, namely self-publication. I hope you will join me in the struggle to bring light and justice to a broken abomination of a deportation machine, our immigration court system.

Table of Contents

Prologue: Why I wrote this book xxix

Introduction: Sexual Slavery In Ghana 1
    Chronology 10
    A Word About Vocabulary 11
    Taking the Bench 12

Part One: Washington, D.C.
    Howard Law: A White Boy's Legal Education 18
    First Exposure To Asylum Law — Jan Pederson 28
    Dissapointing Lesson About Immigration Practice . . . 30
    Central American Refugee Center 33
    Iranian Asylum Cases 43
    The George Washington Law School Immigration Clinic . .52
    Ethiopia 56
    Mafia Pizza Connection Case 65
    Living In Adams Morgan 74
    Richard Lewis 78
    KGB, FBI and Me 81
    Orquesta Candela — Playing In the Band 83
    Orange Jumpsuits 86

The Sixties All Over Again 89
A Preview of the Arizona Law Fifteen Years Earlier 94
Stone Throwing 97
Sexual Blackmail at International Students Office 101
Government Officials Feeding at the Trough 102
The Prosecution of Jonny Tong 104
To Summarize My Teaching Career 113
Nicaragua, and Decision to Become a Judge 115

Part Two: Immigration Judge, Philadelphia

Education of Immigration Judges 124
The Basics – A Primer 127
The Activist Judge 132
IHP Program 139
Jordanian Spousal Abuse 143
The Lautenberg Amendment and Russian Jews 147
Making the Law 148
Prosecutorial Discretion 150
Chinese Boat People — A Great Crisis
Facing Our Nation 156
History of Chinese Asylum Cases In U.S. 159
Philly Courthouse Circus 173
Liberia and Charles Taylor 177
Playing In the Band—Part II 180

Part Three: Immigration Judge, San Francisco

My Judge Day — San Francisco 186
Cuban Detainees – History of Abuse 204
Government Lawyer Helps Prove Case. 208
Gay San Francisco 215
You've Got To Know Your Client. 218
Fraudulent Korean Green Cards 221
Hawaiian Dream Nights 230
Attorney General Massacres
Board of Immigration Appeals 231
Special Registration – Ice Targets Muslim Men. 238
You Can't Win 'Em All. 242
The Most Dangerous Alien In America. 244
Blatant Nepotism In Immigration Judge Selections 252
Time to Leave the Bench. 254
My Approach to Lawyering 255

Part Four: Reforms

Our Mexican Problem – the Bold Policy Statement 265
Immigration Court Reform 269
Drastic Reform of America's Asylum System 281
Legal Education Reform 285

Appendix 289

Acknowledgments 305

Prologue:
Why I wrote this book

THE WASHINGTON POST ON MARCH 13, 2010 reported that the backlog of cases awaiting a hearing in federal immigration courts has reached an all-time high, while at the same time a record number of immigration judge positions remain unfilled. The story went on to state that 228,421 cases were awaiting a hearing in the first months of the 2010 fiscal year and though much of the backlog is due to an increase in immigration cases. The disturbing truth is that successive administrations have exacerbated the situation by failing to fill vacancies on the immigration courts. The Obama administration has even failed to keep pace with turnover of existing judges, causing the total number of judges to continually drop. The New York Times reported this year that over half of the sitting immigration judges are suffering from Post Traumatic Stress Syndrome due to the crushing volume of cases they are required to complete in a system where quality is sacrificed for quantity. What is most disturbing is the vast majority of these cases are asylum-related cases, involving people whose lives are in danger in their own country.

The immigration courts are in a period of intense crisis at a moment in history when America's immigration policy is being challenged and redefined. Congress has debated an overhaul of the immigration system since 2006, but proposals for fixing the courts have been largely ignored. The American Bar Association released a 510-page report in February, 2010, revealing that a total of 231 immigration judges hear more than 300,000 cases a year, an average of 1,200 for each judge, or three times the load of federal district judges. The ABA reported that judges state that they "feel overworked, frustrated, and feel like they are on a treadmill." (Less than a year later, my sources indicate that judges are now expected to handle 1,500 cases a year and receipts of new cases are up 20% over 2010). The judges often feel that their asylum hearings are "like holding death penalty cases in traffic court," said Dana L. Marks, an immigration judge and the president of the National Association of Immigration Judges. As the judges' backlog swells so that most immigrants must wait an average of two years for a hearing, the number of decisions appealed to the federal circuit courts has increased from 9 percent of decisions in 2002 to 26 percent in 2008, the report found, virtually overwhelming the federal courts. Due to lack of training and experience of immigration judges, the report found, their decisions "are often harrowing, haphazard and inconsistent."

Even with recent hires – there are currently about 271 judges in 59 immigration courts located in 27 states and several U.S. territories – the number of judges and court staff would still have to be doubled to have any meaningful impact on the overall quality of justice that is meted-out in these deportation factories. As should be obvious, the money just isn't there for such an increase in these times of global economic crisis.

America is famous for priding itself as a nation of immigrants, but the often shabby and sometimes downright abusive treatment that immigrants seeking asylum suffer in our nation's immigration court system is a well-kept secret. The truth is that our government fails to hire prosecuting attorneys and appoint judges with expertise in the field or even to adequately train them in the law and procedure. But this failure pales in comparison to the even greater scandal that the immigrants herded into these courts are often treated with disdain, disrespect, or even outright contempt by sworn officers of the law. The often needless, lengthy and costly pre-trial detention of individuals who usually do not represent any danger to the community is an everyday and shameful fact of life in our immigration system.

I have spent over twenty years serving both as an attorney representing immigrants in immigration court and as an immigration judge deciding their fates. When I was tapped for the position of Immigration Judge to serve in Philadelphia, and later in San Francisco, I had to adjust to an intransigent bureaucracy, where it seemed most of its employees didn't even remember that all of their ancestors or even parents had come to our shores from different countries, cultures, and languages to be assimilated into the world's greatest experiment – American democracy. President Obama has recently highlighted "empathy" as an important criteria for a judge. If there is one quality that I would have to say is sorely lacking among so many judges and government attorneys in the system, it is empathy.

Perhaps it would be an overstatement to say that the daily abuse and mismanagement I have seen in our immigration courts threatens our democracy; I have no doubt that it threatens our values, as a nation that abides by the rule of law and one that receives the fugitive from persecution with open arms. I have written this book in hopes of preserving that wonderful heritage, which is now in serious danger of being obliterated. The book is filled with true stories illustrating how our current immigration courts are failing, and I provide concrete proposals to alleviate the backlog of cases and to increase the quality of the adjudications.

The names of clients I have worked with and individuals who have appeared before me in my court have all been changed in order to protect their privacy, unless otherwise indicated.

Introduction: Sexual Slavery In Ghana

DOLLY GREW UP IN RURAL southern Ghana, living in her family's compound near the center of the village. She was the oldest of three children in a moderately comfortable household. She had finished high school and had hopes for a bright future; soon she would marry the young Christian man from the city who had shown an interest in her over the past year.

One day while in the courtyard hand-washing clothes, she heard the sound of a diesel- engine Mercedes pull up out in the street, and then a loud banging on the compound door. Hardly had she unlatched the door when it was pushed open in her face, and powerful hands grasped her by the arms. Two strong men, one of them a complete stranger, the other whom she recognized from the village, pushed her toward the idling car, and she only had time to shout out once before she found herself being shoved into the trunk of the car. Her screams were stifled by the thud of the trunk door slamming. During the brief drive in darkness, she cried repeatedly for her parents to save her.

What her parents had never dared tell her, out of shame, was that since she was a little girl she had been promised to the local shaman as atonement for a family debt, a debt of such proportion that, according to the tradition of Trokosi, only the delivery of the family's first-born daughter can appease the gods. In the Ewe language the word *Trokosi* loosely translates as "slave to the gods," or "wife of the gods" and the tradition encourages the village shaman to consummate the marriage between the girl and the gods. The village shaman in Dolly's village was an unwashed, gnarly little man of advanced age, eager to play the mediator to the gods when her time came. After he had tired of using her as his sex slave, he would make her his household servant, the lowest, most abject member in the village hierarchy.

Twice – when she first reached puberty and then three years later – her parents had begged the shaman for a reprieve and paid a comparatively large ransom to forestall the moment when he should finally call in the debt and take possession of her. Her parents had recognized that their daughter was very gifted and had hoped that by periodic payments, they could put off the inevitable until the old man lost interest – but such a man never loses interest. He had seen her recently at the market. When the family was unable to borrow any more for another bribe, he had ordered his henchmen to collect the debt and not to bother being too delicate about it.

I had been an immigration judge in Philadelphia for less than a year when Dolly walked into my courtroom. Dolly's case presented a new theory of persecution in asylum law, and it was therefore the kind of case that every lawyer and judge hopes to run across: a case of first impression.

What is a case of first impression? It is a new animal, either a new theory of law, or a new set of facts which the existing theories haven't had a chance to grapple with before. It is the type of case that can make a lawyer's career, and, when journalists come sniffing around, it can even make the evening news, something that all ego-tripping lawyers yearn for.

Dolly was very lucky to find a conscientious female lawyer who was a seasoned member of the immigration bar. Then, due to a fortuitous conjunction of the planets, her case found its way into my courtroom. A prosecutor was assigned who, once all of the facts about Dolly's case became known, also chipped in and worked with us to find a solution to the poor woman's dilemma.

Dolly would be the only witness in her case. The law allows that asylum can be granted based upon the applicant's testimony alone, as long as it is believable, internally consistent, and withstands the test of cross-examination. It's not the type of case we like to see, where everything has to ride or fall on the poor applicant's testimony alone. Sometimes, a person may be telling the truth but might be so intimidated by the whole process that (s)he gets rattled and doesn't sound believable. On the other hand, some of the most undeserving people are very convincing, colorful liars, who can concoct a story out of thin air, replete with vivid details that move the heart. Especially for a case of first impression such as this, it would have been better if someone else could have come forward as a witness to corroborate what had happened to poor Dolly, but there was no one else.

I set the matter down for a full hearing on my calendar, and Dolly and her lawyer left the court. And I thought long and hard about the case. I had been handling asylum cases, as an attorney, from all over the world for a dozen years. I had seen almost everything under the sun, but this case was something new, presenting a new quality of perversity in the realm of human affairs. It was hard to imagine that in today's world this kind of institutionalized sexual slavery could exist – and with the victim's family participating in her victimization.

Several months later, Dolly came back to court to tell her story. By now I'd had a chance to review the information her attorney had submitted about the practice of Trokosi in Ghana. There were numerous articles from reputable sources, including national Ghanaian newspapers. The evidence showed that the practice existed in rural parts of Ghana, Togo and Benin, that it was indeed as hideous in reality as Dolly had claimed, and that there had even been several failed attempts to pass a law in the Ghanaian legislature outlawing the practice. (It was finally outlawed in 1998 but enforcement is limited due to the strong cultural tradition that still pervades the practice). There was a Ghanaian NGO (non-governmental organization) that had representatives traveling the country roads, visiting villages and purchasing the young women's freedom from the shamans in exchange for either several head of livestock or sometimes a combination of a cow and some cash. (Nowadays a simple Google search brings up dozens of articles about the practice, and the fact that it is still going strong more than twenty years after our hearing).

Half the battle for Dolly had been won – the record now confirmed that this practice existed, that its ramifications were indeed horrendous for the young victims, and that it might possibly have happened to the young woman in my courtroom. The second half of the battle was for Dolly to convince me, the adjudicator, that her particular story was true and that she hadn't just concocted the whole thing. Her story had to make sense, it had to ring true, and she had to withstand the INS trial attorney's attempts, through cross-examination, to shake her credibility.

The trial attorney was a young woman from China, Fen Lu,

who had come to the US after college to attend law school, and then had remained in the U.S., becoming a citizen and landing a job with the INS. It is already an impressive feat to be able to learn a foreign language as an adult, but then to be able to go into court in the foreign country and conduct oral argument, day in and out, represents an incredible mastery of the language. I was impressed by Fen Lu's courage and intelligence.

At the beginning of the hearing, her attitude about the case seemed to be one of routine skepticism. In her eyes, Dolly was probably just another fraud trying to play the system. But in the course of Dolly's subdued but teary retelling of the story, I saw Fen Lu's attitude change.

Dolly was sworn in and took her place in the witness box to my right. She testified in a subdued but steady voice about the events that had caused her to flee her village and brought her to my courtroom.

On that day that she was brought to the shaman by his henchmen, she was dragged from the car trunk into the village square and deposited under a giant baobab tree. A loud syncopated drumbeat terrified her. She looked about for an escape route, but it seemed like the whole village was there, surrounding her where she lay gasping for breath by a bonfire, next to the effigy of the god that the old shaman guarded. Several chickens squawked as they were sacrificed, and their blood was splattered over Dolly's body. The shaman, a revolting man who wore foul animal skins and smelled like a cadaver, approached her and chanted the words of atonement to the gods, and upon his signal she was carried by the other women into his hut. In a last furtive glance at the villagers, many her neighbors, she saw her mother's anguished eyes at the back of the crowd watching her.

Weeks later, after she had been starved and violated continuously, being offered no opportunity to bathe or recuperate, one of the elderly women took pity upon her and helped her to escape. The woman had been in the shaman's household for twenty years and didn't want to see another life destroyed in the same way.

"But do not return to your family," the old woman admonished Dolly.

"Why not?"

"They will return you to the shaman, for otherwise they will still be in shame with a debt to pay. Come with me." Under cover of darkness she was taken to the kindly woman's family, who hid her in a shed in their compound until Dolly's Christian man could be summoned from the city to rescue her.

The young man came and took her to the city, where he left her at the house of some of his Christian brethren. Thoughts of suicide now for Dolly, but she was talked out of going through with it by the kindly Christian family, who in time were able to raise money for her to purchase a fake passport, complete with fake visa, and provide passage to the U.S. She was given the address of other Christians living in Philadelphia to contact upon her arrival. But her visa, though it was convincing enough to get her on the plane departing Ghana, was discovered by an American immigration inspector at the Philadelphia airport to be an obvious fake. She was placed in INS detention in York, Pennsylvania, where an attorney heard of her plight and came to her legal assistance.

For me, one of the most convincing parts of Dolly's story, and you really had to be there, was when she was asked what had happened to her Christian boyfriend who had helped get her out of the village to the city and to the church that eventually smuggled her out of Ghana. "He abandoned me."

"Why?"

"I asked him, why I cannot stay with you?" Tears came to her eyes, and she was reluctant to continue.

"What did he say?"

"He say, 'Woman, you are spoiled and unclean, I will never have you now.'"

I was able to form a conclusion as to Dolly's credibility, based upon her demeanor and the way she related her story, including that last remark. I found that she was credible, that her story was true, and that she was therefore entitled to asylum and the protection of the U.S. government. I announced to the participants in the hearing that I intended to grant the case.

INS counsel Fen Lu agreed with me. She informed me that she would like some additional time to further research, through her own sources, the practice and nature of Trokosi. If her efforts bore out what Dolly was saying, then as a representative of the government she would join in a grant of the case.

For most judges, those would be welcome words. First, it meant that the humanitarian "right thing" was going to be done and that justice would be served. Secondly, it meant that since the government was not opposing the case, it would not be appealed, and therefore the suffering of the young woman would be put to rest earlier. An appeal to the severely backlogged Board of Immigration Appeals could take years to resolve. At least Dolly would leave the courtroom knowing that she wouldn't have to expend any more time and money for lawyers, while living with the uncertainty of possible deportation back to the country where she had already suffered such indignities.

We returned to court a month later. Fen Lu informed the court that she had contacted individuals in the State Department on the Ghana desk, who in turn had contacted our embassy in Ghana. They had communicated with a Foreign Service officer whose bailiwick was human rights in Ghana and who had contributed to the Ghana section of the annual State Department world human rights report. Coincidentally, the year of our hearing was the first time the report included mention of the practice of Trokosi as a human rights concern. According to the Foreign Service officer in Ghana, the practice was one of the embassy's greatest concerns of human rights violations in Ghana. Fen Lu thus felt that she had satisfied her duty to the government to fully investigate and prosecute the case, and since she was convinced that Dolly was telling the truth she could comfortably join with the court in a grant of asylum.

Because for me it was such an interesting case of first impression, I decided to take some time writing the decision in order to reflect and put the facts of the case and their application to the law in perspective. When I rendered my decision, the nation's most influential immigration law journal, Interpreter Releases, published by West Law, learned about the ruling and published many of my remarks verbatim.

Then came the storm: it seems that Fen Lu's superiors in the agency had not heard about the case until the article was circulated. One of the court's clerks informed me that, when the case became known through the press, one of Fen Lu's supervisors came to the clerk's window, insisting upon seeing my decision, and in particular inquired about the appeal deadline. The thirty-day appeal deadline had just passed. My clerk told me she heard an explosion of rage coming from their offices across the hall. But there was nothing for Fen Lu's superiors to do about the case but fume and steam and la-ment the missed opportunity to file an appeal of my decision, which would have kept Dolly in a state of cruel, uncertain limbo.

Frankly, if that case hadn't received the national attention it did, then nothing further would ever have been said about it. The case shows how much the government loves the opportunity to shoot itself in the foot when it comes to publicity. I have often thought about what I would have done had I been Fen Lu's supervisor and if I had been surprised by such an article about the case in a leading law journal. Here's how I would have handled it. I would have called a press conference, inviting Dolly and her attorney and Fen Lu to share the podium. I would have made a grandstanding speech to the press, with TV cameras rolling, announcing "how proud we in the government are to be able to offer this poor abused woman the protection of the United States government, and how our attorneys such as Fen Lu are struggling every day in the trenches to do the right thing and assure that those who deserve protection are afforded it while those who are frauds and abuse the system are weeded out and sent home." I would have recommended Fen Lu for a commendation, which would have given her a chance to visit Washington for a day and have a cheap lunch at government expense and be awarded a medal by the Attorney General. Our government would thus be reported in the press as upholding our sacred tradition of offering refugee to the truly repressed and destitute.

But I suppose that makes too much sense.

Chronology

1. Attend Howard Law School: 1982 – 1985

2. First Legal Job: Senior Attorney, Central American Refugee Center: 1985 – 1986

3. Director, Immigration Law Clinic, George Washington University Law School: 1986 – 1996

4. Election Monitor for Organization of American States, Nicaragua, 1996

5. Immigration Law Judge: 1997 – 2004

6. Election Monitor for Organization of American States, Panama, 2004

7. Legal Consultant, UN High Commissioner for Refugees, Seoul, Korea: 2005

8. Refugee Officer, U.S. Citizenship and Immigration Services, Worldwide travel, 2006-2016

9. Supervisory Asylum Officer, U.S. Citizenship and Immigration Services, 2016-2019

10. Legal Consultant, UN High Commissioner for Refugees, Rwanda, 2019-2020

A Word About Vocabulary

I feel a few words are in order about words used in this book, primarily because it is a legal memoir and as such I make use of legal terminology. For example at times I sometimes use the word "alien" to describe individuals who are in deportation proceedings. I know the word may have an offensive connotation to many people, but at the same time it is a legal technical term, used in the immigration statute to describe "anyone who is not a citizen or national of the United States," whatever that means. Any lawyer dealing with the immigration system will use the word alien, because using the word immigrant or migrant would be incorrect, those words having entirely different legal meanings. So usually if I employ the word immigrant when describing an individual who more properly in legal terms would be considered an "alien" I use the word in laymen's sense.

INS versus ICE. The Immigration and Naturalization Service doesn't exist anymore, having been broken up into three subcomponents post 9-11: CIS, or Citizenship and Immigration Services; ICE, or Immigration and Customs Enforcement; and CBP, or Customs and Border Protection. For the major part of my career covered by this book it was INS trial attorneys who appeared in court as prosecutors. After the break-up of the agency in 2003 those attorneys fell under ICE and are now ICE attorneys. But because I was used to dealing and referring to them as INS attorneys for so long, and because in the popular culture INS is still a living concept, I at times use INS and ICE interchangeably.

Similarly, deportation hearings are now properly referred to as removal hearings, but in popular culture they are still referred to as deportation hearings and I use the terms interchangeably.

Respondent: an individual (the alien or migrant) who is in immigration court "responding" to charges of deportability which are notated on a Notice to Appear, the charging document.

IJ—Immigration Judge

DOJ—Department of Justice

EOIR—Executive Office of Immigration Review, the sub-agency in DOJ that administers the immigration courts

USCIS—United States Citizenship and Immigration Services, under Department of Homeland Security, sub-agency that houses the asylum and refugee programs

Taking the Bench

I put on my robe and pick up the case file. My clerk in the Philly court, Sonya Massenburg, steps inside the courtroom and calls, "All rise." I carry the blue folder with the bold black type, "Executive Office for Immigration Review," and the symbol of the Department of Justice eagle on the cover. When I walk into the courtroom, everyone is standing: the Rule of Law is in action. I gesture for them to sit, calling, "Please be seated."

There may be preliminary matters to discuss. "Are there any issues we can agree on? Can both sides agree that Mr. Gonzalez has been here in the U.S. for ten years, so we don't have to spend an hour taking testimony about that?" We may decide that, out of the ten or twelve witnesses the Respondent has brought with him, we only need to hear from two. Often, when the judge's favorable discretion is necessary, a number of family members will be present. I always like to have them stand and identify themselves on the record, even if we aren't going to have them all testify, as a way of acknowledging their presence, and so they can be assured that the judge *has* taken note of them. We might briefly review evidence that is being presented in the case, get a sense whether either side will be objecting to or has a special concern about any particular item.

Then it's time to start. I push the button on the tape recorder. (Oh yes, the immigration judges have to make sure themselves that everything is recorded). "Today is May 23, 2000, this is immigration judge Paul Grussendorf presiding in the matter of Jose Gonzalez, "A" number…(the "A" number is the government's tracking system for the alien), sitting in San Francisco. Will counsels please state their names for the record."

I said that litany an average of 1200 times a year. Sometimes, on the days we had master calendars, (initial arraignments), fifty times in one morning. Before I became a judge, I never could understand how the judges could say the same thing over and over so many times, day in and day out. When I was a judge, I still couldn't believe it, and looked forward to the day I wouldn't have to anymore.

The tape is running. Maybe the attorneys have some preliminary remarks to address to the court. Then it's time to call the first witness, who most often will be the Respondent. In most cases, an interpreter will be necessary. (The court in San Francisco had four full-time Spanish interpreters and a Hindi interpreter on staff when I was there.) Interpreters for other languages are provided through an agency that contracts with the government. Before we can take testimony, I have to swear in the interpreter, who takes an oath to provide accurate translation.

I've already reviewed the file, and I've organized the hearing in my head before entering the courtroom, so I have an idea of which witness will be most important, and which areas of testimony I want to have emphasized. I can name judges who won't even have opened the file before taking the bench. Then, during testimony, they will be playing catch-up, trying to review documents and read statements at the same time that testimony is being taken in front of them. You can often tell such judges because they continuously shuffle papers during the hearing, trying to understand what is in the file, something they should have done before-hand. Such judges should be fired or reassigned to clerical work.

How did I get to this position, where I dress in the robes of authority, representing the United States, dispensing justice over thousands of people every year? Was it something I aspired to, because I knew deep in my heart that I would be a good judge, and that I wanted that lofty position of power, where I could determine the outcomes of peoples' lives, while having everyone in the courtroom kow-towing to me? Hardly.

My interest in the culture of immigration goes back to my early childhood acquaintance with my grandfather. My father's father immigrated to the U.S. from Germany as a teenager with his family in the last decade of the 19th Century. He came from the little village in Lower Saxony that still bears the family name, Grussendorf, and he settled in a farming community in Grand Rapids, Minnesota, where my father, the youngest of five children, was born. In that new-found paradise, Grandpa ran a farm and taught high school. At that time he was one of the few literate adults in the farming community, and so he assisted his fellow farmers whenever there was a need for someone who could read or write, or crack bad folk-spun jokes. He apparently won quite a reputation as a community leader, because there is a little park named after him with a stone monument attesting to his legacy in Grand Rapids.

When I was growing up in Virginia, my parents would alternate every summer between taking me and my two older brothers to either visit Minnesota and my father's family, or Maine, where my mother's family lived (she was of Scottish extraction). I would have first met Grandpa when he was already in his eighties. He was handsome, a bit like an older Gregory Peck, and incredibly gentle in his twilight years. My Grandma was born in Minnesota of German heritage. In the back of my mind, during those early years, I was always conscious that Grandpa had come from Germany, which is found in Europe, which is over there, across the sea, and that he had come to America like other immigrants in his time to make a better life. Immigration was always about the moral imperative of finding something better for one's family. Surely the seeds were planted for my decision much later, when I was in my mid-twenties, to re-locate to Germany, kind of a reverse migration back to the Old Country, where I lived and worked for five years before returning to the U.S. to attend law school.

PART ONE: WASHINGTON, D.C.

Howard Law: A White Boy's Legal Education

I moved to Washington, D.C. in 1973, right after my graduation from the University of Oregon, to pursue my chosen career in documentary film production. In that first incredibly hot and humid summer, the drumbeat of black liberation was rocking the city. The 1968 riots were a very recent memory. The burnt-out neighborhood called the 12th Street corridor and U Street, once one of the geographic hearts of the black artistic and cultural renaissance, were constant reminders of the still pent-up fury of the disenfranchised black-majority population. During my first tropical summer in the sweltering city I was introduced to the ever-present sight of young black males wearing African dashikis and sporting dramatic Afro hairstyles, who liked to drive past and flash the raised-arm, clenched-fist Black Power salute. People were still getting used to the proud and hard-fought-for moniker *Black* in place of *Negro*. All of this ferment fed into a cauldron of social/artistic/political development and empowerment by/for people who had tasted the bitter fruits of disappointment of unfulfilled promises from the civil rights era. People were justifiably angry.

I was a sax player, and I brought my horn with me when I moved to D.C. I joined my first jazz group, a mix of black, Hispanic and Jewish musicians who rehearsed in a piano shop on 18th Street in Adams Morgan. Under the direction of a tall, gay black band leader, we played free jazz that echoed the chaos of revolution that was in the air. My friendships with those musicians, and the times I spent hanging out in that primarily black neighborhood (it has gone through a remarkable gentrification since then) formed my first introduction into the world of "black people."

During those early years in Washington, while working in the TV news industry for all three national networks and the local news affiliates, I was able to get all around the city. I had a privileged insider's view into the corridors of both national and municipal power, and came into contact with black professionals and working class people of all walks of life. And I visited the main campus of Howard University, which was a fascinating hot-bed of Pan-Africanism. The students built a model of an Ujaama village on the quod grounds, which I remember photographing with a camera crew. Later, before leaving the city to spend five years working in the German TV industry, I visited the campus of Howard Law School, located in a different part of northwest Washington at Van Ness Street, on assignment with a TV crew. I couldn't have possibly imagined at that time, that a mere six years later I would attend law school there.

After five years in Germany I was ready for another challenge. I returned from Europe to Washington, D.C. in the fall of 1982, enrolled in Howard law school, one of a tiny minority of white students at the school. Having spent four years in Washington before my travels, I was already exposed to many of the issues that concerned the black community. The other white students were all from the local area and had mostly chosen to attend Howard for economic reasons – the school offered the lowest tuition of the five law schools in the D.C. area. The economics was also an important consideration for me, but I primarily chose to go there for political and ideological reasons. A year earlier, while still living in Germany but after having made the decision to go to law school, I had visited schools in Texas, and considered my alma mater, University of Oregon, before deciding upon Howard.

Having grown up in the sixties, I always considered Dr. Martin Luther King and Malcolm X to be, not the polar opposites that so many social critics consider them to be, but rather complementary visionaries of the same message. Years later, at my office at George Washington University law school, theirs were the only two portraits that adorned my walls. Today, forty years after their deaths, I still get chills up my spine when I listen to the recordings of either of those great orators and martyrs. And I was delighted to be able to attend Howard, the institution of those giants of legal activism Charles Hamilton Houston and Thurgood Marshall.

I have been asked many times through the years what the experience was like, and how the black students at Howard treated me. I am proud to say that not once in three years did I ever hear a "discouraging word" from a fellow black student. And I cherished the warm friendship and collegiality that was extended my way. We shared so many laughs between classes, and good times between exams.

As an institution whose primary mission is the education of African-American lawyers, Howard Law consciously addresses some of the problems that black students who want to become lawyers face: issues of low bar passage rate and concerns about discriminatory hiring practices once the law school and bar exam hurdles are overcome. And yet the school attracts some of the top black students in the nation, many of whom attended white undergrad schools and who want to indulge in a supportive black community one last time before going out into a still largely white, hostile professional world. But Washington is a great place for a black attorney to start out, or to stay for that matter.

Two Howard professors were especially influential in my legal education: Jerome Schumann and Warner Lawson. Professor Schumann unfortunately passed away in 2004, and Warner Lawson finally retired from the teaching profession in 2014. They both had a very remarkable quality, which was expressed in vastly different styles but was present in each lecture – they had a true love for their students, and they recognized the insecurities that so many law students naturally brought with them to the classroom. Through the use of humor and irony they were both able, in their own ways, to tweak out those anxieties and dispel them during the communal classroom experience.

Schumann, who was the son of share croppers, built his wealth through his knowledge of Property and Real Estate law. He was a heavy-set, handsome man who liked to dress like a banker and always had a cherubic grin on his face. He spoke with the cadence of a southern Baptist preacher, and incredibly he had the talent to use the same dramatic techniques in his Property law lectures. He would start out slow and soft-spoken at the beginning of class, and gradually increase both the volume and intensity of his words, until, fifteen minutes into the lecture, you could have been sitting in a southern church, nodding your head to the rhythm of his words, shouting out, "Preach it!" He chose and enunciated every word for dramatic impact, with as much precision as a Shakespearian actor. I was enthralled each time he delivered his property "sermon." Many of the younger students were cowed by his overbearing persona, which was all a show, but I was old enough to appreciate that I was in the presence of a true dramatic genius. I came out of every one of his classes elated, smiling, thankful for the privilege of having been in his class.

Professor Lawson, my Contracts professor for two semesters, had a completely different style, but one which I naturally appreciated. He brought to the equally daunting subject of Contracts the insights of a liberal arts philosopher and raconteur. He imbued each class with an eclectic array of analogies and aphorisms drawn from a broad spectrum of human experience. A tall, lanky figure, he paced in front of the classroom, chain-smoking cigarettes from an improbable cigarette holder, striking an effete figure of philosopher/jester.

Incredibly, I received the grade of "A" in both of those fearsome two-semester subjects, both of which I had dreaded and would not for the life of me have taken if they had not been required courses. I enjoyed both subjects thoroughly, which I attribute entirely to the teaching abilities of the professors.

I initially concentrated on criminal law at Howard. I interned at the District of Columbia Public Defender Service, at the U.S. Attorney's office, and in the summer of 1984, at the Federal Defenders of San Diego. My two semesters with Howard's criminal law clinic were my introduction to the heady responsibility of defending a client who is facing real jail time.

Like every fresh-faced clinic student I considered myself a crusader. My first client in D.C. Superior Court was a transvestite hooker. He used to ply his trade at Thomas Circle on 14th Street, one of the mainstays of the D.C. skin trade. He was a tall, thin, light-skinned man who I'll call Josh. He'd been busted at night by an undercover cop driving a Ford Shelby Cobra.

I was determined to win his case, and in my research I found an antiquated Court of Appeals decision from the District of Columbia, that basically held that police couldn't convict a homosexual of prostitution without a corroborating witness. The apparent intent behind the decision from the 1950's was that it was so calumnious to imply that anyone was a homosexual at that time that you'd better have a witness to back up your claim.

I went to visit my client in detention at D.C. jail, with my housemate Maurizia, a tall and lovely Italian woman who worked for the World Bank. When we met Josh in lock-up, she complemented him on his beauty-rings. I'd never heard of beauty rings before, and neither had my client, but when she explained that they are the rings that some people have around their necks, and that in Europe they are a sign of beauty, sure enough, he did have them, and he was delighted at her complement. During our interview he confirmed my suspicion that the arresting officer didn't have a supporting witness to back him up. I assured him that I would put on a sterling performance in the courtroom on his behalf.

On the day of my first trial, the arresting cop testified, explaining that he had made a routine bust of a hooker on 14th Street, who then turned out to be a male in drag. After my cross examination, in which the cop admitted that he had been acting alone without a witness the government rested its case. Ball in my court. I then made my brilliantly prepared and executed argument for dismissal based on the precedent decision and the obvious fact that the arresting officer had no supporting witness. The judge wasn't impressed by my argument citing a case from the 1950's, and he denied my motion for summary judgment.

It wasn't my choice, but the faculty supervisor at my side insisted that I put my client on the stand, even though I hadn't prepared him for cross-examination because I hadn't anticipated calling him. We took him through his fairly innocuous story of trying to catch a ride in the evening at Thomas Circle. He testified that he had merely been hitchhiking on 14th Street when the handsome police officer pulled up and offered him a ride.

"What did you do then?"

"Well, I got in the car, of course."

"What happened next?"

"I put my hand on his dick."

When that zinger came out, everyone in the courtroom, except my client, knew that he had just convicted himself. Lesson: Don't let your prostitute client take the stand, unless you are sure that (s)he's not going to talk about male anatomy.

The summer between my first and second year at Howard was spent in Mexico City, attending an international program sponsored by the University of Houston Law School. We enjoyed lectures from Mexican scholars on issues of Mexican-American trade and migration. One of the highlights of that summer was when a group of the students drove to the Pacific Coast, and I encountered the charming beach town of Zihuatenejo for the first time. That summer laid the foundation for my progress in the Spanish language. But the pollution was so bad in Mexico City, I was coughing for months afterward.

My second law school summer was spent in San Diego. I interned for the San Diego Federal Defenders office. The office represented many migrants in federal court who had been arrested and charged with illegal entry, illegal re-entry, and alien smuggling, as well as typical cross-border drug smuggling offenses. I rented a room in the house of one of the nation's most celebrated criminal defense attorneys, John Cleary, who had helped start the Federal Defender's office and had acted as its executive director for a dozen years. A former Green Beret lawyer, Cleary was so rambunctious, creative, and so good at oral argument that the Supreme Court used to draft him for pro bono representations on criminal appeals. (I had the pleasure of seeing him in action before the Supremes a couple of years later). His apartment was in Ocean Beach, a delightful mixed neighborhood of retired Naval officers and bohemian surfers.

He kicked me out of his apartment after I drank the forbidden grape juice, a bottle of juice in his fridge that I had been strictly admonished not to touch. I never knew what kind of bizarre hormones or testosterone treatments he might have dissolved in the precious elixir that would cause such a burst of rage when he found out I had touched the precious juice. (Cleary died in February 2020, the victim of a biking accident. I have to admit that I did not have warm memories of my time in his apartment.)

The office had a legal researcher, Ben Rayborn, who had a colorful background in the annals of American crime. In post Second World War Kentucky, he had been a John Dillinger type figure, the leader of the Benny-Denny gang. His band had a modis operandi: they would walk into a bank and fire submachine guns into the ceiling to get everyone's attention. J. Edgar Hoover once called him "the most dangerous criminal to come out of WWII." While he was incarcerated at Alcatraz, he became an infamous jail house lawyer, where he came to the attention of John Cleary, who was so impressed with his legal skills that the office mobilized to have him released early from a lengthy sentence, so that he could work for the good guys, the Federal Defenders. He joined the office in 1971 and continued to work tirelessly on groundbreaking cases until his passing in 2004.

And Judy Clark, the executive director of the office when I was there, has continued to be a leading light in criminal defense. Her office won the first federal murder trial where the defense employed was 'battered spouse syndrome', a case involving the wife of a Marine sergeant who lived a life of horrible abuse and terror and constant beatings until she finally snapped and blew her husband away with his government-issued .45. Judy has continued to be a pioneer in her field, specializing in death penalty cases, including being appointed defense counsel for Unibomber Ted Kaczynsky. At the time of writing she is appointed counsel for Jared Lee Loughner, the defendant who killed a dozen people and gravely wounded Congresswoman Gifford in Tucson in January 2011.

Mario, who was Judy's deputy and later became director of the office, had been a Navy bomber pilot during the Vietnam War. He was apparently atoning for his sins in Vietnam by representing the downtrodden. From our building we could hear when the military jets on the nearby Naval base powered up and took off. There was always a moment, before take-off, when the sound of an explosion rocked the city. Mario explained, "That's the sound of the afterburners kicking in, that's when the pilot's dick gets hard!"

Every morning I would go across the street to the federal court building with several of the attorneys from the office, to interview the crop of newly-detained defendants prior to their initial arraignments in court. The Federal Defenders stood in for every defendant who didn't have a lawyer. The vast majority of the cases were Mexicans charged with federal immigration offenses, with a number of drug smugglers always thrown in. It is a federal crime to simply enter the U.S. illegally, a violation that carries with it a possible one-year jail sentence; the vast majority of undocumented aliens in the U.S. are never charged with the crime, but at the border the U.S. Attorney's office makes it a point of charging repeat offenders and alien smugglers. Often a re-entry case will be pled down to an illegal entry, or an alien smuggling charge will be pled down to a re-entry. The Federal Defenders were the nation's experts on the interpretation and defense of such crimes and many of the precedent decisions interpreting that area of the law originated in their office.

I was privileged to be allowed to make representations to the federal judge at time of sentencing on such misdemeanors. Arguments by counsel prior to sentencing are referred to as "allocution." By the time I finished the summer internship I had done dozens of allocutions for Hispanics who had essentially committed the crime of trying to find a better life for themselves and their families. I also made my second foray into Mexico, driving down the Baja peninsula to the mid-point at Ensenada and then driving east across the mountains to the Gulf. I knew by then that after law school I wanted to either practice criminal law or some form of immigration law involving Hispanics and the southern border.

That summer gave me an opportunity to work with some of the sharpest attorneys in the criminal defense bar, and I learned a lot of my lessons, especially pertaining to ethics and duty toward one's clients, from my mentors there.

When I left Howard after three years, I knew that I would devote my career to social activism. I never even interviewed with any of the corporate law firms that dangle the big bucks before the noses of anxious law grads. My eyes were set on the burgeoning Central American refugee crisis that was besetting Washington in 1985. I was thankful to Howard for giving me the skills to be a trial attorney and the opportunity to assess the state of the law and figure out what I wanted to do with my career. I was thankful for the dedication of the professors to their students.

Thirty years later to the day that I had first entered the hallowed halls of Howard as a student, I returned to teach a Refugee Law course. In the fall of 2011, while I was working with the UN Refugee Agency at the border of Egypt and Libya on the Mediterranean, I pitched the idea of such a class to the Howard faculty and the idea was approved. I was so delighted to return to that small campus in 2012 and to work with such talented and committed students. I was able to repeat the class in the fall of 2014, but my international travel prevented me from continuing after that.

First Exposure To Asylum Law — Jan Pederson

My first exposure to asylum law — an experience that hooked me forever — came when I interned as a law student in Jan Pederson's immigration law firm in the fall of 1983. I had just returned from spending a summer in Mexico City after the first year of law school. Jan was a solo practitioner at the time, and she had been in the right time and place when the 1979 Iranian revolution kicked loose. She was also a graduate of Howard Law School, which is how I came to see her job posting on the school bulletin board. When I worked for her in 1983, most of her clients were Iranians applying for asylum and other immigration benefits.

The international definition of a refugee, originating in the 1951 Convention Relating to the Status of Refugees, was adopted almost verbatim into the U.S. immigration statute in 1980: *"The term 'refugee' means (A) any person who is outside any country of such person's nationality (...) and who is unable or unwilling to return to (...) that country because of persecution or a well-founded fear of persecution on account of race, religion, nationality, membership in a particular social group, or political opinion."* The concept is popularly referred to as political asylum, but as you can see from the definition, "political opinion" is only one of five possible grounds for a grant of refugee or asylum protection. The foregoing language is a minefield of legal terminology, which gives lawyers and courts enough grist for the mill to keep hordes of legal professionals happily occupied, arguing the meaning of each individual word and phrase. You could say that I have spent my entire legal career doing so.

Before 1980 there was no formal mechanism for someone to present themselves to INS and apply for asylum in the United States. When I worked for Jan, the asylum law was still a very new creature, and the courts' interpretations of it were setting precedent that would have impact for decades to come. It was an exciting time to be entering the field. Jan ran an all-girl law firm. As she explained it, she was willing to make an exception for me because of my background as a journalist living overseas, experience that would be helpful in my delegated role of researching and writing up the asylum applications for her office.

It was my job to conduct interviews with the clients, work their stories into compelling affidavit form, and help document their cases by researching background reports. Over the course of nine months in Jan's firm, I worked with dozens of people who had just fled their homes, many of them having come from wealthy backgrounds before suddenly having to leave with whatever they could pack into suitcases. The Iranian refugees came by way of Cyprus or Europe to the U.S., having no idea of their future — still trying to comprehend their loss. I was their voice. My work helped determine the success of their bid to stay in the U.S. The kinds of people I worked with included former commercial airline pilots, military jet pilots, former generals, colonels, doctors, engineers, scientists – people who had spent their lives scrambling to the top. Now, in their land of refuge, they worked on road crews, construction crews, in parking garages, hotel maintenance – wondering if what had happened to them was Allah's will. I recommend that excellent film with Ben Kingsley, based on the even better book of the same title, *House of Sand and Fog*, for an insight into the lives of Iranian refugees in the U.S.

Jan was a micromanager, so I wasn't just thrown out on my own to possibly mishandle her clients' cases. She reviewed everything I wrote a dozen times, driving me crazy but in the process teaching me how to write a powerful statement – one of the most crucial skills for an attorney.

Another invaluable lesson was she would allow me to sit in on her initial meetings with clients while she evaluated their situations and sized up how to best achieve what they were seeking in the immigration context. She had an excellent manner of drawing the essential information from a client while cutting through the chaff. That is a skill that takes some time to learn, especially in such a complex area of law.

Dissapointing Lesson About Immigration Practice

There is an unfortunate perception in the community, that the practice of immigration law in particular attracts shyster lawyers. It is even more unfortunate that the perception is correct, and such miscreants give a bad name to the many fine attorneys working in the field. I was to learn about such shysters early in my career. Shortly after I passed the bar, in August 1985, a friend in the immigration field called with a tip – she knew a lawyer who was looking for a recent law grad to work in his immigration office, and he might be flexible on part-time work. That was just what I was looking for, because I had already decided that my heart was with the refugees, and that I wanted to work with the Central American Refugee Center in D.C.. They paid notoriously little, and I had student loans to pay, so I thought that if I could get part-time work elsewhere, at a better salary, than I would be able to afford to work half-time for CARECEN. The staff at CARECEN agreed to the arrangement when I pitched it.

I won't mention his name, given that he is among the departed from this world, but he was counsel to the Anti-Defamation League at their D.C. headquarters in downtown Massachusetts Avenue, and so I falsely assumed that he must be a good ethical attorney. He owned a condo just a block away from his office, and that is where he conducted his immigration practice.

I met with the attorney at his office. We negotiated an hourly wage for a twenty-hour work week. He understood my interest in being free to work for CARECEN, and I was happy that he seemed to have the right attitude about everything.

In his practice, he catered to Indian nationals and he had several Indians working for him. He also hosted a weekly immigration law program on radio targeting that community. What I came to learn in the brief course of my employment there, was that he had 3-4 Indians on the payroll at any given time, and that he was holding out the promise to all of them of acquiring their green cards in exchange for them working for slave wages for him. For such a small office to be petitioning for labor certifications for three or more paralegals was fraud and blatantly illegal, given that the business could never have justified the need for so many professional employees. My discussions with the staff revealed that they were all dissatisfied and considered themselves exploited, but they were putting up with it in hopes of receiving the promised green card. But I learned this after accepting the job.

After my first week on the job, he asked for a private meeting with me. He explained that he was happy with my work, but that the office really couldn't support my salary at the agreed-upon rate, and he also threw in that if the other employees knew how much I was making they would throw a fit. Any comparison of my salary with the other employees was ludicrous because I was an attorney, but I really wanted to keep the arrangement so that I would have the time to work with CARECEN, so I agreed to a pay cut from what was already a fairly modest salary.

A week later, when I went in on a Saturday to work, he wanted to have another talk with me. This time he invented a sham reason why he thought my work was not up to par, and he again wanted to push my hourly rate down. I was a new law graduate with a ton of debts to pay, and he must have thought that I could be easily manipulated. I told him that a further decrease was unacceptable and that I would have to take a walk. It was clearly not the answer he was expecting. He cut a check for the time already worked, and on Monday morning I was in line when the bank which held his account opened – I didn't even trust him to not bounce the check.

I later heard from several other immigration attorneys in the city who had had exactly the same experience with him. One of them, herself an Indian national, told me that when the final crunch came with the shyster, and he wanted to squeeze even more on the salary issue, she had refused to even accept payment for the work already completed. But I hadn't been proud, and I had thought it would be doubly outrageous to have him profit for free from the product of my labor.

Central American Refugee Center

My first job after law school was with CARECEN, the Central American Refugee Center, which was established and run by Central Americans in order to come to the assistance of those refugees who were being forced out of their countries by the disturbances of civil wars in El Salvador, Guatemala, and Nicaragua.

During the eighties, hundreds of thousands of Central American refugees came to the U.S. and applied for asylum, only to be told by the System that they weren't genuine refugees fleeing from oppression but rather that they were "economic refugees" just coming to the U.S. to look for jobs. There seemed to be an institutional fix on within the INS and Justice Department to deny the asylum claims of Central Americans. The Department of State cooperated with this culture of misinformation, by assuring members of Congress and government agencies that the alleged human rights abuses in those countries where the U.S. was funding the military action against the insurgents weren't so bad, and that reports of atrocities committed by American backed *Contra* rebels in Nicaragua were nothing but leftist propaganda.

The Sanctuary Movement was an ecumenical response by church activists to the big lie being perpetrated by our government. Its leaders and rank-and-file resolved to come to the assistance of such refugees, who were being shunned by the system, by giving them shelter, what the law calls "harboring aliens." In Texas and Arizona, priests, nuns and ministers were being put on trial in federal court for the federal offenses of alien smuggling and harboring aliens – all because they were answering the call of their consciences and the dictates of the Bible to give shelter to the stranger and the oppressed. CARECEN responded as a legal non-profit, taking on some of the thousands of cases in the greater Washington area. Washington, D.C. became the second-largest recipient of Salvadoran nationals in the country, after Houston, with additional large populations of Guatemalans and Nicaraguans putting a strain on the legal system.

When I went to work at CARECEN in the fall of 1985, the institutional fix was still on, and none of our clients, I mean none, were being granted asylum – out of hundreds who passed through our hands annually. (Congress later rectified this injustice by passing a special law in 1990 allowing all Salvadorans and Guatemalans to remain in the U.S. indefinitely under TPS, Temporary Protected Status. The congressional history of that law and other contemporaneous documents demonstrates that it was passed specifically to redress the injustices of the system in the preceding decade and the institutional fix to deny the Salvadorans and Guatemalans asylum status). In fact, during the 80's there were members of Congress who were agitating against the institutional fix that was on, such as Congressman Joe Moakley.

By joining the office, I became a political activist against the system, a role I relished. CARECEN was in the forefront of pushing for recognition of the masses of refugees coming from Central America. We supported the Sanctuary Movement. I served as CARECEN's liaison to the local office, attending weekly Sanctuary meetings and strategy sessions. The coordinator of the National Sanctuary Movement for the D.C. metro area, the Reverend Phil Wheaton, married me and my lovely Brazilian wife at our apartment. I knew people who were hiding refugee families in their homes, keeping them out of sight of *la Migra*.

I spent a month in Nicaragua, in the war-torn northern part of the country, in the revolutionary town of Esteli at the height of the Contra war in 1985, taking intensive Spanish so that I could function in CARECEN's office. I also made field trips to Guatemala and El Salvador while working at CARECEN.

CARECEN's offices were in an old brownstone on Mt. Pleasant Street in northwest Washington. The Mt. Pleasant neighborhood had transformed itself over the years into a wonderful cultural mishmash of students, African-Americans, and Central Americans, with the latter edging out the others in population. Mt. Pleasant Street itself was like an imitation of a busy street in San Salvador, with sidewalk vendors, Latino grocery stores and clothing shops, and an occasional drunk decorating the sidewalk.

My office, on the second floor at the front, looked out over this surging carpet of immigrants and fringe dwellers, and I knew I had found my home. Our whole staff, except for myself, and Willam Van Wyke, the lawyer I was brought in to replace, was Hispanic. (William became an immigration judge in 1995, retiring in 2015). I have always been grateful for his knowledge and humanitarian commitment to our clients. Sylvia, the director of the non-profit, and most of the other employees were Salvadoran, with a couple of Guatemalans mixed in. It was a Spanish-speaking environment, which I loved. Our offices were full of recent arrivals from the war zones, working with our paralegals to document their stories, while the lawyers prepared their testimony for daily court hearings. Every day we had five-six clients who had to appear for initial matters in court, and we were responsible for an individual merits hearing in court at least every other day, often several.

Roberto's story

One day in the fall of 1985, at our offices of CARECEN, we were contacted by a former Major in the Salvadoran army who I'll call Roberto. He was a handsome young officer whose English was impeccable, having lived during his youth in the United States. He had a story to tell. He had recently fled to the U.S., choosing to abandon his military career and get a job at a restaurant in the States rather than continue to support the kinds of atrocities that he had witnessed back home. He was disturbed by the fact that the war was being waged against peasant families, women and children, in the name of democracy. Massacres of villagers in the war zones were being committed by his military, his fellow soldiers-in-arms, with the support of American funding and training, and the reality of the situation was being denied by all levels of the American government. The particular story that he was eye-witness to was one of torture – he had witnessed the torture of Salvadoran guerrilla suspects by Salvadoran security officials, while an American CIA agent was present and participating in the interrogations. He wanted his story to get out, in order to break the wall of silence. Our government consistently denied that any American officials were involved with such abuses, or that they even occurred.

CARECEN agreed to represent him in his legal matters, and we contacted Ambassador Robert White, the former ambassador from the United States to El Salvador, who was now an outspoken critic of the war and who had founded the Center for International Policy in order to influence American policy in the region. There were many allegations of American involvement in torture floating around town, but until then there had been no really credible witness from inside Salvadoran government circles who was willing to come forward and testify. There could hardly be a more credible witness than Roberto. In addition to having trained at the notorious School of the Americas in Georgia, he had spent a year as an exchange officer at the military academy at West Point. (I always suspected that he might have been more active in the interrogations that he described than as a mere witness, as he claimed, but the important thing was that his credibility was impeccable). It was agreed that Ambassador White would work with him on the legislative front and we would represent him in his immigration matters.

I met with Roberto a dozen times over the course of several months, getting his story in as detailed an affidavit form as possible for use in his legal case. He was always very paranoid about the possibility of spies watching him or even death squads coming to get him. Then, when there actually *was* a death squad killing reported in L.A. against a Salvadoran opposition activist, Roberto decided that CARECEN was too political an organization for him to be associating with, and he bailed on us and hired a private lawyer. But he continued to cooperate with Ambassador White in his campaign to inform Congress.

Shortly before leaving my position at CARECEN, I had an opportunity to travel to El Salvador and see the conditions on the ground. I went with a group of church members and Sanctuary activists who were supporters of CARECEN's activities, including two Catholic priests. Among other things, our trip was enlightening on the topic of U.S. censorship of the news – although it was not technically the U.S. government that was telling the major networks not to run the grizzly stories of military atrocities – and how a major private news organization might engage in self-censorship.

After traveling through many areas of the country that were beset by guerrilla insurgency, we met with a Dutch documentary filmmaker who was based in San Salvador. He had been covering the war for three years. He showed us footage he had shot himself of atrocities committed against civilians by government troops. The same material that was routinely carried by European channels, he explained, was ordinarily rejected by the American networks, even though it was clearly newsworthy. Looking at the footage, and by virtue of that fact that I had worked in the TV news business for a decade, I was able to judge the authenticity of the film material. It was clear to me that, for some reason, perhaps political expediency, the U.S. news networks had decided to go soft on the U.S. involvement and the atrocities being committed in El Salvador's civil war.

We made a road trip, crossing bombed-out bridges, to the embattled town of San Miguel in the heart of contested guerilla territory. Visiting the main cathedral in that town, the Catholic priest, a Spaniard, explained how the army had built its military barracks right next to the cathedral, over the protest of the church, to give the townspeople the impression that the church supported the military's methods against the insurgents.

We visited several small villages in the embattled zone, talking to mayors, city councilmen, and visiting hospitals and schools. Such village leaders tended not to be fans of the Marxist guerrillas, but couldn't condone the harsh methods of the military which targeted innocent villagers. One day we left a village just as a column of FMLN guerrillas was entering from the other side of town.

Arnulfo Diaz

My last client at CARECEN was Arnulfo Diaz (his real name). Arnulfo had been a student activist in El Salvador. He and his fiancé had marched in one of the most notorious demonstrations in the history of the capitol city, in 1980, when, in full view of TV cameras, security forces fired on unarmed students, killing dozens. Arnulfo's fiancé died in his arms that day. Only weeks later, the Archbishop Oscar Romero was assassinated by a government hit squad.

Arnulfo fled into the hills, and after hiding out for several years he made his way to the United States. He was a witness to the kinds of abuses by Salvadoran security forces that the U.S. administration denied were occurring. Once in the U.S., he became an activist. With his Sanctuary movement counterparts, he made public presentations and toured the halls of Congress, speaking to anyone who would listen about the atrocities that he had witnessed, atrocities being paid for with American dollars.

By the time he became my client, he had already been denied asylum by the INS and was in deportation proceedings in Baltimore, where he had the right to re-apply for asylum before an immigration judge. By this time I had been with CARECEN for a year. I had represented hundreds of clients, and not a one of them had been granted asylum — the big lie was still on.

Immigration Judge John Gossart scheduled our hearing in the ceremonial courtroom in the federal district court building, because it was the only one large enough to accommodate the mob of supporters and reporters who had turned out to hear Arnulfo's case. At the first arraignment we discussed such housekeeping issues as presentation of witnesses and evidence, and reset the matter for the big day. After the hearing, I came out onto the steps of the courthouse, to be greeted by a camera crew from a local D.C. station, and I held forth in my first of two TV appearances in the case. Ironically, one of the members of the crew was a guy with whom I had frequently worked a decade earlier, Big John, when I was a free-lance TV news technician in D.C.

The second hearing, in December 1986, was one of those benchmarks in my life that helped shape my understanding of the government and guided my future course. Arnulfo lucked out in two ways – he drew Judge John Gossart as a judge, (Gossart retired from the bench in 2015) and Craig DeBernardis as the INS prosecutor in the case (DeBernardis was appointed to the immigration bench in 1995). Gossart was a hardnosed no-nonsense guy, but he was known to be fair, and so, even though every Salvadoran asylum case that I had been involved with had been denied, I was hoping that the strength of Arnulfo's case, in this particular judge's hands, just might have a different outcome. In addition to Arnulfo, we had one other witness – a staffer from Congressman Moakley's office who had been active with Moakley in trying to affect American policy in Central America and who had recently returned from a fact-finding trip to El Salvador. DeBernardis presented one witness in rebuttal – a Hispanic State Department attorney who had recently spent some time with the U.S. embassy in El Salvador.

When he took the witness stand, Moakley's aide was able to confirm the kinds of atrocities being committed by government troops that he had learned about first hand while in El Salvador. The State Department lawyer who was witness for the government really had nothing to contribute about the actual situation in El Salvador – in fact he confirmed, on cross-examination, that the embassy's human rights expert largely based his reports on news articles that appeared in the local Salvadoran press, and it was irrefutable that the press was heavily censored by the same military government that was committing the abuses. Otherwise, he tried to argue that the Salvadoran Constitution guarantees the right to life and liberty and freedom of speech — something which, as I pointed out in my closing, the Soviet Union's Constitution was also big on.

Arnulfo testified, in front of hundreds of spectators – the feeling in the courtroom was like being in a hushed church sermon — about the simple peasants in the countryside who were being butchered, in a replay of that Vietnam war era nightmare called Operation Phoenix. (U.S. military advisors were in fact on the ground training the Salvadoran military in the use of the same tactics that had brought infamy upon our military in Vietnam; they even called the program "Phoenix").

Something that Arnulfo left out of his testimony, and which I had only learned days after the court hearing, was that while hiding in the mountains of El Salvador, he had himself taken up arms with the FMLN guerrillas against the military. He never lied about it while he was under oath, because he was never asked a direct question "Were you ever a guerrilla yourself, or did you ever take up arms?" I warned him not to lie on the stand under oath – but it would obviously have blown his case if it had come out.

In a dramatic decision, Judge Gossart launched into a thirty-minute review of the evidence and the case law – keeping everyone on the edge of their seats in anticipation. Gossart is able to keep people in suspense, by taking them on a roller-coaster ride: one moment you think he's going to grant the case, the next moment you think he's going to deny. He goes over the pro's and con's, never revealing, until the very end, on which side he's actually going to come down.

In the end, he granted Arnulfo asylum – a decision that made headlines in the local TV and the Washington Post. When I came out of the courthouse with my client, I waited my turn, and once again was interviewed, this time as the victorious crusader. The news coverage showed Arnulfo at home with his family, playing guitar, enjoying a meal, a man whose salvation had finally come.

For a few days I was calling my friends and making sure they'd seen the TV coverage and basking in our victory. But it was a battle that never should have been necessary. It was only such a newsworthy item precisely because there *was* a government fix in, which began with lies and disinformation published by the State Department about the war in El Salvador, and ran all the way down to the lowly INS bureaucrat who was told by *somebody* that all of the Salvadoran and Guatemalan asylum cases should be denied because they were meritless.

(This was five years before the creation of a professional corps of asylum officers within INS, who receive professional training and have access to all the human rights reports for any given country).

The epilogue to the story: the INS prosecutor, Craig DeBernardis, who later became a judge, told me shortly after that hearing about a little investigation that he had conducted on his own. He confessed that he had felt uneasy about prosecuting the case, because Arnulfo's story really did ring true to him, and he was worried about his role in possibly sending someone back down to such a lawless country who could clearly be persecuted upon his return. It was clear to him that such a person, after having been a visible activist against that regime while in the U.S., would likely be targeted by death squads. He said that he had taken a personal leave day and traveled to D.C. to visit the head of the El Salvador desk at the State Department, in order to try and clarify for himself exactly what really *was* going on in El Salvador. And he told me that his conversation with that official had left him convinced that there *was* a problem with the quality of the information that was being disseminated by State, and he was not at all satisfied that he was doing the right thing by arguing in favor of Arnulfo's deportation.

Craig's description to me of his personal quest to learn the truth is one of those rare times in my entire career working with the federal government that I met someone who was willing to buck the system, in this case the 'official lie' and instead follow his own intellectual instinct and personal integrity in arriving at the truth. I can assure you that the system is built to discourage it. Going against the grain and ruffling the feathers of supervisors is not the way to win positive personnel reviews and promotions.

Iranian Asylum Cases

Over the years after my internship with Jan Pederson in her private practice, I continued to be involved with a number of very moving Iranian asylum cases, both as lawyer and judge. My immersion at Jan's office into the history and culture of Iran served as a strong foundation. During the eighties, Washington continued to be a hotbed of Iranian opposition politics, except that now the opposition was not to the Shah's regime but rather to that of the Mullahs. Taking my lunch breaks at Farragut Square, I would frequently see Iranian protest marchers disrupting lunch-hour traffic with their anti-Khomeini banners and loud bullhorns, on the way to the White House – just another Iranian rally.

At the George Washington law school immigration clinic, where I worked beginning in 1986, we represented many Iranian asylum clients, many of whom seemed to live in a cloud of paranoia. Our clients were sure that Khomeini's secret police were on the lookout, monitoring them at rallies, listening in on remarks they made during campus debates, and reporting back to the fundamentalist regime. And I received many indications that their paranoia was well-founded.

For an interesting case that illustrates this point, I recommend *Matter of Mogharrabi*, 19 I. & N. Dec. 439, 445 (BIA 1987). This was a case that originated in Washington during that period, and I knew the attorneys on both sides well. The Iranian student Mogharrabi went to the Iranian Interests Section at the Algerian Embassy, Iran's diplomatic outpost in D.C., when he needed to have his passport examined for renewed student benefits. The individual working behind the counter was another student, and the two engaged in a political argument, with Mogharrabi saying that the Mullahs were religious fascists stuffing their pockets with the nation's wealth, in response to which the embassy employee pulled a gun on Mogharrabi, who noticed multiple cameras on the walls. When he left the building, embassy employees pursued him to his car. This argument, tradition versus the mullahs, was everywhere in Washington within the Iranian expat community, with Iranians convinced that spies were following demonstration leaders to their cars and their homes, making lists for incarceration back in Iran.

Andrea's Story

One of my clients at the George Washington law school clinic was Andrea, a young woman who had been arrested and imprisoned in Tehran several times. In her last arrest, she was whipped in a public square before being imprisoned for a period of eight months, during which time she was brutally tortured. Her crime? Being seen in a car with a man who was not her relative and applying lipstick in public. When Revolutionary Guards later came to search her house, they found political tape recordings and other opposition literature.

Her brother was imprisoned and sentenced to death, but Andrea was finally able to escape from prison, with the assistance of bribes from her family. She fled across the border and out of the country, eventually making it to the U.S.

Andrea got married in Texas to an American, who turned out to be an abusive husband, and when she became pregnant with his child, he beat her until she lost the baby. She divorced him and moved from Texas to Washington, D.C., where she met a wonderful Iranian man, a car salesman who dedicated himself to becoming the stabilizing force in her life.

During the time she was with her abusive husband, she had picked up several shoplifting convictions, and had ultimately suffered a breakdown that required a period of hospitalization. This all made her case much more difficult, because even if she were eligible for asylum on the facts, because of fear of return to Iran, the judge could deny her case for discretionary reasons because of her criminal convictions.

The immigration judge in Arlington who handled the case was my old adversary, Craig DeBernardis, who had been an INS trial attorney in Baltimore. We had shared many cases together on opposite sides in the past. I was assisted in the case by my student Elizabeth Calderon, who later became a very fine immigration attorney in her own right, practicing in Florida. The INS trial attorney on the case was an inexperienced and insecure woman – just one of a parade of such INS attorneys who over the years mishandled cases I was involved in and who abused my clients on behalf of the Department of Justice.

I later obtained a copy of the transcript of the hearing, and the level of the judge's outrage at this inept INS prosecutor was so intense that I used to utilize the transcript as a teaching tool in my classes. Excerpts are included here.

Andrea took the stand and described in excruciating detail all of the things that had happened to her in Iran that had caused her to flee the country. The INS attorney, through lengthy, tortuous cross-examination, made Andrea relive over and over again her degradation at the hands of ruthless prison guards. In the course of a long, hot Friday afternoon, during which the court's air-conditioning broke down, Andrea responded to nit-picking questions, and also was forced to relate the details of her mental breakdown and her imprisonment in a Northern Virginia county jail for shoplifting.

In a case like this, after it became clear that Andrea's story was true, any reasonable attorney for the government should have withdrawn opposition to the case and let the judge enter his decision. Our opponent continued to fight the grant of asylum, which infuriated the judge. He took a break and demanded that her superior, the district counsel named Kevin Smith, come into court to defend the actions of his attorney. The district counsel, who later became an assistant chief immigration judge, came into court, took one look at the case, and bowed out, leaving his subordinate to swing in the breeze under the scathing abuse that the enraged judge heaped on her. I take the liberty of quoting at length from the transcript, a most unique literary work, to illustrate the ferocity of the judge's ire against the government attorneys. The quotes are the remarks of the judge.

"I explained to (government counsel) that in my opinion, not to stipulate with regard to (asylum) in a case such as this, where a woman in Iran has been accused of being a person of loose morals, where a person had been arrested in Iran, etc. — I frankly couldn't understand the position of the Government, and I asked (counsel) if she would be kind enough to ask the District Counsel to come to the courtroom." p. 23 of transcript. "Nobody wants to make a decision, nobody knows anything. This case here, the Government should have come in, the Government should have said, there's no issue (…) with regard to asylum. What does the Government expect to do here? Have every single case and every single possible issue in the case be litigated? I don't see how that benefits the Government. And I can tell you right now, that is not the way the trial attorney's office is supposed to work. The trial attorney is supposed to come here as a servant of justice. As a tool of the Attorney General of the United States to do the right thing. And in this case, when I look at these facts, I mean, how could anybody say that this lady's not been persecuted in Iran? How could somebody say that? I just don't understand it." p. 38 of transcript.

"Not every case is supposed to be opposed by the trial attorney's office. You guys should want to lose some cases. I mean, could you tolerate the idea that this lady could be sent back to Iran? Suppose you were able to convince me to do it. I mean, can you live with that? It's not my purpose to tell you people how to do business, but you know (…) what I find here is very disappointing to me. Everything is litigated. Everything is appealed. This is ridiculous. Just ridiculous. It's time to start making some decisions in the trial attorney's office." p. 39 of transcript.

The main argument that the INS attorney made, as to why Andrea should be denied asylum, was that she had merely been punished in Iran for a routine criminal offense, "powdering her nose in public" as she put it, and that it was therefore not persecution. In his decision, the judge cited at length the State Department's annual report on human rights practices in Iran, rubbing the government counsel's nose in the evidence: "Exhibit 8 in this record, the State Department's Country Report for Iran for 1989, states, and I quote,

'Iran continued in 1989 to be a major violator of human rights.' This is on page 1400. 'Abuses included summary executions of political opponents, widespread torture, repressions of the freedoms of speech, press, assembly, and association, arbitrary detentions, lack of fair trials, continuing repressions of the B'Hai religions community, denial of the right of citizens to change their government, and severe restrictions on women's and worker's rights. (…) I note that, because we have had to listen to the Government argue today that what the Iranian government did to the Respondent and her brother is not persecution; that such acts are consistent with the sovereign right of Iran. That's not what the United Nations says. That is not what the United States State Department says. 'Guards have threatened to torture family members of detainees, and relatives or other prisoners have occasionally been forced to watch torture. A number of prisoners, including young children, have been raped by revolutionary guards. . (…) Brutal common criminals have reportedly been introduced among political prisoners, and incited to torture and rape the other prisoners. (…) At page 1403 it says, 'The government rejects the western distinction between a public sphere, which the state may control, and a sphere of private life, religion, culture, thought, and private behavior, which the state may not properly control. We have had to listen today to the Immigration Service argue that for the state of Iran to impose these kinds of dress restrictions on women, and restrictions on how women could comport themselves in public, is just a matter of their internal sovereignty. That is not what the State Department says." p. 11-14 of trial transcript.

I have spent so much time with this case in these pages, because, in fact, it is not at all an unusual situation to find the government attorneys in such cases taking outrageous positions that are absurd in their posture, except that the results are devastating for the poor immigrants who don't have such a judge as Andrea was lucky enough to have, one who is not afraid to take a stand against such institutionalized idiocy. This judge had spent his entire career with INS, and yet could not contain his rage at the thought that Andrea might be shipped back to Iran. "I'll be frank with you. You're not doing it. It's not the point of the Government to come in here and oppose everything. Conduct three-hour cross-examinations that don't lead anywhere, that keep it so that we can't get any work done here. It's not the position of the Government to come in on a case like this and have no opinion." p. 40 of transcript.

That afternoon, during several court recesses, I noticed in the hallway that two men in "suits" were lingering about, as if they had nothing better to do. I took little notice of them, but something in the back of my mind was trying to tell me that all was not right.

Finally, at five p.m. on that Friday afternoon, the judge granted the case for asylum. We were all physically and emotionally exhausted. Andrea would be able to go home and celebrate with her new family, and relax for the first time in years with the knowledge that she was in no danger of being deported. Her husband had waited the whole time in the hallway. We went to the elevator, in a celebratory mood, and got on when the doors opened. I was congratulating the two of them, when the two men in the suits got on with us, and as the doors closed they pulled badges. They placed my client under arrest for an outstanding warrant from the Northern Virginia criminal court. The allegation was that she had not paid a court-ordered fine after her last shoplifting conviction. Their presence was clearly the result of that INS attorney having made a call to their office.

Because it was Friday afternoon, and the courts were already closed, Andrea had to spend the weekend in jail. I visited her in jail on Saturday and heard the whole story. Yes, it was true she had been ordered to pay a fine, and she had given the money to her criminal defense attorney to pay it. Well, guess what? The attorney had never paid the court!

On Monday, in front of the original sentencing judge, she was able to produce a receipt that she had paid the money to her attorney, and the matter was dismissed. (She was later able to reach a settlement in an action against that attorney for his bungling and/or fraud in the case).

Ms. Voegel's Story

Years later, when I was a judge, I continued to see Iranian cases from time to time in my courtroom. One of the most incredible examples of mule-headed intransigence on the part of the INS attorney that I saw was the case of a poor woman who I'll call Ms. Voegel. She had been granted asylum from Iran in the U.S. years earlier, and had married an American citizen with whom she had several children together. Tragically, she fell victim to the disease of schizophrenia. When she went too long without her medication, she tended to commit petty crimes, which is how she got into trouble with INS and ended up in my courtroom – actually very similar to Andrea's story in the way the process worked.

The nature of her disease was that she would become particularly aggressive and anti-social if she went unmedicated, flinging verbal assaults and obscenities in all directions. On several occasions, when making appearances in front of me for short procedural matters, she started spitting out invectives, as if deliberately trying to antagonize me. Other times, she would sit quietly, staring in my direction as though she were giving me the evil eye. Even though she had a family that wanted to support her, and she was able to obtain the pro-bono services of a very capable attorney, the INS insisted on going forward on charges of deportability, actually trying to get an order to send the poor woman back to Iran.

In our hearing, her attorney presented strong evidence that in Iran, a woman with Andrea's condition would surely be detained and tortured in prison for the kind of behavior that she was exhibiting here, which included taunting the guards with sexual innuendo (that kind of thing would be considered an expression of loose sexual morals). A female Iranian psychiatrist testified for the defense that the state of the art of psychiatric services for such a person in Iran was still somewhere in the Medieval era. That witness clinched the case for me.

I felt that I had heard enough and that Ms. Voegel certainly was worthy of a renewal of a grant of asylum. After all, Iran was now designated by our Commander-in-Chief George W. Bush as part of an 'Axis of Evil.' I granted the case, happy to do the right thing, and reflecting on my experience as a student intern twenty years earlier, when Jan Pederson had taught me about Iranian asylum cases. But the government lawyers didn't see it that way. They appealed the case, keeping the poor woman locked up and separated from her family for additional needless months until the appeals court finally affirmed my decision.

I saw two other Iranian cases as a judge in which the asylum applicant had converted from Islam to Christianity — a crime under Islam called apostasy. The Koran authorizes any devout Muslim to take matters into his own hands and punish someone who has committed the crime of abandoning Islam for another religion. And our own State Department Country Reports make it clear that in Iran the crime of apostasy is likely to be punished by death. Nevertheless, in cases where the evidence was abundantly clear that the Iranian applicant had indeed become a practicing Christian – cases where the evidence included a parade of church members as witnesses – the INS attorneys had the gall to argue, with straight faces, that I should exercise my power as judge and order the individuals deported back to Iran. I could only wonder how they slept at night.

The George Washington Law School Immigration Clinic

In August 1986 I began my new job as director of the immigration law clinic at George Washington University Law School, replacing Richard Boswell in that position. He has been a professor and clinical director at Hastings School of Law in San Francisco for the past thirty years.

During the ten years that I directed the clinic at G.W., we were the only non-profit in Washington, D.C. that would represent so-called "criminal aliens" – migrants who are facing deportation because of criminal convictions. And we were the only ones who would assist migrants with mental problems who were housed in St. Elizabeth's hospital. This in addition to representing as many indigent migrants as possible who were unable to pay a private attorney and were in deportation proceedings.

The hospital, or St E's as it is affectionately called by staff, is famous for housing several notorious nut cases like John Hinckley, President Reagan's would-be assassin, and the poet Ezra Pound after his post-WWII conviction for treason. The hospital also served as the nation's holding cell for migrants and immigrants who were in custody for deportation hearings and who, during their detention, might begin to display signs of mental illness. They would be shipped to the hospital from all around the country for evaluation, where they would then remain while their deport hearing was concluded in the Washington immigration court, located in Northern Virginia. They were invariably penniless and without counsel.

I established a relationship with the social workers at the hospital, and they would inform me whenever a new arrival needed a screening for possible representation. Then I would drive with a couple of students across the Anacostia River to the campus of the hospital, which was set up on an attractive location overlooking the river. Our clients were held in an aging brick building with cobblestone floors in the basements. (This campus will supposedly house Department of Homeland Security headquarters in the near future).

These unfortunates included such mentally disturbed patients as Jose Barsey Duran from the Dominican Republic, who heard God speaking to him and had carved a cross on his forehead to demonstrate his devotion to the Lord. When I was preparing him for his deportation hearing, he told me that God periodically spoke to him. Being naturally curious, I asked him, "And what does he say when he speaks to you?" In a straight voice he answered, "He says not to play with myself and not to eat the pussy."

Although I could appreciate those words of wisdom from the Higher Power, I admonished him to be sure not to tell the judge the words that God spoke to him. Later when we had our hearing before a matronly female judge, I carefully avoided that topic on direct examination. However, the judge herself was curious about what it was that God said to my client, and had to ask him the question, "What does God say to you?" I could only stare at the papers in front of me while he matter-of-factly answered her question.

My Swiss-German client Hans Dieter had a bizarre way of expressing his disorientation. He had escaped from a Swiss mental institution, made his way to Germany, and somehow gotten on a boat that brought him to America. After a year of bumming around the northeast, he entered into Canada, where the Royal Canadian Mounties found him passed-out alongside a highway. When they learned that he had recently crossed the border from the States, they placed him back across the border, and he was detained by U.S. Customs officials and sent to St. E's.

During his period of incarceration at the hospital he had managed to avoid serious evaluation by his captors, pretending that he only spoke German. I could communicate with him in German and I was able to get him to loosen up and tell me what was really on his mind. While talking, he had a fascinating tendency to slowly move and distort his limbs, lifting one leg and wrapping it around his body, putting one arm behind his body and balancing on it, slowly twisting himself into a pretzel, the whole time maintaining steady eye contact and speaking as if nothing odd were happening. I saw him go through this ritual several times.

He was convinced he had been abducted by aliens in Canada. He said he hadn't even meant to enter Canada, but rather had blacked out somewhere in Vermont, and when he came to he was in Canada.

"So that's your proof that you were abducted by aliens?"

"Yes, and because after I woke up, one leg was shorter than the other."

He wanted me to help him to apply for asylum as protection from the space aliens. On my third visit he confided in me that he expected, after being granted asylum, to be put up in an apartment and to be provided for by the State. He thought the conditions were too harsh in the Swiss hospital where he had last been incarcerated, and life should be easy in the U.S. living on the dole as a mental patient. I had to correct his misimpression that the U.S. was happy to just take in and provide for every foreign mental patient that came along. I assured him that there was no provision for the government to provide food and board for anyone, even if they *were* granted asylum, except of course should he remain incarcerated at the hospital, and that in my expert opinion his case was very weak, that the government wanted to deport him back to Switzerland, and that I couldn't imagine any immigration judge granting him asylum protection from the aliens.

After several such heart to heart talks in German, he decided to abandon the façade that he couldn't speak English and was willing to communicate with the doctor and nurses, and on his next court date I informed the judge that Hans Dieter had decided to return to Switzerland, where he felt the food was more agreeable than that provided by St. E's.

I will always remember with fondness the career INS officer who was the supervisor of the immigrant detention unit at St. Elizabeths, Officer Richard Curtis. In my mind he represented the most positive attributes of the INS uniformed services. He had begun his career as a Border Patrol officer in San Diego. He treated his wards with dignity and compassion. On the rare occasion that we actually won a case involving one of his customers, he celebrated with us, delighted that the individual had gotten a fair shake and would be leaving the hospital.

My law clinic students and I appeared in immigration court and at the INS asylum office regularly, representing clients from all parts of Africa, Central America, and Eastern Europe, with a few Asians thrown in.

In addition to my full-time contractual duties of managing the immigration clinic, I also taught the law school's immigration law course, and I created and taught a graduate-level seminar on international refugee law. I felt it essential for my clinic students that they be exposed to the best possible overview of asylum and immigration law. Attendance in the immigration law course was a prerequisite for enrollment in the clinic.

In today's environment of clinical law teaching it is customary for a clinical director to supervise 5-7 students per semester, with a post-grad faculty member to help out, and with each student usually sharing a client, so that the professor might only be responsible for 5-10 clients during one semester. I saw my role much differently – we were an important social service to the community, and if not for us, so many undocumented migrants who were in distress would have had no one at all to assist them, especially during those turbulent years of the 80s when the city was flooded with Central American refugees. In my way of thinking, the best way for students to learn was for them to be exposed to as many clients as possible. This meant that I was often in court five times a week, and managing a dozen students a semester, each with a load of five or more clients apiece, so that I was overseeing sixty or more active cases per semester. Immigration cases can tend to drag on in the system for years, so that our overall case load and the number of clients I was individually responsible for grew into the hundreds. But that was the responsibility that I accepted, and I loved the challenge and diversity.

Ethiopia

The feudalist rule of Emperor Haile Selassie was brought down by a council of Marxist-leaning military officers in 1974. The resulting brutal dictatorship under the rule of Mengistu Haile Mariam became more and more repressive, until the days of the so-called Red Terror in the mid-seventies, when thousands of regime opponents, especially college students, were rounded up and tortured. Through a strange historical twist of fate, the city of Washington, D.C. became host to the largest population of Ethiopians outside of Africa. By the end of the 1980's and into the 90's, the majority of my immigration clinic's caseload were Ethiopian and Somali clients.

Ayalew

Ayalew Agonafer was at first one of our clients, who then became an employee of the clinic and my friend. Ayalew is a handsome man with a slight build, very soft-spoken, who had been a high-ranking official in the Ethiopian government's Ministry of Tourism. He remained in his position after the communists came into power. But he found himself in disfavor over the issue of the *Falasha* Jews in northern Ethiopia.

The name Falasha is Amharic for "exiles" or "landless ones"; the so-called Falasha disdain the name themselves, and refer to themselves as *Beta Esrael* ("House of Israel"). There were between 30-40 thousand Falasha living in northern Ethiopia before the Israeli government agreed to receive them. Ethiopia initially agreed to allow their exodus from the Horn of Africa to the Promised Land. About 12,000 Falashas were airlifted to Israel in late 1984 and early 1985 under the Israeli program, "Operation Moses," and then, for whatever reason, the Ethiopian government halted the airlifts. They resumed in 1989, when about 3500 Falashas emigrated to Israel. Another 14,000 Falashas, practically the rest of the population, were removed with the secret assistance of the U.S. government's "Operation Sheba" program in 1991. When I visited Ethiopia in 1992, I saw a village outside of the northern city of Gondar where the Falasha had recently lived, but the villages were largely depopulated. Some of the simple mud-walled homes had the Star of David inscribed on the walls. (For a Hollywood treatment of this history, see The Red Sea Diving Resort, staring Chris Evans).

In 1986, while still with the Ministry of Tourism, Ayalew had been assigned to accompany a National Geographic reporter to the city of Gondar, one of the fascinating cross-roads of Christianity and Islam in Ethiopia. The reporter surreptitiously did a report about the Falashas in Gondar. At the time, the remaining Falasha population was doing everything it could to depart the country for Israel. The communist government felt that any publicity about that issue was bad press for the government, and anyone involved in disseminating such information, like Ayalew by implication, must be a bad person and an enemy of the State. Thus did Ayalew come under the uncomfortable scrutiny of communist interrogators. He was questioned several times about his complicity with the National Geo reporter, and when he realized that things could get much worse for him, he high-tailed it out of the country, leaving behind twenty years of a distinguished career.

By the time I met Ayalew, he had already applied for asylum and had been denied by the INS officer (there was no official asylum officer corps at that time). He had been routinely placed into deportation proceedings, and our clinic agreed to represent him at his deportation asylum hearing. He had a very strong case and I was optimistic about the outcome. His hearing was scheduled for a day in December when all of the students were out on winter break, so I handled his hearing by myself.

Unfortunately for everyone, an out-of-town judge was assigned to our case at short notice to fill in for a local judge. The judge was in town for two weeks, and he made everyone's life miserable. He was want to abuse and enrage the government trial attorneys as well as the attorneys for the migrants, and he had a special knack for treating the poor respondents who came before him with utmost contempt and indignity. And that was how our hearing progressed. The judge's conduct of the case was an outrage and an offense to the U.S. government and the Department of Justice. After a three hour screaming match, with the judge doing all the screaming, he denied the application for asylum and ordered Ayalew to be deported. Then, incredibly, in passing in the hallway, he said to me, "Don't worry, you'll win on appeal."

Poor Ayalew told me afterwards that the trial had been worse than what he had experienced at the hands of his communist interrogators. The INS trial attorney, a young woman with whom I had a good working relationship, approached me afterwards, personally apologized for the way that Ayalew had been treated, and offered to join in a motion to reopen the case. Rather than us having to take an appeal, which in those times could easily have lasted years, we could have the matter back before one of the regular Arlington judges and approved within a matter of months. And that is what happened.

Later, when I was a judge, I heard from a very good authority that the abusive judge in Ayalew's case had obtained his position as a judge because, when he was an attorney in the Department of Justice, he had made the lives of others around him, including his superiors, so miserable that he had been promoted to the IJ slot to get him out of the office. That's politics for you. That judge finally retired from the Chicago court more than twenty years after Ayalew's hearing.

In 1992 I traveled to Ethiopia because my curiosity about the country had been building since taking on so many Ethiopian clients. I had planned to travel the year before, but then the Tigrean and Eritrean guerrillas were able to sweep into Addis Ababa and force Mengistu from power, so everything was a bit too unstable to make the trip that year. So I went when the feeling of triumph and hope was in the air.

I traveled to the source of the Blue Nile in Bahar Dar. I hiked to the second largest waterfall in Africa, Tissisat Falls, just downstream from the source of the Blue Nile. I spent a few days in the amazing northern town of Gondar, where Christians and Moslems have lived peacefully together for centuries. And I met the monk in the dusty town of Axum who supposedly guards over the Ark of the Covenant. Orthodox Ethiopians believe that the Queen of Sheba was originally from Ethiopia, and that when she returned to their country from Jerusalem, she brought the Ark of the Covenant with her. (See the book, The Sign and the Seal: the Quest for the Lost Ark of the Covenant, by Graham Hancock, for a fascinating but extremely tenuous development of this theory.)

I must say that I was traumatized by the extent of the poverty I encountered in Ethiopia. That may sound self-evident for seasoned Africa travelers, but although I had previously traveled and worked extensively in Central and South America, I wasn't prepared for the level of desperation that I would find in Ethiopia.

During my visit, I was assisted by the family of one of my clients in Washington for whom I had obtained asylum. They were very helpful in making arrangements for me, and I was delighted to dine at their Western-style ranch home in the upscale neighborhood close to the airport in Addis. I met their college-age son, who was applying for a visitor's visa to come to the U.S. Shortly after I returned to the U.S., he was able to come, and he contacted me in Washington. That was when he revealed to me that the family was expecting that I would file his case for asylum in the States as a return favor for their assistance while I was in Ethiopia.

The problem was that I was very familiar with his situation in Ethiopia, and I therefore knew that he had no real problems with the government by remaining in Ethiopia. His family ran a profitable coffee export business, which I had visited, and he helped out there. I told him that I couldn't fabricate a story, and that therefore I couldn't help him with his asylum application. He got the message, and found a local Ethiopian lawyer in Washington who practiced immigration law and was willing to fabricate a story for the right fee.

Shortly thereafter, I also had a visit at the clinic from a young Ethiopian woman who had worked as a staffer at the U.S. embassy in Addis Ababa for several years. I had visited the embassy while I was there, and I knew her working conditions, and I also knew that she had absolutely no case for asylum – in fact, if she admitted to an asylum officer that she had worked at the embassy, it would have led to an automatic denial of her case, because our officials at the embassy would have confirmed that she really had no serious problems that caused her to flee. The only way she had a chance of being granted asylum was by completely concealing the fact that she had ever worked at the embassy. The same thing happened as with the family friend – I told her that I couldn't help her fabricate a story, and she found another Ethiopian lawyer who was more than happy to do it for her.

Exactly 20 years after my visit there, in 2011 I was able to return to Ethiopia to assist with the U.S. government's refugee resettlement program, interviewing Eritrean refugees in Axum and Somali refugees in Dire Dawa. Unfortunately the Horn of Africa is still one of the largest producers of refugees in the world.

Sarah

Toward the end of my tenure at the clinic I was involved in one of the most heart-breaking cases of my career. Sarah was a lovely Ethiopian woman in her mid-twenties who had been traumatized by her communist torturers. During the Mengistu regime, the threat of rape and the infliction of rape upon political prisoners, as a method of interrogation, was common. Sarah was clearly suffering from Post Traumatic Stress Disorder (PTSD) as a result of repeated rapes by her prison guards. When she became our client, she was in therapy and barely able to function. She had been a college student when she was arrested by security officials and accused of being a member of an opposition cell. It was the torturers' methodology to isolate a victim, and over a period of time, to extract confessions, usually fabricated, about their anti-government activities and membership in opposition groups. Under torture, the victim would give up a list of names of other supposed members, who could then be rounded up and tortured in the same way, thus providing an endless list of victims for the torture machine.

When we represented Sarah, it was still a novel theory to argue Post Traumatic Stress Disorder in an asylum hearing. With some victims of torture it was often necessary to make that argument, because otherwise their method of testifying would seem completely incredible – many such victims testify in an emotionless monotone, or "reduced affect," and the unschooled adjudicator might assume that the whole story is fabricated, because they just don't sound convincing. Shouldn't they be acting very emotional if these horrible things really happened to them? Especially difficult was the hurdle of proving, through an expert, that the applicant was actually suffering from PTSD, that the condition had been induced by the abuse alleged by the victim, and that the abuse had been inflicted for political reasons. Establishing credibility of the client was particularly tough, because the last thing such a victim of torture wanted to do was to testify and relive the events in open court.

The timing was good for us, in that right when we were preparing Sarah's case I was contacted by a staff member of the George Washington University Hospital, Jenny, a psychiatric nurse with a background in PTSD, who was looking for an opportunity to help out on one of our pro bono cases. She would gladly appear in court as a witness. Jenny had learned about PTSD through her work over the years with dozens of Vietnam vets. She met many times with Sarah, evaluating her and preparing a medical report about Sarah's condition for inclusion in the hearing.

The female judge at the hearing was clearly impressed by our expert witness, listening attentively and taking copious notes, asking for clarification of certain points. It was the first time that a medical professional had been presented in the Arlington immigration court on a case involving PTSD. I knew this judge quite well, having had years of experience working with her on immigration cases. I had noticed a pattern over the years, that she was inclined to be much more impressed by a witness from the professional class than by a common blue-collar type of witness. I was therefore hopeful that the witness was persuasive enough to carry the day for Sarah.

After our expert witness had testified, Sarah took the stand, relating at length the horror story of the numerous rapes she had endured in prison, speaking in a soft, shaky voice, looking at me and my student for reassurance from time to time. When her hour-long testimony was finished, she was damp as a rag, her clothes soaking with sweat. But she had done what she needed to do – she had gotten her story out so that it could be preserved for the record.

At the end of it all, the female judge ruled that, even if our client had been abused as she claimed, it had not been for political motives, but simply because men are apt to act like beasts. Therefore, she reasoned, Sarah had not been persecuted on account of any of the five protected grounds. She denied the asylum case. The two female students who had worked on the case with me couldn't believe their ears, but by then I was accustomed to such miscarriages of justice in immigration court. Poor Sarah was devastated.

We were able to perfect a strong appeal, and then I referred the case to my good friend and former student, Jeffrey Kantor, who, upon graduating, had entered immigration practice in Arlington. He became custodian of the appeal, because by that time I had left the clinic. The appeal took over five years to be decided by the Board of Immigration Appeals.

Poor Sarah's life was put on hold. She continued her therapy, worked a secretarial job, and lived in constant uncertainty about whether she might at any moment be sent back to Ethiopia – the worse possible situation for a victim of PTSD to be in. She tracked me around the country, keeping in touch with me when I moved to Philly and again when I moved to San Francisco. One day, when I came off the bench after a particularly frustrating case in San Francisco, my clerk Mai told me there was a call for me. When I picked up the phone I heard Sarah's soft voice on the line, "Hello Professor Paul...," telling me the good news that the BIA had granted her appeal and approved her application for asylum.

Several years after Sarah's deportation hearing, when I had become a judge, one of the conference presenters at the immigration judges' annual conference was a specialist in cultural sensitivity issues. He spoke on such court-related topics as how to recognize when a problem with a witness's testimony is due to cultural confusion. I had lunch that same day with the judge who had denied Sarah's case. This particular judge was notorious in our profession for her lacking of any cultural sensitivity. After having heard our speaker, she mused out loud, "I wonder if I've been culturally insensitive?" I felt like responding, "Does a horse have a big ass?" But I bit my tongue. Ten years later, the same judge continued to make headlines with her embarrassingly blind and insensitive behavior that shocked the conscience.

One of the themes of this book is that such incredibly inept, culturally insensitive, and actually harmful judges should not be allowed to "torture" people (an apt and legally correct use of the term) in their courtrooms, with no oversight or censor from management. It would be easy to appoint a neutral panel of experts to investigate such cases. To allow such an unfit person to exercise the power of life or death over foreigners in our immigration courts makes a mockery of the system, and is a perversion of justice, even while we as a nation are trying to export the rule of law overseas.

Mafia Pizza Connection Case

One day in the fall of 1990 I was at immigration court, representing one of the clinic's clients, when the court clerk pointed out a young man in the waiting area and told me that he needed a lawyer. I was always trolling for interesting clients for the clinic, so I approached him and asked him what his story was.

"I don't need a lawyer. They can't deport me, I'm an American citizen!"

So began my working relationship with Frank, the son of a convicted mobster. Frank's Sicilian family had owned and operated a pizza parlor, located only blocks away from the law school and the White House. Several of his family members had been convicted in the notorious "Pizza Connection" case, a Ricco conspiracy case put together by the feds in many cities on the Eastern Seaboard. But the idea of Sicilian mobsters operating in Washington, D.C. was a novelty. Usually Congress had a monopoly on graft and corruption in the capitol city.

Frank had been convicted of the extremely minimal offenses of using a telephone to further a narcotics transaction (the telephone in the family's pizza parlor) and of misuse of prescription drugs. He had served a few months in prison, and he still had several years of supervised parole to complete. But his father, who had been convicted of a more serious cocaine trafficking offense, was serving time in Allenwood Penitentiary in Deerwood, Pennsylvania — a place that I would become familiar with later, when I made appearances there as an immigration judge. Frank was convinced that he was a U.S. citizen, and that all he had to do was explain it to the judge and his deportation case would be dismissed. Frank was wrong on both counts.

I took a look at the immigration court charging papers, and immediately realized that, first of all, Frank was seriously self-delusional about his immunity in this case, and second, that it would be a fun case for the clinic to handle. It became clear that Frank, who was married to an undocumented Guatamalan woman, really didn't have the funds to hire a lawyer, given everything that his family had already been through with the U.S. Attorney's Office. I accepted Frank as a client, and he accepted the clinic as his legal representative, and we were off. Months later, when all the dust had settled, I realized how much, this time, I had misunderstood my client and consequently how I had really let him down.

Frank was a character. He was good-looking in the same way that any of the minor characters on the TV series The Sopranos are attractive; slightly built, about five feet eight inches tall, he swaggered rather than walked. He was full of bluster and bravado that made him extremely irritating to deal with, because he generally refused to listen, even when it was in his self-interest to do so, such as when I was trying to explain to him what his legal case was all about.

He claimed that he was subject to panic attacks, and so he had been prescribed pharmaceuticals to help him deal with them. It was such prescriptions that he had alledgedly abused, by writing scrips when he was too impatient to wait for his doctor to fill the orders for him. His consistently irritating manner was such that I would often say to myself, "This person is an asshole. He's too stupid to know what's good for him. But he's my client, and I'm duty-sworn to provide the best in legal service that I can."

Counterbalancing Frank's ever-present macho bluster, was his sincerely sweet and caring Guatamalan wife, and her little Guatamalan daughter, whom Frank had accepted as his own. She really had his best interests at heart. Unfortunately, because she was undocumented, she could not be of any legal assistance to him in his deportation case, other than to be a character witness for him.

Franks' misunderstanding about his citizenship status was not at all unique in immigration law circles. There are many people who immigrate to the U.S. at an early age, and then go through life just assuming that everything is all right and that they must indeed be

U.S. citizens. In Frank's case, first of all, he had been treated like a citizen most of his life. His parents had become citizens of the U.S. after immigrating to New York from Sicily. He had immigrated with them as a small child.

Under the law, if either of them became a U.S. citizen when he, as a lawful permanent resident, was under the age of 18, he also automatically became a U.S. citizen. The difficulty with his case was that his parents had separated before his 18th birthday, and then it came down to a legal argument as to which parent actually had custody over him and whether that parent had naturalized before his 18th birthday. And that was not an issue that the immigration judge could decide. A judge could only decide to go ahead with the deportation hearing, if Frank could not himself prove that he *was* a citizen. It would take a federal judge in U.S. District Court to make a ruling that overcame the INS charge that Frank was not a citizen, and we immediately launched into action to try to gather the evidence to go into federal court. But we were ultimately unable to prove that, when his parents divorced, his mother, who naturalized first while Frank was still under 18 years of age, had custody of him at the time that she naturalized. Thus, we would have to put on a deportation defense in court. (Years later the law was changed so that it would not have mattered which parent had custody as long as one of them had naturalized – but too late to help Frank).

I assigned a student to work on Frank's 212(c) waiver case. Section 212(c) of the immigration law allowed someone like Frank, with a serious conviction, even a drug-trafficking conviction, to be allowed to remain in the U.S. The immigration judge would look at the relative serious nature of the conviction, and balance it against such elements as Frank's family ties, work history, education, hardship to family if he was to be deported – the so-called equities of the case.

I thought that Frank should have a good chance of succeeding in his 212(c) waiver hearing. First of all, his convictions were relatively minor, even pathetic compared with some of the more serious offenses we routinely saw in court. (Indeed, I had prevailed in a 212(c) waiver case in which my Portuguese client had been convicted of murder of his wife, winning the case and allowing him to remain in the U.S. as a permanent resident). Secondly, Frank's wife would be a really great witness for him. And Frank had drawn Judge Paul Nejelski, one of the most reasonable judges I had ever dealt with, with the caveat that Nejelski tended to be tough on crime, or upon immigrants in his courtroom who had been convicted of serious crimes. The worst thing about Frank's case was Frank himself – he refused to take the possibility of his imminent deportation seriously.

We worked with Frank and his wife for a year. When he had an appointment to see us in the clinic alone, he either came late — which made it very difficult for a student who had a tight class schedule to meet with him — or he even cancelled at the last minute. His wife, in contrast, was always very punctual and conciliatory. Frank always displayed a serious attitude problem, which made him difficult to work with, but I stuck with him for a number of reasons: he had already paid the price for what I considered a nuisance crime by serving time in prison; I didn't think he should be deported for such an offense, if not for his sake, at least for his wife and child's; and we had a potentially good case, if Frank would just wise up and understand the jeopardy that he was in. His attitude was always, "What am

I doin' here? They can't deport me, I'm a citizen. I didn' do nothin' wrong."

One of the problems with the case was the conviction for abuse of prescription pills. I knew that the judge would want to hear all about the background to the abuse, and want to hear about how Frank had reformed. A client's ability to repent and explain how (s)he had constructed a road map for a new life was an important ingredient of such a 212(c) waiver case. Frank's problem was that he hadn't reformed and, like Mozart's Don Giovani, was unlikely to repent even if the Devil was standing over him, with the hell fires opening up, giving him one last chance.

Frank explained that he was subject to panic attacks, and that he needed the pharmaceuticals to control them. We obtained medical documentation from his therapist, who was able to enlighten the court as to the background of Frank's panic disorder. Still, because of Frank's reluctance to talk about it, and his overwhelming macho veneer, I found it hard to take the whole panic attack thing seriously, which was my mistake, and ultimately my failure to Frank.

The day of the hearing. My student, Chris Belvedere, has spent the past forty-eight hours virtually without sleep, preparing the arguments, going over the testimony again and again, with input and modifications from myself, and basically stressing out over one of the most important events in his life so far: a real trial with someone's future at stake. In fact it was three people's future; Frank's wife was pending the ability to immigrate based upon Frank's petition, as a lawful permanent resident, for her. But if Frank were to be ordered deported, than he would no longer have standing to petition for her, and she and her little girl would be unlawfully in the country, with no legal right to remain. Then the choice would become – Sicily or Guatemala?

We had three witnesses to present: the therapist, who could only make a telephonic appearance; Frank's wife, Gloria; and Frank. We decided to take them in that order, in part because the therapist was only available in the first time slot. Then, we would put on Gloria. That way, she could provide sympathy, painting Frank in a good light for the judge, and, after her testimony, she would be able to remain in the courtroom, where she could serve as an important emotional support for Frank. And finally, it would be Frank's turn to perform.

The therapist, as it turned out, was not a great witness. He seemed too emotionally detached from Frank, almost as though he was just showing up to earn his salary whenever he met with Frank. But at least he laid the groundwork for the judge about Frank's manic-depressive swings, and clarified for the judge that the prescription drugs were not the type that your average drug abuser would be taking. Rather, Frank's alleged misuse of the drugs had come about through his natural inclination to cut corners and obtain the drugs in any way that he saw fit, which included, when his therapist was out of town, forging prescriptions with the doctor's signature on them. But the therapist made it clear that Frank was not a narcotics substance abuser – he was just a schmuck.

Gloria was wonderful on the stand, and the judge warmed to her. Unfortunately, under the law, since she had no lawful status in the U.S., the judge could not give much weight to her situation, and he could not even technically consider the consequences of her and her daughter being deported, should Frank not prevail in his case. Rather,

Gloria could only do her best to paint Frank in as positive a light as possible, and throw some natural human sympathy into the case.

Frank. He remained Frank to the end. In his own words, he had done nothing wrong. Sure, he had worked in that pizza place, and maybe on a few occasions he had delivered some messages on the phone that he knew he shouldn't be doing, but he hadn't profited from his activity, and look, now the feds had his father locked up far away from home, he was unemployed, and the whole world was ganging up on him. What did he do, after all? "And by the way, aren't I supposed to be a U.S. citizen?"

This is not the way we had prepped him, naturally, and it shows more of the substance of what leaked through between the lines; his attitude of self-delusional bluster mixed with contempt for the proceedings. And there was something else that the judge didn't appreciate: Frank also didn't have much respect for me or my student. For my part, I was quite accustomed to that kind of attitude coming from clients on occasion; anyone who has worked with criminal defendants knows the score. I was committed to Frank in spite of himself. But the judge got ticked off, because my clinic, and the work I did with the students, and particularly the contribution of the students themselves, was held in very high esteem at the immigration court. For the judge, Frank's attitude on the stand demonstrated a disrespect for all of the hard work we had put into his case, and perhaps, if Frank was too dumb to appreciate what we were doing for him, he was also too dumb to deserve a second chance. I am only speculating from what I observed of the judge's demeanor during Frank's testimony, but I had been working with this judge a long time and thought I understood him reasonably well.

Finally, at one point during the testimony, the judge made a remark that communicated his attitude, namely the likelihood that he was going to order Frank deported. "Will life really be so tough when you go back to Sicily?" What followed next changed my feeling completely about my client, but I realized at the same time that it was too late; I had failed him.

When Frank picked up on where the judge was going with his fate, from that last question, he suddenly regressed into a panic attack. It was as complete a transformation as I have ever witnessed in a courtroom. He went from junior Sicilian mobster bluster, to terrified, helpless baby. He turned as pale as a ghost, began shaking and sweating profusely. Everyone in that courtroom saw the transformation and realized what all of the other macho bullshit was meant to disguise: the man was a scared child.

Unfortunately, the judge was not sympathetic. But I realized, suddenly, why all the years of prescription drug abuse. This man really needed his meds. Up until that moment, only his wife Gloria had realized the real depth of his disorder. I had not comprehended it. My client had needed me to understand, but I had allowed his attitude to put me off. If I had recognized earlier what I finally did on the day of his trail – and I only finally saw the truth because Frank's fear and panic was so loud and clear at that moment — I would have spent a lot more time working with him, breaking down his resistance to cooperating with us, helping to overcome his contempt for the system. Again, this would have been not necessarily so much for his own sake, but for that of the family. The family needed to stay together in America. But I had failed him.

The judge was clearly afraid of my client, even though Frank was completely harmless. He was unsure whether Frank would be able to keep his cool when the bad news was delivered. He told us that we could all go home and "enjoy" lunch, and he would call us at the clinic with the decision to be delivered over the phone. I knew exactly what that meant, because I had seen Nejelski do it a couple of times in the past when he was dealing with violent offenders. He was going to deny the case, and didn't want the bad guy to be anywhere near, in case he decided to take it out on the judge. (The immigration courts didn't and still don't have bailiffs for non-detained respondents). Even though I knew that Frank was a pussycat, the judge hadn't gotten the point.

My prediction proved to be true. After lunch, at the clinic office, my student and I took the judge's call. We received his decision, over the speaker phone, to deport my client. Of course we could appeal, and we did, but given what we had to work with, it was an impossibly high mountain to climb. We had needed to win Frank's case at the trial level.

Incidentally, my student in that case, Chris Belvedere, after graduation became one of the first asylum officers in the new system that was established in 1991, and went on to enjoy a brilliant career as an attorney at the Board of Immigration Appeals.

Living In Adams Morgan

For most of the time that I worked at the G.W. clinic I lived in a one-bedroom apartment in a ninety-year old building in the Adams Morgan neighborhood, at the intersection of Kalorama Street and 20th, facing Kalorama park. It's my favorite neighborhood in Washington, a wonderful eclectic mix of Hispanic, African-American, students and hipsters… The 18th Street – Columbia Rd triangle features club after restaurant after club, and the residential side streets boast leafy old trees and well-tended gardens in front of historic brownstones and apartment buildings.

The neighborhood was in transition. When I first moved into the

2nd story apartment, I would occasionally hear gun fire coming from the park just across the street at night. And sidewalk robberies of people coming home from work at the end of the day weren't uncommon. But over the years things changed in favor of stability and security.

I could enjoy the experience of sitting outside at one of my favorite restaurants in the early evening, and every so often one of my clients or former clients would walk by with a warm greeting and big smile on his/her face for their immigration lawyer, a real affirmation for me!

On the weekend, when the college and professional crowds are out in force to enjoy the sidewalk action, you can hear live music coming out of every third or fourth doorway, from jazz to R&B to hip-hop to African rhythms. After 1997, when I was appointed to be an immigration judge and I had to move out of the neighborhood to move to Philadelphia, I experienced longing for years for that most unique of neighborhoods with all of its incredible characters and cultural offerings.

(Years later, 2015 to be exact, I moved back to the neighborhood, and still love it, although naturally some of my favorite establishments have gone under and been replaced by others).

The Mount Pleasant Riots

While I was living in Adams Morgan and loving the neighborhood, the adjacent neighborhood just to the north, Mt. Pleasant, became the scene of a historic Hispanic riot (first, and to date only one in the city). For two nights cars and stores burned in a major blowout of pent-up frustration and rage against the system by the Hispanic community.

Given that the Mt. Pleasant neighborhood was also my stomping ground, and the street itself was the location of my first legal job with CARECEN, I had more than a passing interest in what was happening there. I heard through word of mouth on the evening of that Sunday that there was a riot going on. Naturally curious both as an inhabitant of the area, but also because there was a distinct possibility that some of my Central American clients could somehow be involved, at least passively, I began walking from Kalorama Park up Columbia Road to the intersection with 18th Street. Once arriving there I was already blocked by a police presence, groups of police dressed in riot gear that were preventing more pedestrian traffic into the area. I watched for awhile, but unable to penetrate any further into the disturbance I turned around.

As I learned the next day, the inciting incident had been an altercation between the police and a drunken, homeless guy and his buddies. When told to move on, he had resisted, and for whatever reason or however it happened, a rookie African-American female cop had shot him in the chest (not fatally). The street erupted with more and more Hispanics rushing in, setting a police car and a metro bus on fire, and starting a good old-fashioned riot.

In that neighborhood, including where I lived, there were an estimated 85,000 Hispanics, including many new arrivals from the Central American countries that were still in upheaval, and apparently many of them who decided to participate in the activities those two nights had experience with violent demonstrations back home. In fact, the next day, after my elderly landlady returned from her shopping, she was exclaiming, "It was terrorists who were rioting last night, trained terrorists!"

That next day, Monday, newly-elected Mayor Sharon Pratt Dixon held a press conference urging calm, there was a peace march down Mt. Pleasant Street including Jesse Jackson locking arms with community Hispanic leaders, and then that evening another round of rioting and looting of shops. More than 60 police cars, 20 metro buses and 30 shops were destroyed.

On that second evening, before it got dark, I walked up again to Columbia Road to observe the city's preparations for what predictably would be a second night of trouble. At the neighborhood Safeway on Columbia Road between 18th and 17th Streets, a group of perhaps fifteen riot-geared police with riot shields were standing in anticipation of trouble. Makes sense, I thought, protect the neighborhood food at least. But a couple hours later, when I walked back to have a look, the police were gone, disbursed to other hot spots, and the Safeway was destroyed. Groups of Hispanic and African-American youth were roaming the streets, looking for something to destroy, and I evacuated back to my apartment. By the next morning, the riots had run their course.

The disturbance actually led to some improvements in community policing and public liason with the police. More Hispanic police were recruited, a community police public affairs office was opened right at the intersection of Columbia Road and 18th Street, the city hired more bilingual employees, money was allocated to social services that represented the Latino community, and Hispanic community leaders were given more resources and opportunity to express their constituents' grievances.

Now, about the actual incident that started it all? There were differing "eye witness" accounts of what really happened. One theory that made sense to me: the police department had recently been equipped with the new-issue Glock 9 millimeter automatic, which notoriously has a hair trigger. The cop involved was a rookie, who probably shouldn't have been pulling her gun in the first place in that situation. There were other cops with her, meaning a combination of nerves and poor training may have resulted in an accidental shooting. The big question, was the drunken man, as the police claimed, pulling a knife at the time he was shot? We all know how common knives are among certain sectors of the population. Some said that they had seen it all, and there was no knife involved.

A short while after all the excitement had died down, I received a visit from one of my Salvadoran clients at the clinic. He came to my office on a routine matter to renew his work authorization. Now this man was an evangelical Christian, and one thing for sure, I trusted his word when he spoke. And he had no interest one way or the other in taking sides. We came to talking about the incident, and he volunteered that he had been there, and that he had seen what happened. And he told me that the man *did* have a knife. For whatever it's worth. My client tragically died in an auto accident on the beltway with members of his family. His asylum application, which had taken years weaving its way through the agency and court systems, was never resolved.

Richard Lewis

Richard Lewis died fighting for the rights of immigrants.

Richard was a law student who had specialized in Russian and East European studies in undergrad. I first met him when he sought a meeting with me in the summer of 1992, before his scheduled participation in my clinic that fall. He informed me that he was spending some time that summer in the Ukraine. Since we had a hotly-contested asylum case from the Ukraine at that time, involving a charming young husband and wife, we arranged for Richard to visit their home village and gather affidavits and evidence during his timely trip to the region.

Subsequently, we went on to win the Ukrainian asylum case,

with Richard acting as student attorney and with the help of evidence that he had gathered in their village. Richard worked in the clinic for two semesters, handling a wide variety of deportation cases. He proved exceptionally bright and motivated.

One evening, I was sitting outside of one of my favorite neighborhood clubs, Chief Ike's Mambo Room, on Columbia Road in the Adams Morgan neighborhood. I was enjoying the summer weather and a beer, happy to be living in such a great immigrant neighborhood. Richard came limping by with a cane. I asked him what was wrong with his leg. He said the injury was the result of a skiing accident, and joked that at least the operation had revealed that he didn't have cancer. That was the first I had heard of any operation, even though we had become pretty good friends by then and were in frequent contact. Richard, in that conversation, used the "C" word in the negative, so I was naively left in the dark. I had taken the reference for a joke, as he had meant it.

But shortly thereafter, he did let it be known that he was fighting cancer. After radiation treatment, and when he was still optimistic about his prospects for recovery, we spent a day traveling out to my house on the Potomac River in Shepherdstown, West Virginia, where we had a pleasant afternoon of discussion in the fall weather. The discussion ranged from popular music to clinic clients to both of our plans for the future. Over the course of that year, his condition sadly deteriorated. I later visited him at George Washington University Hospital, where he was undergoing chemo treatment. I met his parents often, as they traveled back and forth between New York state and Washington, in support of Richard, and I met his sister and his fiancé, who took a year off from work to support him.

Richard always kept me a couple of steps behind the dire news that he was hearing about the failure of his various treatments. When he finally understood the terminal nature of his condition, he faced a decision. What to do with the remaining short time in his life? I know that I would not be brave enough to make the decision that he ultimately did. He decided to continue working for the clinic's indigent clients, up until the end.

By that time he was enrolled in the Civil Law Clinic, and since our clinics shared space, he continued to work with clients just outside my office door. And we continued to share discussions about the immigration clients.

He made a visit to a controversial medical clinic in Texas, in one last attempt to find any possible cure. When he returned, he knew that it was only a question of a few more months that he had to live – and he chose to spend as much of that time as he could in our offices with the clients who were in need.

When Richard passed on, the school established the Richard C. Lewis, Jr. Memorial Award: "Given to a member of the graduating Juris Doctor class who has exhibited extraordinary dedication to his or her work in the Jacob Burns Community Legal Clinics and unusual compassion and humanity toward clients and colleagues." The award is presented every year, and I was given the honor of choosing the first student to receive the award. Richard's example and our friendship continue to inspire me.

KGB, FBI and Me

During the period at the end of the 1980's when Mikhail Gorbachev was loosening up on totalitarian restrictions inside the Soviet Union, the FBI undertook an unusual public relations outreach- they ran a large ad in the New York Post, encouraging any Russians in the U.S. who had ever either worked for or had anything to do with the KGB to come forward and contact them.

That ad was fresh in my mind on the day that a handsome, muscular Russian student came to see me at the clinic in 1990. He asked for our help in filing an application for asylum. He looked like a smaller version of Dolf Lundgren, and I'll refer to him as "Dolf." He was now a medical student in northern Virginia, but earlier, while still a college student in Moscow, he had been approached by the KGB and been given an assignment that he couldn't refuse – he was to report any contacts with American students in Moscow to the KGB. That was all, simply be a neutral observer and file reports. It was apparently a very common practice for KGB to use college students this way, and one that was impossible for a Russian student to refuse to take part in. The KGB had ways to make you cooperate. He had done as told for several years, and then when he was obtaining permission to leave the Soviet Union and travel to the U.S. for school, he was "invited" to continue his affiliation with the KGB in the U.S. But now that the iron grip of authority was disintegrating back home, he had decided to risk not continuing the cooperation. Since arriving in the U.S. he had failed to contact his designated KGB handler.

Thus began a strange collaboration between the FBI and the immigration clinic. After hearing Dolf's story, and remembering that recent New York Post ad, I developed a theory of the case that would prove useful to him and several additional low-level KGB collaborators. If we could convince a judge that Dolf had met with the FBI and given them information about his KGB contacts, then surely it would be persuasive that his life would now be in even greater jeopardy if he were forced to go back home, where the KGB could just have their way with him. (In asylum terminology, this is known as a *sur place* claim, or one that originates in the country of asylum, not in the applicant's original home).

My decision to pursue this strategy on behalf of my clients was a bit of a concession on my part – like many who had come of age in the 60's, my attitude toward the FBI had not been a positive one. In the early seventies I had been arrested and held overnight on three separate occasions while merely taking part in peaceful demonstrations. On all three occasions the charges were either dismissed or I was subsequently found not guilty. As was later revealed during Congressional hearings into FBI activity during that period, the agency had engaged in blatantly illegal and unconstitutional monitoring and harassment of such demonstrations and the organizations participating. Such COINTELPRO activities by the FBI were found by Congress to be unlawful, leading to reforms of the agency. In fact, I had only recently obtained through a Freedom of Information Act (FOIA) request my FBI file, which contained 40 pages of much-redacted material but made for fascinating reading. I was therefore not predisposed to buddy-up with the FBI. But now I was in attorney mode, trying to think of the best solutions for my clients.

I contacted the local Washington FBI office and was referred to an agent who I'll call Charlie. We arranged for Dolf to be debriefed at my office, in my presence. Charlie and his buddy who showed up for the interview were right out of Central Casting – young and handsome, in business suits and all-business. They were thankful for my having put them together with Dolf. In the end, the interview was rather anti-climactic, Dolf repeating essentially the same story that I had already heard and responding to a few questions that I can't divulge. A key to the success of Dolf's asylum case was that the agents were willing to confirm for the judge by way of an official statement that they had indeed debriefed him.

That was the first of half-a-dozen such collaborations between my office, our Russian asylum clients and Charlie's FBI team. Charlie showed his trust in me by contacting me on occasion and asking for the clinic's help in some cases, such as when a certain witness for his office was undocumented and needed some counseling or assistance with their immigration case.

Orquesta Candela — Playing In the Band

In 1989, my friend Peter, a piano player, joined a salsa band in Washington. When I went to hear them play at a local club, the music was so dynamic and rapturous that I was converted, deciding that I also wanted to play in a Latin band. But what instrument could I even play to provide access to such a group? My piano skills were way to paltry. What came to mind was the saxophone. But I hadn't touched a saxophone since my early days in Washington back in 1973. I purchased an alto from a pawn shop and spent some time reacquainting myself with the horn. I responded to an ad in the City Paper — a Central American group named Orquesta Candela was looking for horn players. The group rehearsed in a town house in a relatively dangerous block of 13th Street Northwest (dangerous at that time, now fully gentrified). On a steamy July night I went to the audition. I was jumpy just walking from the car a full block to the front steps of the townhouse, where a group of Hispanics were hanging out and shooting the breeze. All of the musicians were from various Central American countries except for the lead singer, Josephina, who was a beautiful, chocolate-skinned woman from the Dominican Republic. The rehearsal space was the cramped living room on the first floor, and we had to play without air conditioning in Washington's notorious code orange summer heat. I passed the audition, and for the next four years I played with the same musicians in different configurations of dance groups in the clubs around Washington. We had work every weekend, sometimes playing clubs both Friday and Saturday nights and then a wedding or *quinceanera* party on a Sunday.

Often a member of the dance audience would come up to me during a break and inquire, "Professor Paul?" and sure enough, it would be one of my clients from the law school clinic.

It's a funny thing about human nature – that thing called inertia. There were always several members of our band who were undocumented. Even though they knew that I was an immigration lawyer, and I invited them to come by the clinic in order to assist with their status in the U.S., none of them ever followed up on it. Sure, I would be bombarded with questions during rehearsal about how does one go about doing this or that to get the green card – but they could never find the time during the day to actually commit to having their situation resolved.

When I was a judge, I saw the same mentality repeated a hundred times. People who had been in the country for years, but who couldn't be bothered to take steps to legalize their status, suddenly encountered *la Migra*, and then they were hauled into my court, and it was too late, and all that I could do for them was to sign the order sending them home.

One of our percussionists from Nicaragua decided, after a year in the U.S., that life was just too tough for him here, and he returned home. A year later, when I was visiting Nicaragua in 1993, I walked into a club in Managua and there he was, leading his own band!

Even in the Washington area, such clubs weren't necessarily the safest places to spend a lot of time. At one club in Silver Spring, Maryland, we finished playing for the evening, and I had a beer at the bar before leaving for the night. It was my practice to always stayed absolutely sober during our performance, but then after the gig I liked to kick back and have a beer or two before driving home through the late night. A smallish, dark-skinned man, obviously Central American, came in and sat down at the bar next to me, ordering a Tecate beer. After a while I left and drove home. Fifteen minutes after I'd left the club, that nondescript man shot dead another patron at the bar and fled. The police speculated that he was a contract killer, hired by a jealous husband.

We were often witness to knife fights that broke out in the clubs, sometimes right in front of us while we were playing on the bandstand. Sometimes the disruption might only last minutes, or the performance might have to be interrupted for a half hour while things cooled off. Once, at the King Kong Club in Langley Park, Maryland, we were in the middle of a song when the lights were suddenly turned on and the power to our amps was cut. I looked up to see what the deal was – a group of State troopers were clearing the club, having gotten an emergency call from management about a violent altercation.

One Friday night, while the band members were relaxing outside, taking a break from a gig at Cristina's club in Alexandria, we heard gunshots from the next block over, and soon a young man went limping past where we were standing on the sidewalk, looking furtively in our direction, blood dripping from a bullet wound in his foot. Fifteen minutes later and we were back on stage, me playing my sax solo from Juana la Cubana.

Orange Jumpsuits

As mentioned in Dolf's case, the disintegration of the Soviet Empire led to a new fertile field of asylum applicants in the U.S. – those individuals fleeing Soviet satellite countries, who were finally able to get out because of loosened restrictions on travel. Early one fall morning in 1994 I received a call from the Arlington immigration court clerk. There were two newly-detained Albanian stowaways who had been caught in a container ship at Norfolk while hiding inside a container. They had been transferred to Manassas county jail in northern Virginia, and were on that day's court docket. They needed representation. Were we interested?

You bet we were. We were known as the go-to clinic for detained migrants, especially if the case was interesting. Since the fall of the East European communist states, Albania had been in a free-fall, and lots of interesting cases were being generated from that region. I grabbed two students who happened to be in the clinic that morning, and off we went to court. We met with our two new clients in the detention cell down the hall from the court on North Fairfax Drive. They were dressed in orange jumpsuits from the county jail. They explained that they had boarded the container ship at a port in Spain, and had been concealed inside the tight container until their arrival at Norfolk, where they had to make a racket in order to get noticed – and detained by INS.

They spoke little English, but could get by in German, and since I am fluent in German we could communicate. There would be no

Albanian interpreter at court that day, but one would be needed for the merits hearing later. After a brief meeting, I decided that their cases were potentially strong, and that they would be fun for the students to work on.

At our initial appearance before Judge Bryant, he asked if we could be ready for trial in ten days. He was fast-tracking the cases because they were held at Manassas county jail due to overcrowding. With grins on their faces, my two students shook their heads in the affirmative, and we were set. We met with our clients again in the holding cell, and then on the weekend my students made the trip out to the county jail with an interpreter to complete their asylum applications and prepare their testimony.

Ten days later I met my students at the court for the Albanian hearings. We put the cases on that morning, one after the other, the judge withholding decision until both cases had been heard, because the facts of their cases were intertwined and the two Albanians were witnesses in each other's case. The government had assigned a different prosecutor for each case. We finished both cases before noon. After a brief recess, Judge Bryant returned to the bench and announced that both applicants were granted asylum. The government attorney waived appeal.

The INS guards surprised us by indicating it was their intention to release our clients right there in court, in their orange jumpsuits, rather than making the trip all the way back to Manassas on a Friday afternoon. Usual protocol would have been to take them back and out-process them from the county jail. The students and I would have returned to the clinic and celebrated and gone home for the weekend. Instead, we found ourselves with two Albanian refugees in orange prison jumpsuits on our hands.

I drove them back to the clinic, and we had a team of students working the phones, trying to find someone in the metro area to take our two refugees for at least a couple of nights until further arrangements could be made. By the end of the afternoon, we had struck out. No one wanted to take them in or had space for them. No refugee or religious charitable organization or church group was willing to volunteer their assistance on such short notice. There was already a surplus of needy refugees and homeless people in the city. It was disheartening to realize that we couldn't get a single positive response.

I finally thought of a solution. I remembered a family of Albanian Pentecostal Christians who had helped out as witnesses on another case, who lived way out in Maryland between Hagerstown and Sharpsburg. Coincidentally the location of their house was only a fifteen minute drive from my house in Shepherdstown, West Virginia, which is basically across the Potomac River from Sharpsburg. On that Friday afternoon I loaded our two orange jump-suited refugees back into the cab of my Toyota pickup truck and drove an alternate route to my house, by way of Rt. 70 west to Sharpsburg Pike. The housing development where our host family lived was just down the road from the Antietam battlefield. When we found the house, the Christian family came out to greet the two fellow countrymen with open arms. It was a joyous union.

I drove on to Shepherdstown elated, ready to enjoy the weekend and share the story with my friends. I was so happy to have found a refuge for our refugees.

On Tuesday the next week, I was in my office when Norma, our receptionist, buzzed me on the phone. Our two Albanian refugees were in the reception area, wanting to talk to me. I went down the hall to find two frustrated men, no longer in orange jumpsuits but rather in worn but clean and freshly-ironed slacks and button-down shirts. We had a heated discussion in German. "Good to see you, but what are you doing here?" "We can't stay with that family." "Why not?" "They are always reading the Bible to us, they want us to become Christians." "Well, can't you just listen? After all, it's a place to stay." "No, we cannot stay any longer, too much about Jesus." "But we couldn't find you any other place!" "We have a place." "Where?" "In Chicago." "You have a place in Chicago?" "Yes, we finally reached our friend there, on the phone." "But how will you get to Chicago?" "We don't know, we have no money."

It took another day of phone calls to raise money from different good-hearted people so that we could put them on the train to Chicago.

The Sixties All Over Again

In the fall of 1993, after having worked at the GW clinic for seven years, during which time the clinic's national reputation had been firmly established, I received a letter in the internal school mail from the Dean. It came without any forewarning, a complete shock out of the blue. In two sentences he informed me that, because of budget constraints, he had decided to eliminate the immigration clinic, which meant that my services would no longer be required. However, due to the little technicality that my contract required a one year advance warning prior to termination, I could stay on for one more academic year.

Under the faculty regulations, the Dean couldn't just decide to eliminate a program on his own say, he had to present the proposal to the full faculty and obtain a majority vote. But in this case, aside from the eight clinic professors and a few of our allies on the faculty, such as Roger Schecter, Tod Peterson and Jonathan Turley, most of the law professors sat shamefacedly silent at the next faculty meeting, where the elimination of the immigration clinic was treated as a done deal. The Dean held significant leverage over even tenured faculty members in the way of discretionary summer bonuses and research grants.

However, Eric Sirulnik, the director of all the clinical programs, said upon hearing the news, "We can't let him get away with this!" and organized a rally. Several days later a group of two hundred students and representatives from other community immigrant organizations, such as Ayuda and Hogar Hispano, convened on the quad right outside of the dean's office window, for a rally with bullhorns in support of the immigration clinic. Students carried placards with such slogans as "Deport the Dean."

The Dean gave an interview on local TV defending his decision to slash the immigration clinic, where he claimed there was no interest or need for the program. Just the fact that the incident had already caught the press's attention was a blow to his plans to effortlessly eliminate the program. He had a hard time explaining to the reporter that in a city with the second largest Central American population in the country, and with the largest population of Ethiopians outside of Africa during a time of immense upheaval in the Horn of Africa, the immigration clinic's services were not that important. But as was typical of such short-sighted managers, he had completely ignored the interests of his most important constituency – the students, some of whom had only decided to attend G.W. law school because of the national reputation of the immigration clinic. Indeed, earlier that same year, when a committee from the American Bar Association had conducted a periodic review of the school, it had harshly criticized many of the shortcomings in the school, but had especially lauded the contribution of the immigration clinic.

Round two: only months later the Dean, under pressure from university management, then announced additional cuts to programs that affected many of the other law students. That did it. The whole law school student body went on strike. On a sunny fall day they marched to the administration building, Rice Hall, and sat down in the public street that runs past it, blocking traffic – and they refused to move. They demanded to speak to the president of the university, and when told that he was out of town they announced that they weren't going anywhere until they could speak with him. Again, signs that they carried included calls to save the immigration clinic. When I saw the rally I was reminded of the sixties anti-war demonstrations, some of which I had taken part in, during a time prior to the birth of most of these students.

Although I had nothing to do with that spontaneous mass action by the students, some of my students were among the ringleaders, and were also active in student government. By mid-afternoon, when the students continued to shut down the campus and disrupt traffic they caught the attention of the press. Then a contingent of the student leaders, including two of my students, were invited upstairs to meet with the president of the university, who was supposed to be out of town, and with several members of the Board of Directors of the university. The main concern of the school administration was to persuade them to disband the demonstration and stop causing a focal point for the evening news.

In the course of that meeting, the law students were made a remarkable offer. For legal reasons I can't divulge which high-level official said it, but they were told that if they would call off the strike, jobs could be found for them in K Street law firms. (K Street is Washington's main business street where commercial law firms have their offices). The students declined the opportunity to sell their souls in that shameful manner so early in their careers, but they did agree to further negotiations with representatives of the administration. In subsequent meetings it was agreed, in order to quell the wrath of the students, that in spite of the budget cuts, the school would provide the law students with an annual discretionary fund in the amount of $70,000 for the next three years at their disposal, the funds to be used in whatever way the student body chose. The students had won!

If the law school faculty had proven to be spineless worms over the issue of the elimination of one of the school's most valued offerings – the immigration clinic – the students on the contrary rose to the occasion, demonstrating the true spirit of socially-conscious future lawyers. For the next three years, up until the time of my departure from the university, every time that the student government convened to debate and divvy up the annual $70,000, the students allocated $30,000 of that amount to the operation of the immigration clinic. That meant that with some additional fundraising from outside "soft-money" sources, we were able to keep the clinic open and continue to serve the community, in the face of the Dean's attempts to shut us down.

Finally, after those three years, the dean admitted defeat, confessed that the clinic had proven more popular than he had realized, and reinstated funding for it from the school budget, guaranteeing the clinic's longevity. It's hard to think of anything more satisfying than to have the Dean of the law school try to fire you, only to be overridden by the President of the university because students pressured him to keep the immigration clinic.

That Dean must have really not liked me! He got creative with the rules again and pronounced that since the clinic was being added to the permanent law school offerings as a new program!! the law school would have to conduct a national search for a director of the clinic. Again the faculty was mostly silent about that flagrant assault upon their intelligence. So I was put in the unique position of having to compete against the nation's finest for my own job!

In the context of a national search, a pool of fifty applicants was culled down to three by the faculty appointments committee. At least I made that cut! Then each of the three candidates was expected to do the traditional song and dance to persuade the faculty to hire them. But frankly, my heart just wasn't in it any more. We had fought the good fight and preserved the clinic. But having to put up with the constant antagonism from the administration over a period of years was getting old. And I had another dream.

For some time now I had wished for the opportunity to go abroad and do international humanitarian work in some tropical country with lots of jungles and biting insects and fatal endemic diseases. At the end of every school year I would feel a bit like the character in the film Mr. Holland's Opus, when some of my students accepted really fascinating jobs with the United Nations and other international organizations and I was left behind to plan for another school year. So although I nominally threw my hat into the ring, I didn't even do the traditional grip and grin where the candidate contacts all of the members of the faculty for brief visits to taut their qualifications. And the divided faculty chose another candidate.

Another factor in my decision was that the Dean, although proving unable to cancel my program, had managed to submit the whole clinical program to the indignity of being ejected from our modern space, which was situated in the main building underneath the library, in order to make way for more books! The clinics were moved into an old brownstone building, with cramped offices and facilities and which was fully inadequate for the demands of a modern law office/clinical setting, and even without any handicap access. I had chafed at the conditions for a couple of years already.

So the immigration clinic lived on under new management and that wonderful institution still serves the community. But what if Eric Sirulnik hadn't called out the resistance to the Dean's power play? And what if my students hadn't heeded the call and gone into the streets to protest?

A Preview of the Arizona Law Fifteen Years Earlier

In 2010 the great State of Arizona disgraced itself by enacting a racial profiling law, SB 1070, the Support Our Law Enforcement and Safe Neighborhoods Act, which at that time was considered the broadest and strictest anti-illegal immigration measure in the nation. The measure was drafted by perennial white nationalist Kris Kobach and supported by Arizona governor Jan Brewer. (Kobach was later a "birther" challenging president Obama's citizenship, and called for a registry of Muslims in the United States. His anti-immigrant activism is legendary. He just lost the Republican primary for U.S. Senator from Kansas.) Among other things, the Arizona law authorized state law enforcement personnel to stop and inquire of an individual's immigration status based upon "reasonable suspicion" that the person may be an undocumented immigrant.

For those in the immigrant advocacy community the law was a giant and unconstitutional overreach. Even if most police officers would try to carry out their jobs in a professional, objective way, who do you think they will be inclined to ask about papers when they make a routine traffic stop? The blonde-haired Swedish student in a bikini?

By mere chance I had a startling look into the kind of racial profiling that already routinely goes on throughout the Southwest. One day in 1995 I received a call from the law school administration. I was told that a group of one hundred gifted Hispanic high school students was visiting the university, and someone had decided that I should be on the group's itinerary for that evening, that the school needed to find someone to entertain them. I was dumbfounded.

"Let me get this straight – these are high school students, not law students?"

"That's right."

"And I'm presuming they are U.S. citizens, or at least most of them, right?"

"That's also correct."

"So why should I be talking to them? I'm the immigration guy. People come to me when they are *not* citizens, to find out how to become one or to avoid deportation."

"I'm not really sure, just that someone upstairs said we need to find a faculty member in a hurry who can spend time with them tonight."

Although it was totally out of my area of expertise to entertain a group of high school students, presumably in order to maybe give them a good impression of the university, still I thought it could be fun to meet them, so I accepted the challenge. But I had no idea what to talk to them about. I got together with one of my Hispanic clinic students, Marta, explained the situation to her, and we talked about possible options. Finally I had an idea. I just needed something to get the ball rolling, to open the forum up for discussion. I was hoping that one or two of the visiting students would be motivated enough to jump in if they heard an interesting theme.

I said to Marta, "This is what we'll do. Just a little roll-play to get things going." I summarized my idea, and she agreed that it was worth giving it a try. "Then we'll see if anyone has had a similar experience or would like to comment."

"Sounds good."

That evening at 8 pm we met the students, one hundred especially gifted young Hispanics who were visiting Washington for the first time, most of them from southwestern states. They were all well-dressed, with the buoyancy and optimism of youth. I was impressed that, on their short visit to the nation's capitol, someone had decided they should waste an hour of their time with me, and I was afraid they would be bored to death.

I introduced myself and Marta, explained we were going to do a little roll play. "This is Marta, for our roll-play she's a student and I'm a policeman, and we're ready to start." Marta then began walking like a nonchalant pedestrian across the front of the classroom until she reached me. I tried to look particularly menacing, and speaking in an artificially brusque voice, I said, "Hold on right there, young lady, you look like a Mexican, let me see your papers!"

The whole class of one hundred students broke into loud pandemonium! Everyone was raising their hand, shouting for attention, some standing to make sure they could be heard, talking cross-wise, wanting to share their own experiences. I learned that fully three-quarters of the students in that room had had exactly that experience back in their hometowns. It was just a little peak into the kinds of harassment that Hispanics, even U.S. citizens, put up with in their daily lives. Fifteen years later, when I heard that the State of Arizona was considering a law that would sanction such warrantless stops, I remembered those students and what they had taught me.

Stone Throwing

One of my cases involving a young Palestinian man was memorable for the comic way in which he found the mercy of the court. Hussein was a seventeen year old student who had been living in the West Bank at the time of the First Intifada, between 1987 and 1993, a period of unified resistance to Israeli occupation. He traveled to the U.S. on a fake visa to visit his mother, who was a lawful permanent resident here. He had been stopped at immigration inspection and put into deportation (technically exclusion) proceedings. His other family members in the U.S. included several uncles and aunts on both his mother's and his deceased father's side. After arriving here the family decided they wanted him to apply for asylum.

When I first met with Hussein and his mother, I had no idea what I was getting myself into, but later, when we brought in all of the uncles to prepare for his deportation hearing, I realized that I was dealing with the type of family where all of the male adults felt that they should be calling the shots. They wanted to influence the way that I prepared and put on the case, and of course I wasn't about to allow that to happen. I wanted to present Hussein's mother and one of his uncles, who had been present at the time of his father's death during a clash with Israeli soldiers, merely to establish the fact that he had indeed been killed. We needed to persuade the judge that the father's death had been a significant trauma that would give rise to Hussein's "well-founded fear of persecution," and the fact that he had been killed and the manner in which it occurred was something we needed to establish through personal testimony.

At that time the nightly news featured graphic images of the violence arising from the clashes between Palestinian resisters and Israeli soldiers, and the sight of youthful stone throwers became an iconic image of the Intifada. It seemed that everyone who had a chance was throwing stones at Israeli soldiers, it became a badge of courage, and the press loved to feature photos of brave Palestinian boys standing up to the soldiers, like modern-day Davids to a Goliath.

In the course of my preparations with Hussein it became clear that he had also participated in the stone-throwing. It was something that I wanted to prevent the Jewish judge from hearing about, if at all possible.

I knew and respected Judge Joan Churchill on many levels. (Subsequent name change to Joan Arrowsmith). She had been kind enough to let me intern with her during my last semester in law school, teaching me a lot about the inner workings of an immigration court. At that time, in 1985, the court, which is now in Arlington and counts five or six judges, consisted of just one judge, presiding in the former lobby of an old hotel on Eye Street just a block from Union Station. I had conducted research for her, sat in on a lot of cases, and input data into the court's Wang computer, the cutting edge at that time.

So I knew her well enough to know that she wouldn't appreciate an asylum applicant who had been throwing stones at Israeli soldiers. Apart from the issue of where her political sympathy might lie, I knew she would consider it an act of aggression equivalent to terrorism. When we prepared Hussein and his family the night before the hearing, I did my best to reason with the proud members of the clan who wanted to politicize everything in the hearing, whereas I wanted to tone down everything and only highlight my client's fear of return.

"Listen, no matter what happens tomorrow, I don't want this judge to know that you were throwing stones. You understand? That won't go well for you. If anyone asks you a direct question, then you have to answer honestly and admit to what you were doing. Otherwise, we're not going to bring it up. You were there at the demonstrations, you were a sympathizer, but don't volunteer the information that you were throwing stones! Only if asked. Is that clear?"

Hussein seemed to understand what I was getting at, but several of the uncles still wanted to let the court know, to let the world know that their nephew had bravely faced down armed soldiers by throwing stones. I wasn't planning to put any of the more aggressive ones on the stand, and I debated with myself about keeping them out of the courtroom, but firstly they were insistent on attending, and secondly, I usually like to create a presence by having as many of the family members in the audience as possible. I just kept my fingers crossed that all would go according to script.

The next day, we put on Hussein's mother and his uncle who had been present at his father's death first, to set the stage for why Hussein had decided to come to America and was fearful of returning. Then Hussein, this thin seventeen year old kid with peach fuzz on his face, took the stand and described the frightful events that had happened in his neighborhood and that he had been a witness to when he was a mere sixteen years old. All was going well. Miraculously, the INS counsel didn't ask Hussein on cross if he had participated in the stone throwing. It almost looked like we were going to get him off the stand without the fateful question being asked. But when INS counsel was finished with his cross, Judge Churchill indicated that she was still curious about something. Inwardly I groaned, I knew what was coming.

The judge asked in a slow, precise tone, "Now, at any of these demonstrations you have described, were you by any chance…(pregnant pause)… throwing stones?"

Hussein looked at his mother in the audience, he looked at me, he looked around the courtroom. I could practically hear my admonishment working through the gears of his mind, "I don't want her to know, but if you are asked a direct question you have to tell," I had said.

Hussein responded. "Could you repeat the question?" It was a good feint, because everything was going through an interpreter, and that gave him another thirty seconds to try to figure out how to answer. The judge again,

"Were you by any chance throwing stones?"

The tension in the audience was palpable, the half-dozen family members all knew what I had told Hussein, they all knew what the answer *should* be now, because they all knew that he *had* been throwing stones, but if he told the truth it would be over for him.

Remarkably, Hussein still feinted. "I'm not sure I understand the question."

I knew that Judge Churchill wasn't going to stand for that. But before it could go any further, one of the overly boisterous uncles stood up in the audience, and at the top of his voice he ranted, "He wasn't throwing stones! He should have been throwing stones! We are all ashamed that he did not throw stones, but he wasn't!"

His performance was so over the top that it was comical. Everyone was at first shocked, and then when Judge Churchill burst out laughing, we all laughed in a release of tension. Somehow the judge accepted that response as the answer and didn't insist on a follow-up from Hussein. He never answered the question under oath, and she dismissed him from the stand. Of course, I knew that the uncle's version wasn't the truth, but he wasn't under oath to tell the truth and I didn't see any ethical duty to correct an outburst that didn't come from my own client. Asylum was granted!

Sexual Blackmail at International Students Office

Most universities have an office that represents the interests of foreign students enrolled at that school, including handling the intricacies of the issuance of student visas so that the students can enter the United States and study at that institution. Such an office works for the benefit of the school administration, and has not intersection with an immigration clinic. Shortly before I left G.W. a scandal hit the front pages involving the university's director of that office.

Rumors had apparently been circulating for some time that the individual was on the take, accepting bribes for the promise of a student visa. When a police sting netted him in an attempt to solicit a certain type of bribe, the talking heads had a field day.

One day an Arab national came to his office, asking for assistance. The director said, "Let's go take a ride and we can talk about your problem." He invited himself into the young man's convertible, and as they were driving around the Foggy Bottom area, the director demanded sex in exchange for the guarantee of a visa. When the prospective student demurred, the official reportedly asked, "What's the matter, you people all go for that stuff!" Unfortunately for him his remarks were being taped in a sting operation and were made evidence in a prosecution for attempted bribes.

Now and then various international student offices on campuses make headlines when conspiracy to issue fraudulent student visas comes to light. In spring of 2011 a school administrator in Lancaster, California was sentenced to jail and fined a hefty amount for involvement with fraud and collusion in the issuance of student visas.

Government Officials Feeding at the Trough

In 1990, Congress amended the immigration statute to include a provision for immigrant investors, the so-called millionaire green card provision. Critics had long charged Congress with being recalcitrant, given that other industrialized countries, including Canada, had a provision to allow immigration of an individual who was willing to invest large sums in the nation's economy. Congress finally caught up, with a provision that essentially allowed anyone who was willing to invest one million dollars in a new company, in an urban area, that employed a certain number of U.S. citizens or permanent residents, to immigrate as a lawful permanent resident; for investment in a rural area, only $500,000 was required.

Shortly after the passage of the bill, I began to see, in the Washington Post's Want Ads, an advert for immigration lawyers to join a firm based in Greenbelt, Maryland. The associate would travel all over the world recruiting potential investors for the new program. It caught my eye because it was the kind of job I had always dreamed about doing – international travel, staying in five-star hotels while meeting with interesting people in exotic locales – except I had a clinic to run. One of my students, a recent law-grad, responded to the ad and was hired.

My student, Joachim Tremols, contacted me after being on the job for several months, and voiced his concern about the ethics of the job, asking if he could come by my office and talk to me. Joachim was a native of Cuba. We had worked together in the clinic on a tough Peruvian asylum case, and I had grown to trust his judgment and maturity. Prior to attending law school, he graduated with an MBA and worked for a while in the banking industry. In other words, he was better at math than I am, and he knew about accounting practices.

I was shocked, upon seeing him, at how conflicted and shaken he was with the information that he wanted to discuss. Turned out the company in question had been created by several former government officials, including a former Commissioner of INS, a former General Counsel of INS, and a former U.S. Ambassador to Brazil and Columbia. Joachim explained his job to me, and at the end of the summary, he declared, "This looks like a pyramid scheme to me!" He was being sent overseas to recruit investors, not to invest the full one million dollars as required, but apparently to invest only $125,000 into the recruiting company, much of which then remained with the company as legal fees. The client/investor was then expected to assist with the recruitment of additional investors, so that as long as more investors were chipping into the pot the company would be able to put up a million dollars per client. Clearly not what the law intended.

Although the relative legality of the scheme was not at all clear to me, it certainly sounded fishy, and I knew someone who might be able to provide an answer. "Why don't we call my friend, Maury Robinson, and run it by him?" Maurice Robinson was a venerable immigration law specialist, Editor-in-Chief of the leading immigration journal at that time, Interpreters' Releases, a former judge at the Board of Immigration Appeals, and, in his senior years, perhaps the most respected person in the field. He always graciously accepted my invitations to address my immigration law class each fall semester. I called him and he invited us to come right over.

Joachim repeated his story in Maury's office, and the old lion of the law reacted as I had; unclear what's going on, but where there is smoke, there is often fire. He asked Joachim if he would be willing to meet with authorities in Department of Justice, including the General Counsel of INS, and Joachim agreed.

Thus were the first stones overturned in what led to a major investigation into corruption of past government officials, who, as the government later charged, were not only involved in a classic Ponzi scheme, but were using undue influence to get current government officials within INS to approve applications without the proper scrutiny. The Baltimore Sun ran a lengthy article about the investigation on February 20, 2000, entitled, 'Cashing in: Immigration Official Insiders Siphon Millions Selling Green Cards to Wealthy Foreigners.' Among the findings of the investigation was the zinger that some of the ex-officials doing the cashing-in had been instrumental in the formulation and passage of the 1990 law. Also involved in the company was a certain Prescott S. Bush, the brother of the president who signed the law.

Afterword: In 2013 I accepted a job with the agency's Immigrant Investor Visa Office, the folks who administer the EB-5 visa program. The program had undergone tremendous reorganization, largely due to the exposures recounted above, including the circulation of this book in 2011. The team included a tremendous team of economists and adjudicators, and I thoroughly enjoyed working with everyone there and was elevated to a supervisory position after one year. But I still longed for overseas refugee work, so after exactly two years of working with huge files of financial documents I accepted a 30% reduction in salary to return to the Refugee Affairs Division of USCIS.

The Prosecution of Jonny Tong
(name changed to protect his identity and my life)

In the summer of 1995 I received a call from a prominent white collar criminal defense firm in D.C. – Nixon Peabody. They were representing a Chinese immigration attorney, a naturalized American citizen, who was charged with conspiracy to commit fraud with sham marriage applications, and they wanted me to be a defense expert on the issue of the ethics of the procedures of preparing marriage petitions in immigration law practice. As a professor, one of my duties included teaching in the tricky area of the ethics of immigration law practice.

This case presented one of those great ironies in life, because ten years earlier, when I was clerking at the immigration court as a student intern during my last semester of school, I had met Mr. Tong and taken a liking to him. He was an affable character, an immigrant from Taiwan with a very busy practice representing Chinese clients. He had grown up in Taiwan when the island was under Japanese occupation, learning Japanese in the school system until the end of the 2nd World War, while speaking Mandarin at home. He had come to the U.S. in 1960, getting his law degree at Columbia, and had set up a one-man shop in the D.C. area. He could be seen at the INS building daily. I had observed him in court, and so I knew that he was not the most eloquent when expressing himself in English – the problem was that with his heavy accent, he sounded like a bad imitation of the Hollywood caricature Charlie Chan. Before I graduated and while I was still anxious about finding a job, I had approached him and "generously" suggested that he hire me to be the front man in court hearings, because I considered myself a natural litigator and an eloquent orator. He listened politely to my offer that he hire me and declined.

Tong had been charged by the U.S. Attorney with 32 felony counts of fraud and conspiracy. One evening the FBI and INS had raided his office and carted off boxes of files, including what the prosecutors claimed was evidence of fraud. A number of Tong's former African marriage clients were now cooperating government witnesses against him. They had provided statements that Tong had coached them in their allegedly fraudulent immigration interviews. Forensics evidence proved they had submitted such false documents as fake passports and fake birth and marriage certificates from Africa to Mr. Tong, which he had then submitted to the agency as part of their green card applications.

There were a lot of wild allegations being hurled at Tong about the way that he worked with and prepared his clients for their marriage interviews, which upon examination I knew were outright false or misleading. For example, one of the documents the government had seized from his office and now was introducing as evidence against him was a list of typical supporting documents to be submitted along with a marriage petition. When I examined it, I revealed to defense counsel that in fact it was a photocopy of a sheet that was routinely handed out at the INS office! This snafu, and equally troubling allegations, such as that it was somehow improper to prepare a client for the interview, caused me to believe that somehow the prosecution team just didn't get it and was seriously overreaching in Mr. Tong's case.

It appeared incontrovertible that the African clients in question had indeed lied about their alleged marital relationships and in their interviews at INS – the question was, to what degree was Tong complicit? Tong's basic defense: until recently, he had only worked with Chinese clients. When African clients started being referred to him, he didn't have the cross-cultural skills to know they were lying to him. He couldn't know that documents they had submitted were false; after all, he wasn't a qualified forensics document examiner. It was a reasonable defense, but he had a big fight ahead of him.

A female Vietnamese immigration lawyer who had her practice in Fairfax had also been charged at the same time in exactly the same type of scheme. She and Tong had nothing to do with one another, her office was in northern Virginia and his was in Maryland, but apparently, zealous prosecutors were on the lookout for foreign-born immigration practitioners. She had pled guilty considering the prohibitive expense of mounting a defense. Such a conviction would result in the loss of her license.

We had two sessions at the offices of Nixon Peabody to prepare my testimony. We practiced my recitation of certain precedent cases that were standard in the industry and might be enlightening to a jury. Courts had held that a marriage was not a sham if the parties *intended* to form a life together *at the time of the marriage* — that we couldn't expect a marriage involving a migrant and a U.S. citizen to be any more perfect than between two U.S. citizens. Additionally, a lot was being made of the fact that Tong would prep his clients for the marriage interview. Well, in fact, an attorney would be incompetent if they didn't prep their client for any such interaction with a government official, either in an administrative context or in court. What is *verboten*, of course, is to prep them to give false testimony, but otherwise you want to give your client some practice in responding to the types of questions that can be expected, because even the most honest church-going member of the community can get nervous and freeze up when being interviewed or even interrogated by an official government representative.

For example, a few years earlier I had agreed to pro bono representation of the director of CARECEN (Central American Refugee Center in Washington) in her bid for a green card based upon her marriage to a U.S. citizen, a nice chap I knew from my time when working at their office. It was just a routine, mundane interview and they had been involved in an intimate relationship for years. Nevertheless, when we got in front of the examiner in Baltimore, the poor guy started shaking in his boots like he was on trial for murder. I had to talk him down during the interview! and persuade him that no one was going to think he was being untruthful. The petition was granted.

Mr. Tong's week-long trial was held in the Eastern District of Virginia, located in Alexandria, a traditionally conservative court — the same court where the "American Taliban" was tried and convicted in 2002. In the past I had argued several federal habeas cases there on behalf of clinic clients.

I had to go down to the courtroom twice, because the first time, when I sat and waited in the witness room during the afternoon, I wasn't called. I met the other government witnesses who were being called against Mr. Tong. The expert forensic document examiner was going to be able to prove that some of the African clients had used false passports and other documents to gain entry into the U.S., and then submitted them with subsequent applications for the green cards. But that didn't prove Tong's culpability. An attorney is given and receives documents in good faith from his clients.

Some of the INS examiners who I knew from my daily routine representing immigrant clients were also waiting to be called. As it turned out, they only had good things to say about Tong: that he was such a nice gentleman, how they had always enjoyed working with him; that he had on occasion fallen asleep during an interview…not a very strong case to show a cold, calculating conspirator. But their testimony was necessary for the government to authenticate the fact that certain of the marriages and subsequent INS interviews based on those marriages in which Tong had appeared as counsel had later turned out to be shams.

I was the only witness for the defense. And the defense team had decided not to put Tong on the stand. When practicing with him, it had become apparent that he was just too nervous to be a good witness. So a lot was riding on my shoulders. On the last day of trial I was called from the witness room. I crossed the hallway and entered a large ornate traditional courtroom with wooden paneling. My eye located the witness stand. In order to reach it I had to cross the full length of the courtroom. Time for everyone to watch the witness walk. But I was only halfway across when the court clerk appeared in front of me and shoved a Bible in my face. "Put your hand on the Bible. Do you solemnly swear....so help you God?"

I personally found such an intrusion of religion into the proceedings offensive, but I wasn't about to object in front of the jury, and I dutifully put my hand on the Bible and swore to tell the truth. (As a judge, the oath I have always administered is, "Sir, do you swear that everything you say in this hearing will be the truth?" without any mention of God or the Bible.

The judge, a plump, elderly white man, invited defense counsel to begin his examination of me. The attorney proceeded to take me through our prepared testimony. But every time I tried to cite a relevant case, as we had practiced, I was met with an objection from the prosecutor, which the judge sustained without even looking up from his notes. After the third such objection, it became clear that the judge didn't want anyone in the courtroom interpreting the law except himself. But the major part of the defense strategy had been that they would use me, a law professor specializing in this area of practice, to bring out how loosely the courts had interpreted legitimate marriages in the immigration context, which would take a lot of the heat off of Mr. Tong. I felt like turning to the judge and saying, "Look, who's the expert here, you or me?" but I restrained myself.

I was afraid the wind had been taken out of my testimony and I was letting Mr. Tong down. However, we did score a few good points, by my pointing out that the one supposedly damning document that Tong used to show his clients how to "cheat" was in fact an official INS handout. And I was able to explain how, in my view, any competent lawyer *would indeed* prepare his client for the interview, just as we practiced with the law students and our clients before such interviews.

I explained, "For example, a question that is always part of the exam is, 'When is your wife's birthday?' You wouldn't believe how many men can't answer that, and so it helps to practice it." A lighthearted chuckle from the jury.

I had been avoiding looking over at the jury. I couldn't figure out how to do it without it looking really obvious, but when the prosecutor was coming to the podium for cross, I did steal a glance. I was only able to discern that it was a group of all white men and women – they seemed like a decent enough bunch. I wondered how they were taking in everything, whether they found this kind of trial interesting or boring.

The Assistant U.S. Attorney was a white gentleman in his midthirties. I subsequently learned that this was his last case before leaving office to take up a teaching career at a prestigious law school. Naturally he was intent on winning his last case and going out with a bang.

His method of cross-examination was to posit several hypothetical questions and have me comment on whether I thought such practice or action would be improper on the part of an attorney. He gave several obvious examples of misconduct:

"Would you say that it is unethical to encourage a witness to lie?"

"Yes, of course."

"How about, representing a client at a hearing on a marriage petition for a green card, when the attorney knows for a certainty that the marriage in question is a sham?"

"Yes, that too would be unethical."

The answers were easy enough, because that kind of conduct was clearly unethical conduct, but it was not what Tong was directly accused of having committed. But by leading me in that way, he created the impression that he was on a roll – here I was responding affirmatively to each of a series of questions. Mr. Tong was being tarnished with the brush of innuendo.

But then he blundered and tripped, or as someone said once, "he hung himself on his own petard." He asked me if I would consider it improper if the attorney advised his clients, when the citizen spouse (petitioner) was living in Washington, D.C. and the alien spouse (beneficiary) was living in Maryland, to file the petition in the Baltimore INS district office rather than the northern Virginia district office, which had jurisdiction over Washington.

I understood immediately what he was getting at. Among the local immigration practitioners it was well-known, at that time, that the Baltimore INS office was better managed, more efficient, and had a much quicker turnaround than the Virginia office, which was constantly plagued by mismanagement and huge backlogs. In fact, while I was practicing law in the area, so many managers were brought through to try to correct the problems in Virginia that I lost count. Hence any competent attorney, if he could get the Baltimore office to assume jurisdiction over the case, would do so – it was only in the best interest of the client. The question, in the way it was put to me, suggested that Tong had been improperly forum shopping for his clients by somehow fabricating jurisdiction with the Baltimore office.

Without hesitation I cited the regulation, which the prosecutor was obviously not familiar with. "The regulation clearly indicates that, where the two parties reside or are domiciled in two different jurisdictions, it is proper to choose either of the two jurisdictions in which to file the petition." I enunciated loudly and firmly, a professor lecturing the assembled multitude, and a big departure from when the judge was sustaining every one of the prosecutor's objections about my testimony.

Upon hearing my answer, the prosecutor's mouth hung open. Clearly no one had bothered to point out that aspect of the law to him. There was a "pregnant pause" in the courtroom. One thing you don't want, as a litigator, is to be so surprised by a witness that you stand there with your mouth hanging open. He then indelicately rushed to wrap up his questioning, and I was dismissed from the stand.

After my testimony, I was able to remain in the courtroom to hear closing arguments. Defense counsel Laura Miller did an excellent job, and in her remarks she brought out several crucial points that I had not been aware of. The African witnesses for the prosecution had all been granted immunity and the promise to be able to remain and work in the United States, even though they were technically illegal in the country, and had all admitted to committing the crime of marriage fraud. Tong, on the other hand, who maintained his innocence, would, if found guilty, be stripped of his license to practice law and would see the end of a career of thirty years of hard work. He wasn't a big fish with a huge practice on K Street, he just ran a modest store-front office with his wife as assistant.

Johnny Tong thanked me on his way out of the courtroom. He looked shaken and depressed from the experience. The jury deliberated in the afternoon, and returned the next day with a verdict of not guilty on all counts. When I heard the outcome, pride burned in my chest that I had been able to help out this little guy who I had known all those years, in a case where the government had so clearly overreached. He continues to practice law in the Washington area.

I thought about the case and where the government had gone wrong, and I came to the conclusion that they made one fatal error – they never consulted with an expert in immigration law, and lord knows they had plenty of attorneys working with DOJ with whom they could have consulted. They had presented two INS investigators as witnesses, but excuse me, they tend not to be experts in the field. Their job is to investigate and make arrests, not to interpret the ethics of the legal practice. They were not legal experts, but rather police officials, but the prosecution had relied entirely upon them for understanding and interpretation of the law. I didn't see any indication that the prosecutors, who were versed in criminal law, had bothered to really figure out what was the state of the immigration law, or, in particular, the way that issues of sham marriages were being dealt with by attorneys and the immigration courts. If they had, then surely that soft-ball question about domicile, which was turned into a home run for the defense, would never have been lobbed my way.

To Summarize My Teaching Career

I taught immigration law at three different law schools a total of fourteen years, and refugee law for twelve years at two law schools, and had the intensive but satisfying role of directing the immigration clinic at George Washington for ten years. How to characterize the role of teacher, and the satisfaction that this noble calling gives? I refer to an old Mexican folktale.

A priest taught Spanish grammar to elementary students in a remote village in the Mexican Yucatan. He lived alone and his best friend was his pet parrot, a beautiful scarlet macaw, which accompanied him on his shoulder in the classroom for years, sometimes swinging from its honorary perch in the corner, singing along to nursery rhymes while mimicking the children's voices. Over time the priest neglected to clip the parrot's wings, for where would it go? They were dependant on one another, so he thought.

But one day the parrot *did* fly out the door of the classroom and was gone. The priest was heartbroken. He waited for the parrot's return. Days passed, turning into weeks and months. He finally realized that his friend would not return.

One day the following year, the priest was travelling through the jungle on a burro to visit another village five miles away. When he was at midpoint in his journey, he began to hear strains of music coming through the thick jungle underbrush. As he rode along, the sound grew louder, until he could make out the distinct voices of children, and he soon realized they were singing the song he always used in his class to teach the alphabet. He was perplexed, because he was unaware of any schools in this remote part of the jungle. After a while he came upon a clearing, and to his astonishment, he saw his old friend, the parrot, leading a group of twenty multi-colored macaws in the sing-song alphabet melody. The parrot saw him and flew to perch on his shoulder, calling, "Master, master, now I have my own class, aren't you proud of me?"

Nicaragua, and Decision to Become a Judge

One afternoon at the end of November in 1996, I came off of the hot dusty streets of Managua, Nicaragua into the air-conditioned office of the electoral observation mission of the Organization of American States (OAS). I had spent the day, as I had practically every day during the past three months, working in the streets of that "transitional democracy" (OAS terminology) assisting in preparations for the upcoming presidential election. A phone message was waiting for me: call Washington immediately. I called the number on the memo, and was connected to Assistant Chief Immigration Judge Kevin Smith. Kevin had been District Counsel in Arlington for a period of time while I was representing immigration cases in the Arlington immigration court. He told me on the phone that I had been approved for a position as an immigration judge.

My deployment in Nicaragua with the OAS was one of the hardest, but most rewarding, experiences of my life. In 1996, Nicaragua saw its second free and fair election, transitioning out of the decade of Sandinista rule of that country. In 1990, during the first election that was a result of an internationally-brokered peace process, in a surprising reversal of fortune the popular Dona Violeta defeated Sandinista President Daniel Ortega, forcing the Sandinistas to withdraw from the presidential palace. They still retained considerable power, however. They still held control of the Ministry of Defense, and they had a significant representation in the National Assembly and were still holding power across the country in major municipalities. 1996 was a benchmark election. Political observers considered that a second peaceful election and transition of government would assure the international community and investors that democracy was now sufficiently entrenched in the country, such that the return to power of the Sandinista dictatorship would be unlikely. The OAS electoral mission was thus important to officially sanction a fair election.

I had been in Nicaragua exactly a decade earlier, during the height of the Reagan-backed *contra* war against the Sandinistas. I had spent a month learning Spanish in the northern city of Esteli, a city which was always subject to encroachments of *contra* guerrilla forces. Over the years the war had ground to a military stalemate, and finally the UN and OAS had brokered a peace agreement, which included demobilization of the guerrilla forces after the first free election in 1990. Later, in 1993 I had returned for a month to prepare an assessment of the human rights situation in the country for the Research and Documentation division of the asylum office in the Department of Justice. During that trip I traveled from Managua to the southern parts of the country, discovering the fascinating colonial city of Granada and the little paradise city of San Juan del Sur on the Pacific coast. On my third trip in 1996, I was able to get to many other parts of the country, including the autonomous Atlantic zone, where the native Miskito and Rama populations had been granted political autonomy and were in control of the local governments.

Objectives of the OAS mission leading up to the election included monitoring the issuance of voter I.D.s to those eligible to vote; monitoring of the various voting precincts and polling places around the country, to assure that staff contracted by the electoral commission were doing their jobs and the polling places were accessible to the public; observing electoral rallies and monitoring all press coverage related to the election; and on election night, being at preordained polling places to monitor the actual voting and the activities of other election monitors to insure the integrity of the vote.

I gained some unwelcome notoriety during my deployment as an election observer. One day in October I went into a polling place in the highly political city of Masaya, south of Managua. Masaya had always been one of the centers of Sandinista support. Just as I was about to enter the school where the polling place was situated, I met a middle-aged female AID employee who was monitoring the election for the American embassy, who had just been inside talking to the poll workers. She said, "Those people are really worked up in there." I went inside to discover that the poll workers were angry because they hadn't been receiving their daily salary and food allotments as promised by the government's Election Commission.

Protocol required that whenever an election observer entered a polling place, their name and electoral commission ID number should be entered in a log maintained on the sight. As I was chatting with the angry poll workers, I routinely wrote my info on the ledger. They mentioned that they were going to have a demonstration at the local office of the election commission that evening, and asked if I could attend. I said that I wasn't sure, but I would inform headquarters about the rally and see what they said. Observing such rallies was part of our normal duties as election observers. That particular day, we ended up not attending that rally.

The next day, after the morning briefing at the office in Managua, I was already on the road with my Nicaraguan driver, heading back to the same city to continue the work. I heard my name being called over the short-wave radio. It was the director of the Managua office inquiring of my whereabouts. I told him where we were, and he ordered me to pull my vehicle over to the side of the road. It turned out that he was in a vehicle right behind me and he had been trying to chase me down. He said that the morning's paper contained allegations that I had been agitating the poll workers in Masaya to go on strike, and that at the demonstration the night before they had become extremely rowdy and riot police had been called in to quell the demonstration.

The story of any involvement on my part was absurd, of course, but I was told to turn around and report to headquarters, where the head of the OAS mission was waiting to question me about my involvement in the unrest in Masaya. Because an OAS worker was accused of having gotten involved, it had turned into an international incident which could be very embarrassing for the mission. During the interview at headquarters, I naturally maintained my innocence and I was excused, but with the caveat that I shouldn't return to Masaya.

That evening, at home, I was watching the nightly news as usual. Ever since my years of work in the TV news industry, prior to law school, I have been addicted to the nightly news. I especially like to watch it whenever I travel. I think of it as much as an anthropological pursuit as a quest for the real news; you can learn a lot about a country by the way the news is presented.

During the broadcast, I was astounded to see a close-up of my passport photo flashed on the TV screen, while the announcer reported that an OAS worker had been accused of inciting the local poll workers in Masaya to riot. He mangled my last name, but still there was my picture being broadcast nationwide so that any potential troublemaker could be on the watch for me. Who could say how many crackpots might like to have a chance to make a point by taking a shot at me? What was also disturbing was that the photo could only have come from one of two sources – either our own national office, which meant that one of our own workers would have been paid off to betray me – or the office of the Electoral Commission, and it would have been a crime for anyone there to have given out that information. And what was the motive to expose me in that way? At any rate, it was the kind of fame that I didn't need.

After that incredible news broadcast, the head of the OAS mission decided it was too dangerous to leave me in the area, and instead I was "exiled" to the Atlantic Coast, where I would spend the next three weeks – the two weeks leading up to and the week following the election – in the town of Puerto Cabezas in the northern Atlantic Zone. For me, being sent there was kind of like the fable of Brer Rabbit, where he pleads, "Please don't throw me in the briar patch." I had wanted to go there all along.

The Atlantic side of the country is an area populated by several indigenous tribes and black Caribbean peoples of African heritage. The locals speak English, or their own dialect of same, and also an interesting dialect of Spanish. Puerto Cabezas is the only significant town in the north, the center of power of the Miskito Indians, and Bluefields is the city in the southern zone, the center of power of the Rama Indians, and also the zone where the black population is dominant.

I was stationed in Puerto Cabezas with an OAS organizer from Venezuela. Carlos, a charming young black man, lived in New York with his American wife. He had a tremendous sense of humor and we got along splendidly, living outside of the immediate reach of the OAS bureaucracy in Managua. For diversion, we gave each other nicknames. In Nicaraguan Spanish, the word "Chelli" is slang for white person. And everyone in Nicaragua knows that most people in Bluefields are black. As terms of personal endearment, I called Carlos "Commandante Bluefields" and he called me "Commandante

Chelli." There was nothing to do at night in that dusty little town that was right out of a wild west novel, except to drink beer at the only local disco, where insanely loud, blaring music tortured the surrounding streets until late in the evening. We drank enough beer during those three weeks to supply a Sandinista regiment.

On the night of the election I was assigned to a remote polling place in the jungle, at a primary school without electricity, where the local Miskito Indians counted the ballots for the first hand count by the light of kerosene lamps. Their conversation shifted between the Miskito and Spanish languages. I was in awe that I was even able to be there and witness the event.

The Sandinistas lost the presidential election to the conservative opposition candidate, Arnuldo Aleman. (After his six year presidency, he was tried and convicted of accepting bribes and kickbacks during his term of office. As of this writing he is still battling to stay out of jail). The Sandinistas demanded a recount.

Thus I was witness to the same kind of tedious recount that that other tropical State, our state of Florida, would go through only four years later. Commandante Bluefields and I were assigned to remain in Puerto Cabezas while that municipality conducted the recount. The same thing was going on in every city across the country. All of the ballots were brought to a warehouse in the center of the city, and members of each party had observers on full-time watch as the contents of the bags containing the ballots from each individual polling place were opened and the contents recounted. The whole process took several weeks.

The Sandinistas had won the election for mayor of Puerto Cabezas, and they still controlled the police force of that city and they had significant influence within all local branches of government. But they had lost the local election for governor, and they had trailed in the Presidential vote there. One week into the counting, the army was tipped off that the Sandinistas were hatching a plot to storm the warehouse where the ballots were kept at night and to steal all of them, thus depriving the opposition candidate, the notorious former Miskito *contra* leader Steadman Fagoth, of his predicted victory as governor of the province. A tally sheet of the hand count of each polling place had been used to report the first unofficial election results to Managua, and those were the results which the Sandinistas were now contesting.

The local representative of the Election Commission was alerted to the plot to steal the actual ballots. He and my superiors in Managua hatched a scheme to protect the integrity of the count. At midnight, I was entrusted with a briefcase containing the original tally sheets from all of the polling places in the northern Atlantic zone, and I was picked up from my hotel by military jeep and driven to the military airfield, where the hulking body of a huge Soviet army helicopter awaited its only passenger. I felt a bit like Jonah in the belly of a whale in that helicopter. Thus was I spirited away from Puerto Cabezas, returning to the capitol earlier than anticipated. At the airport in Managua I was again met by a military escort and driven to OAS headquarters with the briefcase containing the results of the electoral mandates of all of the Miskito Indians in Nicaragua.

After I received that phone call in the Managua office from Judge Kevin Smith in Washington, I had a big decision to make: whether I should accept the offer to become an immigration judge. My other interest, after having been stateside bound at the university for ten years, was to continue to seek overseas employment. That had been my original game plan, and the reason why I had been happy to turn the reins of the immigration clinic over to another lawyer. I had been chomping at the bit to do international work. In my grand scheme, this Nicaragua contract was just the start of a new career for me.

On the other hand, there were obvious strong arguments in favor of accepting the position as a judge. First, it was a natural progression in my career. I knew the law, especially in the areas of asylum and deportation defense, as well as anyone. It would be a position from which I could help develop the law in crucial areas that could be meaningful to a lot of people. The downside – little opportunity to travel; a strict nine to five regimen; and being a cog in the federal bureaucracy. Nevertheless, all of my friends encouraged me to accept the judge position, citing issues such as professional stature, and that I could always do other things later that would fulfill my desire to travel and work with people abroad. But I confess that the ultimate consideration that pushed me into the pro-judge camp – I knew how proud it would make my parents, especially my father, who was a retired Marine Corps officer.

But still, when I returned to the States after the OAS mission, I interviewed for a job with the Agency for International Development in Peru, for a two-year "promotion of democracy" contract. They wanted me for the position, and it was very tempting, especially after already having had a taste of the Brazilian Amazon jungle years earlier, and now the jungles of Nicaragua – I imagined being able to spend considerable time in the Peruvian Amazon as an offshoot of that job. But after discussions with my friends, I was persuaded to decline the offer and accept the judge position.

PART TWO: IMMIGRATION JUDGE, PHILADELPHIA

Education of Immigration Judges

Obviously most Americans never clutter their minds with the question of how immigration judges are trained or prepared for this most sensitive and responsible of jobs, but I suspect if they ever had to contemplate the issue, they would feel certain that the Department of Justice affords the IJs the highest level of intensive training. After all, the immigration law code is widely considered by the legal profession to be the second most complex area of law in the American system, subordinate only to the tax code in level of intricacy and opaque convolution. Then you have to throw in the many difficult factors of adjudicating hearings with people from all over the world, whose lives are at stake and hanging in the balance upon the decision of the judge. And think of the vastly different conditions in each country of origin that judges have to grapple with when ruling on a claim for asylum. Surely our government would guarantee that the judges are highly trained experts in their field. **Think again.**

The agency had established at that time a relationship with the National Judicial College on the campus of the University of Nevada at Reno, Nevada. I trained there with the first group of immigration judges who graduated from that venerable institution. During our week-long residence on campus, the college was also training traffic court judges. I loved the run-down, frayed-at-the-seams quality of that gambling town. I jokingly commented that the IJs were being trained in Reno in order to test their legal skills during the daytime and their moral resolve at night. I had personal knowledge that more than one of the budding judges, in addition to spending their evenings in the casinos gambling, made visits to the notorious bordello called the Mustang Ranch on the outskirts of town.

We spent four days listening to lectures by a staff of immigration judge faculty, giving us inside tips about how to navigate certain tough situations that might arise on the bench, such as always remembering to turn on the tape recorder when starting the hearing. (At one of our conferences it was revealed that one of the judges had neglected to do so in hundreds of cases, requiring each case to be retried). Every day at lunch time we sat around picnic tables at an outside verandah, eating the chicken and tuna-salad sandwiches provided by the college, and sharing our anxieties about the job. We each had the opportunity to participate in a mock hearing, where we actually wore a black robe and read from prepared scripts while pretending to be judges. And we each received a handsome embossed certificate lauding the fact that we had undergone the rigorous Reno boot camp for IJs.

Four years later, I was invited to serve on the faculty of the training camp in Reno for new judges. I presented lectures on the topics of asylum law, section 208 of the Immigration and Nationality Act, and withholding of deportation, section 241(b)(3)of the Act. One day of lectures, a total of four hours when you take into account lunch and coffee breaks. Naturally, asylum law is that aspect of the immigration law that is dearest to me, it is the motivating reason that I decided to become an immigration attorney and later to become a judge. It was appalling, and ludicrous to imagine that these future judges would be well-equipped to make educated decisions on such complex issues of law after such a brief introduction. In comparison, asylum officers, those officials who receive the initial applications and conduct interviews of asylum applicants, for half of the salary of immigration judges, routinely receive six weeks of training on the asylum law and procedure alone. Any new judge who had not already been practicing in the field for at least several years would be helplessly lost and bound to bungle multiple decisions while learning on the job.

I am informed that recently the training has been overhauled and lengthened. A new IJ now starts off in his own court observing and being mentored by an experienced IJ, then receives two weeks of training instead of the one week that I received, and then is assigned to a different court not his/her own for two weeks to begin doing cases while under mentorship of another judge. I still consider this to be woefully inadequate given the complexity of the law, even if narrowed down to only those aspects of the law involving deportation hearings and asylum law. IJ's should still be plugged into an intensive asylum law training, perhaps a streamlined version of what new asylum officers receive. I am also informed that judges complain that they receive way too little administrative time for refreshing and catching up on the state of the law and new developments in their field; and that the ratio of law clerks to judges is still vastly inadequate. When I was an IJ in San Francisco we typically had one Department of Justice research clerk (an entry-level attorney position) assigned to 16 judges. I felt so sorry for the individual that I tried to never call on him for assistance but rather did all of my own research and writing.)

"Judge Terence T. Evans of the Seventh Circuit Court of Appeals offered one of the best descriptions of what it's like to be an Immigration Judge.

'Because 100 percent of asylum petitioners want to stay in this country, but less than 100 percent are entitled to asylum, an immigration judge must be alert to the fact that some petitioners will embellish their claims to increase their chances of success. On the other hand, an immigration judge must be sensitive to the suffering and fears of petitioners who are genuinely entitled to asylum in this country. A healthy balance of sympathy and skepticism is a job requirement for a good immigration judge. Attaining that balance is what makes the job of an immigration judge, in my view, excruciatingly difficult.'" Quote by Judge Paul Schmidt, from

Guchshenkov v. Ashcroft, 366 F.3d 554 (7th Cir. 2004) (Evans, J., concurring).

The Basics – A Primer

With an estimated 11 million undocumented migrants in the U.S., the enforcement of our immigration laws and the practice of immigration law by attorneys and their staff guarantees that there are job opportunities for tens of thousands of people in this field. Attorney membership in the American Immigration Lawyers Association alone is roughly eleven thousand lawyers, and surely there are an equal or greater number of lawyers who practice in the field without joining this reputable organization.

In my career, I have emphasized two specialized areas of the practice – asylum law and deportation defense. There are lawyers and law firms that specialize in bringing highly skilled workers, managers and professionals to the U.S. – boring! Some lawyers specialize in assisting people to immigrate based upon either offers of employment or family-based petitions – also boring. Those areas of the practice can be much more lucrative, but lacking in the human drama that asylum and courtroom work offers.

Asylum Law

When Congress passed the Refugee Act of 1980, it provided for the first time a procedure to allow any foreigner in the U.S. to fill out a form, called an I-589, and apply at the local INS office for asylum status. The Refugee Act incorporated the definition from the 1951 Geneva Convention on the Status of Refugees into U.S. immigration law. The asylum applicants were guaranteed an interview by an INS officer and a decision on their claim. For the first time, there was a market of asylum seekers that allowed a growing number of lawyers to specialize in the field. When I was a student intern at Jan Pederson's office in 1984, approximately half of her very successful practice involved representation of asylum applicants.

Typically, if an asylum application is rejected by INS (now USCIS) the applicant has an opportunity to present their story to an immigration judge in a more elaborate hearing, where they can present testimony and witnesses and be subject to cross-examination by a government attorney. Then, if the judge denies the case, it can be appealed to the Board of Immigration Appeals, and eventually up to the Federal Circuit Court of Appeals, and even on to the U.S. Supreme Court. You can see the myriad opportunities for lawyers to get involved.

Importantly, the new asylum law created an avenue for new lawyers who wanted to be involved in an area of human rights law. Many immigration lawyers of my generation got involved because of the urgent need for lawyers to represent the tens of thousands of refugees coming from Central America in the 1980s. There are few things more compelling than working with someone who fears persecution and torture, to understand their case and to shape it with them to present it in the most effective way possible, for presentation to either the asylum officer or the judge.

Deportation Defense

Deportation defense is the other area of immigration practice that affords the lawyer an endless supply of very meaningful cases, and a professional life filled with compelling stories, human drama, and an ability to really make a difference in people's lives. Especially for someone who is interested in other cultures and languages, this can be a very rewarding area of practice. It's an area where there is always an opportunity to get involved, with approximately 260 judges, thousands of court support staff, and thousands of government attorneys and their support staff involved in the system. There are lawyers who specialize in Spanish-speaking cases, or African cases, or Indian or Asian cases, and there are lawyers like myself, who loved the challenge and diversity of working with people from all over the globe.

If someone is in the country in an undocumented status and the government wants to deport them, there are only a few limited avenues of defense:

1. Asylum: the former asylum applicant can renew the application for asylum before the court, or anyone can potentially raise a claim for the first time in court.

2. Cancellation of removal: if a person has been in the country for at least ten years, and has qualifying relatives to whom they can show that it would cause exceptional hardship if that person were deported, they may qualify for cancellation of removal; or if they have been a lawful permanent resident (LPR) for at least five years and have been in the country for at least seven, they may be able to qualify for cancellation.

3. Adjustment of status: if someone already had a visa petition to become a permanent resident pending with the

government, it may be possible, depending on the timing and the circumstances of the petition, for the immigration judge to grant the adjustment of status, and the person can walk out of the court with a document showing they are a Lawful Permanent Resident.

4. Already U.S. citizen: you'd be surprised how many people who are put into deportation proceedings *are* U.S. citizens and don't even know it. Possibly they were born in the U.S. and their parents moved back to their country at such an early age that the individual was never made aware of it, as happens frequently with births along the southwest border; or citizenship was passed along by a parent through operation of law.

5. Torture convention: if a person can show that it is more likely than not that he would be tortured if returned to his country, he may qualify to stay in the U.S. under the Convention Against Torture.

6. Battered spouse under the Violence Against Women Act (VAWA) – if an alien spouse of either gender has been the victim of abuse by a U.S. citizen they may qualify for cancellation of removal and eventual green card.

If the above quick primer seems complicated, believe me, it's much worse. When I was directing the immigration law clinic at George Washington, I wouldn't let a student near a case until they had spent a full semester in my immigration law class, reviewing the concepts and sample cases. Then, in my clinic we had additional lectures about procedure and conducted mock hearings to prep the students before they ever got near a live client, after which everything had to be done under my supervision. Yet new immigration judges are given a crash course in immigration law, during which time they spend perhaps one day, at most, on the issue of asylum law. This includes judges who have never had any exposure to immigration law before. Then they are set free to decide people's lives.

The above list and explanation is an extremely simplified overview. In practice, the language of the law, and the analysis of that language, is very complicated. Immigration lawyers spend countless hours attending conferences and workshops in order to understand ways and strategies of dealing with the intricate statute and regulations. What makes it worse is that every year Congress either amends the law, or new regulations are promulgated by the various agencies involved. It is possible for the best-intentioned and most experienced lawyer to make a mistake.

The practice of deportation defense affords a lawyer the opportunity to live the courtroom drama, to act essentially as a defense attorney for their client. In reality most lawyers are not very good at it, because they never have the chance to really hone their evidentiary and cross-examination skills. The best way to do that is to work as a prosecutor or in a public defender's office for a few years.

The lack of skills on the part of government lawyers appearing in immigration court is equally noticeable, and all the more regrettable because they have so much power and are officially representing the interests of the U.S. government. The newest group of ICE prosecuting attorneys, at this writing having been trained in December 2019 in Dallas, were exposed to a week of book training and lectures and didn't have a single session on courtroom practice or procedure.

The Activist Judge

Authority of immigration judge: The immigration judge shall administer oaths, receive evidence, and interrogate, examine, and cross-examine the alien and any witnesses
Immigration and Nationality Act

Conduct of hearing: The immigration judge shall receive and consider material and relevant evidence, rule upon objections, and otherwise regulate the course of the hearing.
Title 8 Code of Federal Regulations

My appointment to the immigration bench led me to Philadelphia. I didn't know a single soul there except for Judge DeBernardis, the same man who had been the INS trial attorney on the Arunulfo Dias case back in my CARECEN days. Craig was from Philadelphia, and had been appointed an IJ in the early nineties, but he had been required to move to Arlington to accept the position. Finally, in 1996, a position opened up for him in Philly and he moved back. I was sent there to fill a new third slot that was created when the work load for the court increased.

I first moved into a sublet at 13th and Spruce, in the bohemian heart of Center City. At that time, a serial rapist was stalking that section of town. The Philly police looked for him for several years without success; he was later caught and convicted in Colorado, where he had moved to stalk a college campus community there. Aside from the rapist, it was a great neighborhood to live in as an introduction to Philly; artists, musicians, and gay hipsters populated the streets. And there was a vintage guitar store right next to my building, where I spent many hours trying out the guitars.

After six months, I moved into a row house in Roxborough, a working-class neighborhood in Western Philly. The house was rented by Anne Marie, a strong, very political woman, who had quit the profession of union organizer after ten years to become an elementary school-bilingual teacher in one of Philly's toughest schools in the northeast part of town. Nearly all of her students had lost a parent or close relative to drug-related violence. She rented me the room on the front part of the house that faced Wissahickon Park. The park had great trails where I could go running along Wissahickon Creek after work.

In Philly, at the time that I started my tenure there, the INS trial attorneys were all young and relatively inexperienced. They tended to be drawn from state prosecutor's offices after one or two years of experience. I learned, upon my arrival in summer of 1997, that none of the INS attorneys had any background in immigration law or, according to my informal poll, had even had an immigration law course in law school, and most of them fancied themselves as tough-guy prosecutors. Many of them dreamed of moving on to the U.S. Attorney's office to prosecute federal crimes. As a result, most of them treated the immigrants who came into my courtroom as criminals who had to be broken down and humiliated on cross-examination. And of course it was management that set the tone in the office. (At this writing, I have heard that most attorneys in that office are still recruited from state prosecutors' offices).

I had seen that mentality in INS attorneys many times in the past: take, for example, the INS attorney who was notorious for being just an outright asshole (actually, there are more than one, so if you happen to be a government attorney and you think this applies to you as you read this, think of that Carly Simon song, "You're so

Vain"). Once, when I was still director of the GW clinic, I was representing a young Ethiopian woman in her asylum hearing. She had a very strong claim to asylum, but while in the U.S., she had committed the "cardinal sin" of having included dependants on her tax returns who shouldn't have been there, such as cousins or nephews who weren't actually living in the household (let's see a show of hands for all of you readers who have done something similar). Most likely she wasn't even aware of the entry on the form but had rather just signed off at the preparer's recommendation.

It was her day in court, and the INS attorney was cross-examining her. He thought that this tax matter was excellent proof of her propensity to lie, and that therefore it would destroy her credibility about the merits of her claim of persecution. Judge Cary Copeland was clearly sympathetic to my client, and I felt certain that we had already won the case, based upon her testimony on direct examination. The attorney kept harping on the same line of questioning about the taxes, in spite of my objections of "asked and answered." He refused to let go, and he approached her where she was sitting in the witness chair and leaned over in her face, continuing to badger her; a particularly ugly scene.

I objected. "Your honor, I request that counsel step back from my client."

The judge was in the middle of responding, "I think that's about right," when my client fainted on the stand, clearly from the overload of stress that this clown had been heaping on her. It was as if her body turned to jelly, and she slid down off the chair onto the floor. Luckily one of the court clerks was a trained paramedic, and my client came around shortly, but we had to interrupt the trial upon the judge's orders.

But that particular attorney got his come-uppance. I heard from one of my former students, Antoinette Rizzi, who was later in private practice, that she had been in a deportation hearing with him at the Powhattan Correctional Institute in Virginia. Her client was a particularly big and mean convict who was being deported for his criminal history. The INS attorney was up to his old tricks of verbally abusing the client on cross. Finally, the client-convict had enough, and he rose up out of the witness chair and began chasing the attorney in circles around counsel's table and had to be restrained by the guards. My friend had to suppress her laughter at the sight, and she especially appreciated the look of terror on that attorney's face.

(Two decades later, I encountered one such INS/ICE lawyer by chance on facebook. I connected with him, and told him that, believe it or not, those times we had clashed in the courtroom together had been some of the most memorable and enjoyable times in my career. I was disappointed to see, under the Trump administration, his nativist and anti-Muslim rants in alignment with the new administration, and I had to "unfriend" him).

A prosecutor who appeared before me routinely for three years had a particularly nasty, grumpy, unrelentingly anti-immigrant attitude. Spending so much time on a wide variety of cases with him, I naturally wondered what might have happened in his youth to leave him so twisted. Once, during a hearing in which the migrant's request for relief was suspension of deportation, I noticed during a particular line of questioning that he seemed to know a lot about the functioning of dairy farms. The migrant had worked on a dairy farm in Pennsylvania, and the nature of his questions displayed more than a laymen's knowledge. After the hearing, I asked him if he had any background with dairy farming, and he affirmed that his family were dairy farmers in Western Pennsylvania. I later learned that his parents, as owners of a large dairy farm, had recently been sued by a dozen former herders and dairy production workers who had lived at their ranch. Allegations raised in court stated that "the housing was deplorable. There were mushrooms growing on the carpets, holes in the roof. When they went to the employer and asked him to fix it they were fired." The workers received a settlement of $335,000.

That information said a lot about where he might have gotten his contempt for migrant workers: from mother's milk, so to speak.

Even if the young attorneys weren't particularly mean-spirited, they still tended to be woefully lacking in knowledge about the conditions in the countries from where the respondents in court had come from, and lacking in life experience that would give them the tools to understand and relate to the plight of the asylum seekers. The author John Le Carre' put it amazingly succinctly in his novel, A Most Wanted Man, Scribner, 2008, which features as a backdrop the German asylum system. He refers to the frustrations of an attorney for an asylum applicant having to deal with low-level bureaucrats with such power and whose only experience outside their country is on holiday cruises. How many times have I been that attorney, listening to inept government prosecutors haranguing the asylum seekers, or later as a judge, when I had to bite my lip to not hurl invectives at them for exhibiting such a petty kind of thinking when discussing life-and-death events involving the people before them.

(After much deliberation, I have eliminated the names of the "bad guys" in this memoir. Even though, as a work of non-fiction, the names should properly appear, I finally came to the following conclusion: first of all, to put their names in print really wouldn't improve or correct anything; their supervisors already know exactly who they are. My point is that it is the system itself, management, that needs to be indicted for allowing such grossly incompetent and malicious people to continue in positions of trust and power. To name them here would only embarrass them in the eyes of their mothers. Second, everyone else in the professional community who has to deal with them on a daily basis knows who they are, and if those practitioners have occasion to read this book, they will know exactly who I am referring to.)

Some of the young attorneys in Philly were equally abusive. In one case, Judge DeBernardis decided to grant the application for asylum of an Egyptian Coptic Christian. The man's wife, who was undocumented but was not in deportation proceedings, was sitting outside the courtroom with their infant son. If her husband was granted asylum then she would by operation of law also be entitled to asylum protection. When the judge signaled that he was planning to grant the case, the INS attorney asked permission to leave the courtroom for a break, then went upstairs and persuaded an INS agent to come down and arrest the woman because of her undocumented status, while she was holding the baby in her arms.

At first, in my new role as a judge, I had a very hard time with that mentality. As judges, we of course are supposed to remain neutral, but as I saw the kinds of abuses taking place in my courtroom by government lawyers, including a general lack of respect for, and a calculated attempt to demean and degrade the individuals who were on trial, I came to see these young, overzealous attack-dogs as the enemy, and myself as a protector of the migrant's rights. But that meant that the workday would be filled with fights and recriminations, which leads to high blood pressure and anxiety. I realized that in the long term it would be unhealthy for me and ultimately unproductive.

I have never been known as a radical, quite the contrary my colleagues would confirm that I have always been quite the moderate by temperament and in my professional life. But I couldn't go on seeing unrepresented migrants, who were typically common laborers, being abused in such contemptuous and unprofessional ways in my courtroom. Something had to be done.

After a few months on the job, I re-evaluated the situation, and after discussions with some of my friends in the profession I adopted a different approach. These abusive INS attorney "kids" were young and inexperienced – they didn't know any better. And was I not, after all, a professor? Hadn't I just spent ten years teaching law students who were close to the same age as these INS attorneys, about the ethics of immigration law practice, helping to instill in them a respect for the dignity of our clients? I decided that part of my role as judge should be to teach these INS attorneys; to fill in where their education and experience in the field was so clearly lacking and where their superiors in government had failed to provide proper training. I made the conscious decision to view them as my students, rather than as arrogant, proto-fascist bureaucrats who abused their power. I began seizing the opportunity to talk to them after the hearings in private, explaining my view of the cases, engaging in dialog with them, using the cases like classroom exercises. And in a very short time I began to notice a difference. With many of the young attorneys, their attitudes and the way they conducted themselves in court changed markedly. In the long term, I came to enjoy working with most of them, and we developed a good professional relationship. I was actually sad to leave them when I moved from Philly to fill a spot in the San Francisco court in 2001.

And I suppose that a measure of my success was the fact that, when my departure from Philly was announced, the District Counsel, that is, the managing attorney for the INS lawyers, sought a private audience with me to ask if I would reconsider. And this was not someone whom I had considered my friend.

Actually my decision to intervene in the way that I did is not as radical as it might sound. An immigration judge is given broad discretion, per statute, regulation and case law, to assure that the rights of the migrant respondents in court are protected. As the statute section quoted at the head of this chapter indicates, an immigration judge is authorized to play much more of an active role in hearings than in traditional criminal or civil proceedings, including "interrogate, examine, and cross-examine..." And a judge must ensure that a migrant who is without counsel is informed of all her rights in the hearing, including any avenues of relief from deportation. This sounds more like a judge in the European Civil system than an American judge operating in the Common Law system who is much more of a neutral observer. It seems to stem from the earlier history of deportation hearings when the judge or "special inquiry officer" was both judge and prosecutor in the case and rarely would a respondent have an attorney representing him. It wasn't until 1982 that the judge's role was made separate from that of the prosecutor and the Executive Office of Immigration Review was established as a sub-agency to house and administer the immigration courts and judges.

IHP Program

One of my responsibilities in the Philly court was to handle the Institutional Hearing Program docket, by way of video link-up with the Allenwood, Pennsylvania federal penitentiary, at Deerwood, PA. Inmates at Allenwood had federal felony convictions. The immigration law requires that aliens who have such convictions and are deportable because of their convictions should be moved through the deportation process while they are serving their time in prison. That way their ultimate deportations won't be delayed another several years after they are released from prison by further lengthy deportation hearings and appeals procedures.

We had an elaborate video system set up in one courtroom which allowed me, from the bench, to move toggle switches in order to pan the camera, and zoom in on the inmate or witness who was sitting in front of a camera in a secure location at Allenwood, and they in turn, from their monitor, could see me or a witness on screen. Even though, technically speaking, it was possible to conduct the whole hearing, both preliminary and trial phase, over the video screen, I felt it was important to make an occasional field trip out to the site, what we call in government "showing the colors," in order to inspect how the facility was managed and to receive any complaints from the inmates about access to the process. I arranged through our excellent court administrator, Elliot Edwards, to conduct twice-yearly visits and to have a government attorney accompany me, and we would do a few days of hearings at the site. We toured the three facilities, maximum, medium, and minimum security.

Allenwood is one of those federal institutions that houses a lot of mobsters and convicted politicians (what, there's a difference?), the kind of place that is often referred to as Club Fed. The facility has a big wood-working and furniture production factory where inmates are employed. I noticed that the court bench and other furniture in our courtroom in Philly bore the same labels that were being affixed to the furniture in the factory there — UNICORE.

One of my first Allenwood cases was an Italian immigrant who had kidnapped himself in order to collect a ransom. That's right, Ricco was a resident of twenty years in the U.S. His luck had run out and he had become unemployed, and so he decided to fake his own kidnapping and try to extort money from his brother-in-law, who was a successful lawyer in New York. In his bogus ransom note, Ricco threatened to harm himself if the money was not delivered. Unfortunately for him, his brother-in-law became suspicious and called in the cops. Ricco was convicted of extorting money with the threat of violence. The conviction was arguably a deportable offense because of the threat involved, which made it an "aggravated felony." Ricco had spent several years in jail for his offense. He had no family or ties back in Italy, and I wanted to cut him some slack, reasoning that Congress, when it wrote the aggravated felony law, surely couldn't have intended it to apply to someone who threatens to harm himself. I threw out the case, or "terminated" it, but on appeal the Board of Immigration Appeals overturned my decision. The appellate court reasoned that a threat of violence is a threat of violence, no matter whom it is made against.

One day, during the Allenwood video hearings, I looked up from the file in front of me to see a young man, thin, Arab descent, looking into the camera from the small room at the prison. I called the case name, "This is the case of Salim …." I had hardly finished when the INS lawyer, Kurt Saccone, rose and handed me a document.

"Your honor, we are making a motion to recuse."

I saw that he had a decision from the Board of Immigration Appeals, dated several years earlier, with this young man's name as the appellant, and my name as the attorney on the case. It all came back to me. At the law school clinic, we had worked a miracle to get this man a 212(c) waiver, in spite of his convictions for possession of heroin with intent to traffic. We had put on a noble defense in immigration court, lost, and prevailed at the BIA, an outcome practically unheard of with that type of conviction.

With a crestfallen voice, I addressed my former client. "Salim, it looks like you've gotten yourself into a fix this time." He was up on an aggravated felony charge for drug trafficking, and the type of waiver that we had won for him had since been eliminated from the statute by Congress. The eventual outcome of the case was a forgone conclusion. But I could only recuse myself from the case, having been his advocate in an earlier proceeding.

On the lighter side, in the year 2000 the warden of Allenwood held a press conference to announce that investigators had uncovered a most heinous conspiracy right on the grounds of the prison facility: Some of the Italian mobsters who were imprisoned there had arranged to have prison guards smuggle their semen out of the prison, to be handed over to their girlfriends or childless wives. As "juicy" as this story was, I couldn't understand what was really illegal about the supposed activity. Besides the fact that it made for a wonderful story of human initiative, I didn't see where the harm lay. The New York Post was one of the papers to publicize that the mobsters, who were paying guards to smuggle their semen out, included George "Georgie Neck" Zappolla, a Lucchese Family capo; Frank Pontillo, a soldier in the Colombo Family; and Antonino Parleveccio.

Jordanian Spousal Abuse

In one of my most memorable cases I also played a bit of an activist role, but it was really only in helping to sort out and assess what evidence was really crucial to the case. I had to insist that the attorney for the respondent do a bit more homework to assure that the evidence she had submitted was sufficiently corroborated in order to build a strong record.

The woman on trial was a Catholic from Jordan, who had fled to the U.S. after years of abuse at the hands of her husband and his family. In a country where honor killings are all too frequent and well-documented (approximately 40 a year are reported), Sally's husband thought that he could beat her and knock her to the floor in front of his family, for such insubordination as working outside the home, even though he freely enjoyed the monetary fruits of her labor. Sally's siblings had immigrated to the U.S. years before she came, and she had visited them in the U.S. once before, and told them of the kind of abuse she was receiving. At the time, she had felt it her duty to return to the family in Jordan and submit to further abuse. It was only when her older brother visited her in Jordan and saw with his own eyes the kind of indignities that she was suffering, and realized that in fact her life was in danger by remaining in her own household, that he persuaded her to return to the U.S. – but this time for good.

When Sally left Jordan the second time, and then did not return, her husband went to the Ecclesiastical Court in Amman, Jordan, and filed a complaint against her. The Court in turn sent her a summons to appear. She had no desire to return. Then the Court sent her a set of interrogatories, questions to be answered in response to her husband's claims that she was a bad wife and had abandoned the family. She responded in writing. Then the Court issued a verdict, which essentially said that the evidence had shown that her husband tended to beat the crap out of her, but still it was her duty to return to the family and continue to submit like a good wife.

During Sally's immigration hearing in Philly, she and her brother who had visited her from the States and seen the abuse that was heaped upon her were witnesses. They were both credible and rock-solid in their testimony. Everyone in the courtroom was visibly touched by Sally's testimony of the kinds of beatings she had endured, and by the remarks that her own mother-in-law had made, such that her husband should kick her and jump on her head while she was down because she was too independent. Sally's lawyer submitted a mountain of documents about the conditions in Jordan, including evidence that honor killings are common in Jordan. In that pile of papers, I dug out the Ecclesiastical Court's summons of Sally to give testimony, and its decision in her case. Other than submitting it, sandwiched in among all of the other documents, her lawyer had made no further mention of it.

The main problem with the case was that, at that time, spousal abuse was a very controversial issue upon which to base a grant of asylum (still is). The BIA had ruled that spousal abuse was usually not a strong enough ground for a grant of asylum, because, aside from the abuse the victimized spouse was suffering, other ingredients necessary for asylum, such as the hand of a state actor or state persecutor, was missing. Sally's attorney was making a straightforward spousal abuse argument, without giving sufficient emphasis to the power of the Ecclesiastical Court in Jordan over her life.

During a break, I conferred with a student law clerk whom I had invited to observe the hearing. Lt. Alicia Galvany was a third year law student and a reservist in the army. I liked to jokingly refer to her as Lieutenant. I spoke with her about the way that I saw the issue shaping up, that namely the Ecclesiastical Court's involvement was the key to the case – if we could show that it was acting in a quasi-official or governmental capacity, that fact would distinguish Sally's case from other spousal abuse cases. I recruited the Lieutenant's help in researching and writing the decision. Then I went back into the courtroom.

"This ruling by the Ecclesiastical Court is the key to your case – this is how we can distinguish this case from the BIA's rule that spousal abuse is usually not a grounds for a grant of asylum. I need you to take some time and submit further evidence of what exactly this ruling means in terms of Jordanian society. Report back to me with whatever evidence you can find, and then you'll get your ruling."

I had already decided to grant the case. I was only helping the attorney and her client shape the case and the argument so that it would withstand appeal. After several months, during which time the Lieutenant also conducted her own research, new evidence was submitted which showed that in Jordan such an Ecclesiastical Court had the power to imprison someone who disobeyed its order – that Sally could be confined, and would remain so until she agreed to return to her husband so that he could continue to treat her like a human football. The evidence of the Ecclesiastical Court's power to impose such a sanction was what the case needed to distinguish it from the BIA's general rule against spousal abuse as a ground to grant asylum. The Lieutenant and I conferred further, and then I invited her to write the opinion.

She did such a persuasive job that the government attorney declined to appeal. We issued the decision just a day before Christmas, so that Sally and her Christian family would have something extra to celebrate that year. The case was reported by the leading immigration law journal, Interpreter Releases, published by West Law.

Afterword: Finally, sixteen years later, the Board of Immigration Appeals issued a precedent decision, in a Guatemalan case, establishing that women who are battered in their relationships and unable to seek the protection of police and/or courts in their country may under certain circumstances qualify for asylum. *Matter of ARCG-*, 26 I&N Dec. 388 (2014). I'm proud to say that my former student, now Board Member Charles Adkins Blanche, wrote the decision. And hats off to many tireless advocates in this area of practice including Professors Karen Musalo and Deborah Anker, who have toiled for years in the trenches to make this decision a reality.

Post-Afterward: Attorney General Jeff Sessions, among other outrageous and unlawful indignities that he imposed upon the immigration court, also assigned to himself (certified) a case, *Matter of A-B-* 27 I&N Dec. 316 (A.G. 2018), which was his mechanism for re-interpreting the above case-law. In an incompetent but damaging way he attempted to outlaw the theory that such women, or spouses in general, can qualify for asylum based upon the theory as developed over decades of jurisprudence. This was part of the general scheme of the Trump administration to severely limit the ability for migrants to qualify for asylum. Litigation is ongoing. Two years later several federal circuit courts have already overruled or severely narrowed the import of his decision and we are confidant that in the future it will be rolled back in its entirety.

The Lautenberg Amendment and Russian Jews

Northeast Philly has a large Russian population, and many people from the former Soviet Union have settled in Pennsylvania. Early in my judge career I had to grapple with an issue I knew well from being an advocate for refugees. Asylum applicants from the former USSR made up the third largest group, after Chinese and Mexican nationals, on the Philly court docket. Advocates for asylum applicants from the former Soviet Union argued that the courts should follow the same principle that American refugee adjudicators in Moscow applied. According to an act of Congress, known as the Lautenberg Amendment after its author Senator Frank Lautenberg from New Jersey, anyone presenting themselves to the U.S. embassy in Moscow or other consulates in former USSR countries, who could show that they belonged to a group that had traditionally been persecuted in the USSR – which included Jews and Pentecostal Christians – could be granted refugee status. (An amendment made to the 1990 Foreign Operations Appropriations Bill established a presumption of refugee eligibility for certain categories of persons from the former Soviet Union and Southeast Asia).

The argument being applied in immigration court, which was based on the Equal Protection clause of the Constitution, was that if that rule applied to refugees overseas, it should also apply to asylum applicants in the U.S. who could otherwise show that they belonged to one of the selected groups. I had made that same argument myself when representing several asylum applicants at the law school clinic – but now I was a judge with the fates of hundreds of such individuals in my hands.

I wasn't the first IJ to conclude that the Lautenberg Amendment should apply in immigration court. John Gossart, a very fine judge and mentor in Baltimore (and the judge in the Arnulfo Diaz case) had issued an excellent written decision applying the same reasoning. I adopted the same position, naturally very controversial and unpopular with the INS attorneys, that any asylum applicant in my courtroom from the former USSR, who could prove through birth records, passports, ID documents or other persuasive evidence that they were Jewish, would be granted asylum – which was in line with the Lautenberg Amendment. The problem for our Jewish applicants from that region was that they had often spent a lifetime trying to conceal their Jewish identity because of prevailing prejudice and persecution in the USSR. But they usually managed, one way or another, to comply with the requirement. The ranks of the Russian Jewish population in northeast Philly continued to grow.

Making the Law

I handled a case in Philly that opened my eyes about just how quixotic the development of the law can be. The issue involved whether a certain felony conviction for counterfeiting qualified as an "aggravated felony." That term was added by Congress to the immigration law statute in 1990.

First, a little background: the early history of immigration law in our country is largely one of Congress – mostly white males – compiling lists of undesirable people to keep out. Initially, in 1875, convicts and prostitutes were barred. In 1882, lunatics, idiots, and those "likely to become public charges" were added to the list. In 1891, the "diseased," "paupers," and "polygamists" were added. In 1903, epileptics, the "insane," "beggars," and "anarchists" were added, and in 1907 the "feebleminded" and persons with certain physical defects were added to the list. (See the excellent resource, Immigration Law and Procedure in a Nutshell, by David Weissbrodt). Then Congress began restricting immigration from certain East European and Southern European countries, and in the 1920s Congress banned outright immigration from Japan. A whole book could be written on the famous Chinese exclusion cases, beginning in the late 1800's, when the Supreme Court upheld legislation to exclude and summarily expel Chinese nationals. (This was always a favorite topic of mine while teaching immigration law in San Francisco). The notorious McCarran-Walter Act of 1952, passed by Congress over the veto of Harry Truman, included the exclusion of persons for their beliefs or party affiliations, most notably the Communist Party. And on and on, to the present day.

In 1996 Congress added considerably more kinds of offenses to the list of aggravated felonies, including counterfeiting, but arguably, the kind of counterfeiting Congress was referring to was that which we traditionally mean when we say the words money or currency.

My case: a German man was convicted of affixing fake pharmaceutical labels to vials of pills and selling them for what they were not. In the vernacular, he had committed a kind of fraud. But the federal government, for whatever reason, indicted and convicted him under a federal counterfeiting statute – he had been "counterfeiting" the labels.

After serving his federal prison sentence, he was brought into my courtroom in an orange jumpsuit, accompanied by federal agents. He happened to have retained a very fine lawyer, Thomas Mosely, who was a former Department of Justice attorney. Mosely argued that the provision of the immigration law, the aggravated felony section under which the INS was trying to deport his client for counterfeiting didn't apply, because that section only referred to "monetary instruments."

I liked the argument, and gave both sides an opportunity to brief it. Then I issued a decision in which I agreed with the defense.

In this case, the government wasn't going to be able to deport their man, because he had been convicted for counterfeiting pharmaceutical labels, not monetary instruments. I terminated the case. The government appealed.

I heard how the rest of the drama played out from the INS attorney who handled the case, Jeanine Linehan. She told me that she briefed the government's argument to the Board of Immigration Appeals, and that the government's appellate counsel in Washington had even commended her on what a fine job she had done. But then the INS found out which three-judge panel of the Board of Immigration Appeals was going to handle the issue. (see chapter on massacre of BIA). When they learned that Lory Rosenberg, one of the most liberal (and competent) judges, was one of the three judges on the case, they got cold feet. They predicted that Lory's panel would uphold my decision, and thus make it the law of the land that the definition of aggravated felony could not be extended to types of counterfeiting that had nothing to do with monetary instruments. They withdrew their appeal, thereby letting the German guy off the hook, but at the same time leaving the issue unresolved for future confusion.

I was surprised and disappointed to hear that the government had taken this round-about method of court shopping in order to avoid the implications of my decision.

Prosecutorial Discretion

Over the years I've never ceased to be amazed at how some of the INS attorneys, who are persons enjoying positions of great privilege and power, earning upwards of $160,000 a year, can be so callous and lacking in humanity – sometimes just downright bastards. Are they all the victims of early childhood abuse? Are there special training schools where the government takes normal people and turns them mean? It's funny, I've met many ICE attorneys and officials who are just mean, ornery individuals. I've never met an attorney working for a non-profit or NGO who is mean and ornery.

Of course I have worked with many fine INS attorneys, and of those individuals, I have admired their legal skills and their humanitarian inclinations. But somehow too many disturbed and twisted people get through the initial job screening, to enjoy life-long appointments where they can abuse their authority and make other people's lives miserable while acting in the name of the Department of Justice or Department of Homeland Security.

The irony is that, given the way the system is set up, the ICE attorneys have much more power to give someone a break than the judges do. That's because of a concept known as "prosecutorial discretion." If the government chooses to charge and bring a case in immigration court, the judge can't say, "Well I think this case just isn't worth worrying about, this pathetic little old lady isn't doing anyone any harm – case dismissed!" But the prosecutor *can*!

There are so many cases of serious criminal offenders who deserve to be deported, and the INS agents are so overworked investigating and rounding them up (today's ICE), and the immigration courts are so backlogged with such cases – I often wonder why they don't agree to let the undocumented migrant workers and day laborers, or the little grannies who just want to stay here with their families have a break. Such individuals may technically be in the country illegally and subject to deportation – but someone in the government should have the sense to say, "Let's see here, I've only got so many lawyers, and so many days in the week and hours in the day – I think I'll let this one go, concentrate on the bad guys." But in my seven years as a judge, and eleven years prior as an attorney, I never knew of a government attorney who decided to withdraw the charges on a particular case after the papers had been filed and concentrate their fire on more worthy targets. This is one of the major complaints of most judges that I know.

Usually, when you read the daily paper and learn about a whole family of wanna-be immigrants who have lived in the U.S. for the past twenty years, and even though their kids all went through the school system and are now straight A college students, and the family is contributing so much to the community, and the daughter was just offered her first acting job on Best Years of Our Lives – the law finally caught up with them and they've gotta go back to the Philippines or Mexico – it's not the judge who is insisting they go home. If they're here illegally, all the judge can do is sign the order. But the INS attorney could, if (s)he wanted, cut that family a break. Who is going to gain anything by uprooting them from their local community where they are paying taxes, and sending them back to a developing country where they have to start all over again?

When I was relatively new on the job, I had a heartbreaking experience that illustrates this point. A family from Eastern Europe was in deportation proceedings. They had to drive several hours to get to court. One of their daughters, in her early twenties, suffered from cerebral palsy and was confined to a wheel chair, unable to even lift her head. Her father was eventually going to be able to immigrate through his high-tech job, based upon a labor certification which had already been filed, and then he would be able to petition for and bring in the rest of the family legally – but it was a time-consuming, tedious process, and in the meantime, because they had all overstayed their tourist visas, the government wanted to kick the whole family out. Everyone in the courtroom knew that the family and their lawyer were going through the motions, filing applications in order to buy time, while the eventual labor certification wound its way through the system.

The second time they all came into my court, and I saw again the young woman who was confined to her wheel chair, and heard from the young INS attorney that the government insisted that the whole family show up for every appearance, I remembered the tradition in American jurisprudence of prosecutorial discretion. I naively thought that I could do some good by arranging an amicable chat with the attorneys involved in the case, including the INS attorney's superior. I called them all into my chambers. The conversation went something like this:

"This lady obviously has a very difficult health condition, and I'd like to spare her and her family the hardship of having to travel two hours to court every few months just so that she can eventually be told that she has to go back to her country. I personally don't see any sense in going through with her case, since down the road she'll be able to immigrate anyway through her father's petition. I was thinking maybe we could all agree to terminate her case, but still proceed with the rest of the family. I just wanted to share my thoughts with everyone and see what the government thinks about it."

There was an uncomfortable silence. The supervisory prosecutor had a frozen smile on his face. He looked at me like I was from another planet. "We're not interested in any kind of a settlement." That's when I knew that *he was* – from another planet, that is.

That was the extent of the conversation. I had no choice but to go ahead with the case and eventually order that the whole family leave the country. The consequences were that they would all have to return to Eastern Europe, but later, because the father's case was on track, they would eventually be able to return legally. I didn't have a magic wand to wave and say, "Don't worry, you can stay here after all." But the prosecutor did.

In fact, not too long after that conversation in my chambers, President Clinton's Commissioner for the INS, Doris Meisner, issued a directive to the field and the INS attorneys, reminding them of their prosecutorial discretion, and encouraging them to exercise it in compelling humanitarian cases. The directive was a follow-up from an initiative from a group of 28 members of Congress who had called upon the INS Commissioner and Attorney General Janet Reno to exercise discretion in such hardship cases. Meisner consequently sent out a message from headquarters to the field, because of the frequency in which the kind of scenario that I just described was being repeated all over the country. Yet I never saw any evidence that it was taken seriously by INS supervisors in the field. I could easily imagine that, for example, of those that came before me, perhaps at least one case a week should have been a good candidate for the prosecutor to withdraw the charges, for obvious humanitarian reasons, such as a single mother of U.S. citizen children, or single wage-earning father in the family, or serious health reasons, or serious mental problem of the respondent.

Indeed, when I was still in law school, and I interned with the U.S. Attorney's office in the District of Columbia, in Superior Court, I saw the very same principle being applied there. Early every morning, an Assistant U.S. Attorney would review, with the police officers who had been out all night making arrests, the kinds of cases and evidence that they had. On the spot, the decision would be made not to charge certain cases, even though they might be legitimate arrests, for several reasons, including the purely discretionary decision that "this case just ain't worth the trouble it would take to prosecute it." This is the procedure called 'no-papering.' When the defendant appeared in court at arraignment later that day, the case would be called, and the court clerk would announce, "This case has been no-papered, sir, you are free to go, " and the would-be defendant would walk out of the court with a huge grin on his face.

In June 2011 the head of ICE, John Morton, issued a memorandum on prosecutorial discretion, essentially making the same points that I make and encouraging the ICE attorneys to look for opportunities to exercise the power in immigration court. However, observers of the system claim that even if this position is well-intentioned, the good effects are more than nullified by a substantial increase of round-ups and deportations of simple migrant workers and undocumented laborers and mothers of U.S. citizens under the current administration.

(As mentioned in the forward to the 2nd edition of this book, on August 18, 2011 the Obama administration announced sweeping changes to the way that court cases are prioritized, essentially echoing my recommendations word for word.) (See my recommendations for reform below.) ICE attorneys across the country were charged with the task of reviewing their case loads and identifying cases that were good candidates for the exercise of prosecutorial discretion. Although in the eyes of most practitioners, these ICE prosecutors were still way too timid in their exercise of discretion, it was still an important starting point. The point was made that law enforcement resources should be concentrated on the bad guys rather than on the low-lying fruit.

Postscript

On May 18, 2018, white nationalist Attorney General Jeff Sessions overturned decades of practice in immigration court by essentially eliminating the practice of administrative closure which has been an option for immigration judges when both sides agreed for humanitarian reasons to put a case on hold. This boldly added an approximate 350,000 cases to the current backlog of a million and a half cases in immigration court.

Chinese Boat People — A Great Crisis Facing Our Nation

The fact that thousands of Chinese migrants are being smuggled into the U.S. by the sophisticated and deadly Chinese organized crime networks called "snakeheads" is a problem of crisis proportion, which has not been adequately addressed by our government. The U.S. State Department estimates that approximately 30,000 to 40,000 Chinese are smuggled in each year. According to news reports, Fujian City, where many of the smuggled aliens come from, has become a boomtown of new construction and businesses, based upon money from those who manage to make it to the U.S. and hold out long enough to begin sending revenues back home.

For a close-to-home look at how pervasive the problem is, residents of any major urban area in the U.S. need only open their local City Paper or variant, the weekly free newspaper that is distributed on sidewalk newsstands. Turn to the back pages, to find dozens of ads for Asian Massage Parlors, or Asian Acupuncture Salons. 90% of them use women who are being held in servitude, having been smuggled into the country and not being free to leave the location without escort, until they pay off exorbitant fees plus bogus interest that they are charged. Recently, in the San Francisco Bay area, federal and local police have been targeting such brothels, with frequent raids demonstrating that the women are virtual sex-slaves who are being held against their will.

Guam

On a Friday in July 1999, I departed Philly on a Continental Airlines flight to Guam, arriving at five p.m. two days later (the international dateline pushes travel to Asia one day forward). I was on an emergency deployment to preside over the first of hundreds of hearings involving Chinese boat people. INS had detained more than five hundred Chinese on Guam and on the neighboring island of Tinian. There had been a mini-invasion of smugglers' boats into Guam's waters, after one such boat, laden with its human cargo, was disabled during a storm and towed into Agatna Harbor by the U.S. Coast Guard. In that instance, the dozens of smuggled Chinese who were found on-board were flown to Seattle for further processing. Word apparently got out that all the smugglers had to do was get their clients, who had contracted to pay upwards of $40,000 each, to Guam, and they would automatically end up on the U.S. mainland. Boats began converging upon Guam like it was the promised land, and the Coast Guard only had one cutter, based out of Honolulu, to try and intercept them.

In order to counteract the invasion, INS, in cooperation with my agency, EOIR, decided to detain everyone in tent cities, letting them swelter under the tropical sun, and to complete all of their hearings on Guam. I arrived in the first group of rotating judge details, with three other IJs, to begin the hearings.

EOIR had always maintained a court in Guam, which was staffed out of Hawaii on regular details by the IJ there, but that part-time operation had never been intended to handle such a massive influx of customers. On a wartime footing, additional courts and personnel were equipped and staffed in Guam.

I landed on a typical day of balmy weather and took a cab to the

Marriot on Tumon Bay, where all court personnel would be housed during the six months of the mobilization. I would be meeting the other three IJs the next day. I found a convenient bar on the beach to enjoy the sundown on the waters of the Philippine Sea. I felt like I had really arrived, delighted that the government had paid to fly me out to this tropical paradise. The next two weeks were a combination of hard work and personal satisfaction with the job. The stay would also give me an opportunity to pay homage to my recently deceased father, who had landed with the American invasion force as a company commander with the 4th Marine Division on neighboring Saipan and Tinian islands in July 1944.

I got up early every morning and went for a run along the beach, one mile down the cove to the Hilton Hotel and back again, ending my run with a dip in the warm water before dressing for court. The first thing I did every afternoon when returning to the hotel after court was to go for a swim and then change into more comfortable tropical clothing.

One evening, after enjoying one of the incredible sundowns that bless the western side of the island every night like clockwork, and not having anything else to do for the evening, I strolled across the street to one of the island's many strip clubs. I discovered that my three other IJ comrades were already seated there, beers in hand, enjoying the show. They were still wearing their business suits and reveling in their shared forbidden pleasure. I was the only one of our group who was not married. Their interactions that evening reminded me of the wonderful John Cassavettes film, Husbands, in which three men, played by Cassavettes, Peter Falk and Ben Gazzara, go out on the town without their wives and try to have a good time, but are ultimately too guilt-ridden to enjoy themselves.

Most of the strippers were Asian, as were most of the customers. After a while, a group of drunken Japanese tourists came in and grabbed the front row seats. When an extremely attractive Asian stripper approached the front of the stage, one of the men leapt up and dived on top of her, pushing her down and pawing her all over. Her reaction was to take it in stride and let him feel her up for a bit, before regaining control of the situation and separating herself from him. Later, a Korean stripper approached one of the IJ's, took off his glasses and, with a priceless move rubbed them against her vagina, and then used his tie to clean the smears on the glasses, leering into his face at close range as she did so, then placing the glasses back on his face. When he turned back to us, he had a look of mixed embarrassment and pride, as though he had just made a conquest.

One of the CBP agents who was on the Guam detail later told me that INS frequently raided those strip clubs because so many of the girls dancing there were undocumented. I thought what a great news story it would make, if during one such raid they discovered four immigration judges in the audience salivating over undocumented strippers.

History of Chinese Asylum Cases In U.S.

First was Tiananmen Square – June 1989. After the massacre of Tiananmen Square, Congress passed the Chinese Student Protection Act of 1992, which granted automatic permanent residency to those Chinese students who could show they had arrived in the U.S. before April 11, 1990. One of my former students, Laura Foote Reiff, drafted Executive Order 12711, which was a temporary ban by the Bush administration on the deportation of Chinese nationals. The CSPA – Chinese Student Protection Act – made the provisions permanent – the stated purpose of the Act was to prevent the persecution of Chinese students who were in the U.S.

Naturally there was a lot of incentive on the part of Chinese asylum applicants to try and prove that they had somehow been involved with the political turmoil of the summer of 1989. Suddenly every young Chinese national in deportation hearings was claiming they had been involved. Then, after the CSPA was passed, there was even more incentive to prove that they had entered the U.S. prior to April 11, 1990.

The next popular kind of claim to asylum arising from China involved the one child policy, the Chinese government's attempt to curb its population growth by mandating that each family could only have one child. Stories abound of local enforcers carting women away, either to be forcibly aborted or forcibly sterilized. In 1996, Congress amended the asylum law, to include under its coverage anyone who had been forcibly aborted or sterilized, or had a fear that such forced measure could occur. The language was clearly intended to address the Chinese government's mandatory one-child per family policy, and it was widely considered to be a maneuver by the pro-life faction in Congress. It was a terrible mistake to tinker with the asylum law in this way (until then the language in the statute had tracked almost verbatim the language of the 1951 Geneva Convention on the Status of Refugees), and the U.S. asylum system and immigration courts paid for the mistake in the form of drastically increased applications from Chinese applicants.

Suddenly, every female Chinese arriving in the U.S. claimed to have been forced to abort a child. Part of their applications in immigration court included evidence from OBGYN's in the States that the woman had undergone an abortion. But as anyone familiar with life in China can explain, abortion has been the favorite method of birth control in China for decades. Many women endure multiple abortions by choice in their lives. It is thus impossible to tell if an abortion was coerced or voluntary – all that an adjudicator can go on is the woman's story. The legislative blunder remains in the statute at this writing.

When the Chinese government foolishly banned the Falun Gong movement in July 1999 (a quasi-Buddhist belief system founded by a charismatic preacher who lives outside China) thousands of Chinese asylum applicants wanted to take advantage of the sympathy of U.S. asylum officers and judges. Suddenly, every Chinese applicant was able to demonstrate the quasi-tai chi movements of the Falun Gong practitioners and recite the pseudo-Buddhist philosophy about the wheel that is located in the abdomen and rotates sometimes clockwise, sometimes counter-clockwise. Every supposed practitioner could recite incidents of miraculous healing, including cures of cancer, and of horrible government repression of their belief.

In Philly, fully fifty percent of the immigration court docket consisted of Chinese cases – mostly from Fujian province. The court employed contract Fuzhou interpreters, as well as Mandarin and Cantonese, to handle all of the cases. Due to this overwhelming exposure to the Chinese cases, I became fascinated in Chinese culture, and began studying Mandarin at the local community college and traveling to China during my vacations every year.

Later, when I was a judge in San Francisco, many detained Chinese, who had been stopped by INS inspectors at the airport because they were in possession of fraudulent travel documents, were brought into my courtroom. I heard many asylum cases, based upon Falun Gong membership, alleged Tiananmen Square activities, and the Chinese family planning program. But a new type of case presented itself numerous times, always from very young female Chinese. When I heard the story the first time I was intrigued, but as the story was repeated by one after another young woman, I became convinced there was an explanation for the pattern.

The standard story always involved a girl from a small village. Either the village headman or his son developed a fascination for the girl, and began approaching and harassing her, insisting upon either sex or marriage. Sometimes the headman wanted her for his son. Sometimes a brief kidnapping was involved, during which the girl was held at the headman's house or a secret location, until a miraculous rescue or escape occurred. The girl always escaped to the larger city of Fujian or Shanghai, and paid a smuggler to bring her to the States.

I was curious how this story, which we were hearing too often to find credible, was propagating itself among the female detainees. Finally, while speaking with a Chinese friend one day, I explained the situation, and immediately got the response, "Oh, that is the plot of a very popular soap opera in China!"

I also heard some colorful stories from the Chinese applicants during my visit to Guam. One afternoon, sitting in the hot, humid courtroom in Agatna, I was witness to a remarkable, classic courtroom confession, the kind which is usually just the stuff of crime-writer fantasy. A Chinese respondent was the bereaved husband of a woman who had allegedly been forced to have an abortion because her second pregnancy violated the one-child family planning law. He was testifying about how, after arguing with the local population control police against the threatened sterilization of his wife, he was arrested and thrown into a makeshift jail in a storage room behind the local police station. After sitting around and agonizing over his wife's fate for two weeks, he decided to escape through the flimsily boarded-up window. So far this story wasn't that unusual, in fact it was fairly routine for the kind of thing that we were hearing in Guam

– the miraculous escape from detention story. But then came the twist – while he was escaping out the window, a guard entered the room and tried to restrain him. They fought, and in his fear of being caught and punished even more severely, he killed the guard.

The INS attorney protested that the applicant had not put that part of the story, about the death of the guard, on his written asylum application; indeed, this was the first time that he had told it to anyone. I wondered why he had included it now at the hearing, when it wasn't strictly necessary in order for him to make out a case for asylum. If what he had already related up to that point about his wife's forced sterilization was true, that would be grounds enough for a grant of asylum – but he was confessing under oath in a court of law that he had killed a man. He answered that after he had taken the oath in our court, he realized he had to tell the whole story. I asked him again why he believed that, and he repeated the same answer several times.

Finally, because I still wasn't satisfied with the answer, I said, "Sir, I don't believe you. There must be some other reason that you would come into court and confess to a murder, when there was no need for you to do so." He broke down and began to tremble. With shaky voice he answered, "If I did not tell the truth about the guard, his ghost would come to haunt me." All of us in the courtroom began looking around the room, expecting to see a ghost materialize in front of us.

Another man made an equally startling statement in court. He had participated in a demonstration in his village against the excesses of local police authority in overtaxing the villagers. After a scuffle with the police, he and several others were arrested. He was looking at a lengthy sentence for opposition to state authority, or a free trip to a reeducation camp. His wife went to the police station, begging for his release. Given that she was young and attractive, and that men are beasts, the police worked out a deal with her – a couple of them would have their way with her in exchange for her husband's release, but then he would have to flee the area. She reluctantly submitted to the ordeal at the station, and he was released and fled to the neighboring city, where he made arrangements with a smuggler to leave.

After hearing his story, I asked him if he had had any contact with his wife since leaving China. He answered no.

"Well, if you are allowed to stay in the United States, will you want to bring her here to join you?"

"No."

I was naturally surprised by the answer, given the sacrifice she had made for him. "Why not?"

"After what she did with those policemen, I don't want to have anything more to do with her."

I was astounded. I thought I'd heard everything there was to hear about Man's inhumanity to Woman. But I still had a decision to make. If his story was true, he qualified as a political refugee. I had the power to grant him asylum. What would you do?

In another case, a young woman from Fujian province told me that her husband had been smuggled to the United States by snakeheads, that the boat had been seized by U.S. customs, and that some of the Chinese on board, including her husband, had been persuaded by U.S. prosecutors to turn State's evidence and testify against the smugglers. Then, back in her village she had been contacted by the smugglers, who had told her that if her husband testified against them in New York, they would kill her. Later, when she heard a car pull up in front of the house and looked out the window, she saw four young men with the obvious traits of the gangster snakeheads coming to her front door, and she fled out the back, and proceeded to make her way to the U.S.

As I listened to her recounting her story, I realized that it was identical to a novel by a Chinese author that I had just read, called A Loyal Character Dancer, by Qiu Xialong, published by Soho Press. The similarities were striking, right down to the same town in Fujian province, and the four gangsters getting out of the car to catch her, while she fled out the back door. I asked her if by any chance she had read the same book. She claimed not to have heard of it. But that didn't mean that her New York lawyer hadn't read or heard about it and fed her the story.

How had she gotten out of China to come to Guam?

"I paid smugglers."

"So you paid snake heads to bring you here?"

"Yes."

"How much?"

"Forty thousand U.S. dollars."

She couldn't explain, though, if snake heads had threatened to kill her in order to stop her husband from testifying, why she would be willing to pay them such a large sum of money, and trust her life to them to bring her to the States safely.

I don't purport to be an expert on China or to be a "China hand" by any means, but as mentioned, after my exposure to so many Chinese asylum cases in Philly, I had been learning everything I could about the country and culture. I made four trips to China, at my own expense, in four years. And I met with document experts at the U.S. consulate in Shanghai and with the INS Officer-in-Charge at the U.S. embassy in Beijing, who had spent fifteen years in China, and who I really would describe as a "China hand."

That officer had a lot of insight into the political situation in the country, and some interesting theories on the kind of people who make it to the United States and file for asylum. I must say that I concur in general terms with the evaluation. As we all know, there is a lot of repression and persecution of dissidents in China, but the ones who are being persecuted aren't, for the most part, the same ones who are coming to the U.S. – they tend rather to be languishing in prison cells or reeducation camps.

Under our asylum law, if someone is granted asylum in the United States, they have the right to petition for their spouse and dependent children to join them in the U.S. and the family is also granted asylum status. I heard credible stories of family members who came to the embassy in Beijing to process their applications to join their spouses, who had been granted asylum in the United States: women in fur coats, driving Mercedes, asking to defer travel to the U.S. until after their child's school year was finished – hardly the actions of someone who fears persecution, or whose husband has been persecuted.

In the States, there are so-called consultants, and even licensed attorneys, who help their Chinese clients prepare false asylum claims, right down to giving them video tapes to practice their answers to the judge's questions at home. Two attorneys in New York, Robert Porges and his Chinese wife, were indicted and convicted of cooperating with the smuggler snake heads. They were accused of having filed over 6000 fraudulent Chinese asylum claims, earning $13.5 million over a period of seven years for such cases. Their clients were often held hostage at gunpoint by the snakeheads, and beaten until they came up with the money they owed the smugglers. The lawyers were alleged to have actually helped to hold the Chinese applicants in virtual slavery, until the debt their clients owed the snake heads had been paid off, while filing blatantly fraudulent asylum claims for them. Porges was sentenced to 97 months in prison and fined $125,000.

A local San Francisco attorney who appeared in my courtroom representing Chinese cases was caught on video tape by a local news channel that was investigating such fraudulent practices – his office handed out instruction videos to clients on how to learn the Falun Gong exercises, so that they could present bogus claims that they belonged to the persecuted group.

My Trip to Saipan

Decades after the war, the Japanese have returned to Guam and the Northern Marianas in a more modern invasion force. They come to shop. They now inhabit the luxury hotels strewn across Tumon Bay, Guam's version of Waikiki, deploying at early dawn in well-coordinated platoons for their shopping sprees and to occupy golf courses. The more adventurous can go to shooting galleries and fire the kind of automatic assault rifles that are banned in Japan. A Japanese tourist can easily make up the cost of a package deal, air and hotel inclusive, with the money they save in taxes during their exhausting shopping binges. This exquisite embarrassment of consumerism begs the question: which side has been dealt the greater ironic blow - the Japanese soldiers who so bravely holed up in caves and fought to the last man, or the Americans who gave their blood to liberate the islands, only so that years later the lovely, perpetually thin Japanese ladies could reclaim them in the spirit of hedonistic shopping euphoria.

I was lucky to be in Guam in July, when the island celebrated Liberation Day. The humidity in Guam easily matches that of the North Carolina swamps. I chose that day to visit the invasion beaches where the Marines landed, shortly after they took Saipan and Tinian. Japanese gun emplacements still loom silently over the beaches and the languid surf. During the traditional parade down the main street of the old section of town in Agatna, the local crowd treated several American WWII veterans who were on hand that day like royalty. You could actually see and feel pro-American sentiment in Guam's residents.

I spent the next weekend visiting Tinian and Saipan. It takes an hour to fly from Guam to Tinian on a turbo-prop plane. My visit reversed the order of battle in 1944 due to the flight schedules of today's commercial carriers: Guam-Tinian-Saipan rather than Saipan-Tinian-Guam.

Tinian is a tiny island with a population of around 3,100 people, 75% of whom are ethnic Chamorros (down from an approximate 40,000 at the time of contact with Europeans.) The battle for Tinian, on the heels of the American capture of Saipan, lasted from July 24 to August 1, 1944, and from an 8500-man Japanese garrison only 313 survived.

The island was especially important to the Americans because of its airfield. Located 1500 miles from mainland Japan, it was used to stage daily bombing raids to Tokyo. The Navy Seabees (civil engineers) built the largest airbase of World War II, covering at that time the entire island. It is the airfield from which the Enola Gay departed for Japan to put a final apocalyptic ending to that generation's bloodiest struggle. But in comparison to Saipan, a much larger island which was captured first, Tinian was only lightly defended and the Japanese soldiers couldn't offer up much resistance. The Navy faked out the Japanese and landed the Marines on a different beach than the one they had anticipated and had been more heavily fortified.

There was only one major hotel on Tinian. My flight landed at sundown at the tiny airport. Our plane was met by buses sent from the Malaysian-owned hotel to shuttle the expectant guests, most of whom had come for the gambling offered up at the hotel's casino, the few miles to the hotel. We drove along a dark boulevard, peering out into a vast blackness, barely perceiving the tops of palm trees against the sky. Then, suddenly, the sight of garish lights and blinking neon signs came into view, like something out of Apocalypse Now - we had arrived at an oasis of impossible excess and gambling dementia on this otherwise idyllic tropical island.

For me the entertainment value at the hotel was in the exotic character of the staff and guests. The employees were mostly Philippine, Indian and Bengali, all of whom apparently could be contracted very economically. The gambling halls were populated by a most colorful mélange of Asian characters.

I only needed a day, starting at the break of dawn the next morning, to visit the island's several landing beaches, Japanese bunker systems, and the captured Japanese airfield which was converted by the Americans for their air campaign against Japan. The once-busy airfield now lies cracked and deserted. The concrete loading bay where the only A-bombs ever used on humans were loaded onto a B-29 Superfortress bomber stands lonely, forgotten, baking under the tropical sun in the heavy humid air.

Then I went to catch the mid-day flight across the channel to Saipan. When I arrived at the little airport I only saw one other potential passenger in the waiting area, a somewhat frail-looking woman of perhaps sixty years of age. When the airline representative announced that it was time to board the plane, she and I walked out onto the tarmac to the single-engine Piper. To my surprise, she climbed up into the cockpit. *This could be it*, I thought to myself, *the big dip into the Big*

Sleep. I buckled myself into the two-seated passenger area with a seat belt that was too loose and too old to be adjusted. Without a single encouraging word from the pilot, such as, "Hi, I'm the pilot," or "Here we go, enjoy the flight," we taxied down to one end of the runway and turned around to take the runway at take-off speed. There was no place for me to grab onto, no handholds on the fuselage or above my head, such as those afforded in the cab of my Toyota pickup truck. (My father remarked once, how ironic it was that during the Pacific campaign he had been dive-bombed by Japanese Zeros, and now, in Oregon, he drove a Dodge truck built by Mitsubishi, the same company that had manufactured the Zeros.) I flailed about in my loose seat as the plane was buffeted by updrafts from the channel. But then I forced myself to relax and enjoy the view of the steep cliffs over the channel. I figured the pilot had probably been flying the same route for years, and after all, how hard could it be to take off and land again on the other side? We flew over Banzai Cliff, where, toward the end of the battle, hundreds of civilians either threw themselves off into the jagged coral rocks or were pushed by Japanese soldiers who didn't want their Korean slave laborers to fall into American hands.

If Tinian was a relatively easy campaign for the Americans, Saipan by contrast was a hard bloody slog. My father was awarded the first of two Silver Stars on Saipan. He was a captain in command of an infantry company with the 4th Marine Division. He was wounded during the landing, evacuated to a hospital ship where he was patched up, and returned to the battle. He lost half of his company during that battle, between June 15 and July 9; not at all an unusual casualty count for the brutal island warfare in the Marianas. After the fighting in Tinian, he continued on to the battles a year later at Iwo Jima and then Okinawa. It is impossible to say how much that passage through hell changed him. Was he ever able to share it with anyone? He did not with my mother or any of his children. He passed away in May 1998.

The defending Japanese garrison in June 1944 on Saipan numbered 30,000, of which 29,000 thousand were killed in action or committed suicide. Americans lost 3,400 killed and over 10,000 wounded. In the fierce fighting 20,000 Japanese civilians died.

Today's Saipan has an economy buttressed by sweat-shop textile factories. The workers are mostly Chinese and Philippine women who live and work in self-contained barracks, producing clothing with the Made in America label for Gap and other trendy outlets. It is that industry, coupled with the highly developed tourist industry – which like Guam caters mostly to Japanese – that makes Saipan an overdeveloped but fascinating island.

I had made arrangements to meet Oscar Martinez, the Officer-in-Charge for Immigration and Naturalization Service in Saipan,. I volunteered to go out with Oscar on his weekly jaunt through the jungle in search of souvenirs. He was a Vietnam vet who fought during the Tet offensive. When I agreed to go with him I didn't know how much of a fanatic he was about his Japanese war memorabilia. He had a self-appointed mission – to explore every inch of the Saipan jungle, especially those cliffs and caves where the Japanese had holed up until the bitter no-surrender end – before he was transferred from the island.

He picked me up early that Sunday morning, and we drove to an area close to the so-called Suicide Cliff, where thousands of soldiers threw themselves off rather than being captured by American soldiers (not to be confused with Banzai Cliff, which is on the same side of the island.) From the road, we walked several hundred yards along a trail through dense undergrowth, before commencing a climb up the side of the rock-face, which eventually led to the cliffs. Oscar's methodology was to trace a jigsaw pattern up and down the cliff-face, looking for traces of Japanese encampments and caves which might reveal any treasures in the eyes of a Sunny Surplus souvenir collector. The jungle turned out to be surprisingly benign. By that I mean we did not encounter any biting insects, and there are no poisonous snakes on Saipan.

Once we had climbed several hundred feet the undergrowth thinned out. But the area where we spent the morning exploring was often so steep that we had to always have at least one hand firmly gripping a tree branch before advancing, or we might go plunging over the side of a cliff. To make matters worse, it started to rain, a slow warm drizzle. We saw many illegal coconut crab snares (the coconut crabs are a protected species) made from coconut husks by the locals.

I followed Oscar's lead as we climbed up one rock-face and down another, moving slowly and exploring a dozen different former Japanese camp sites. Oscar had a technique of hanging canteens and mess kits from his webbed belt, so that by the end of the morning he looked like an itinerant tinker with all sorts of vintage metal vessels hanging from his body. He showed me how to identify the WWII vintage stamp of the Japanese Navy on the bottoms of cups and mess kits. I was content to carry out a very nice, large vintage sake bottle with a milky bluish tint, and a brown beer bottle which I later gave to my brother Mark, a Captain in the Navy.

Finally we'd had enough and it was time to find a way off the cliff. We headed downward, only to discover that we had already traveled laterally so far that we were immediately above the steep drop that overlooks the tourist parking lot for visitors to Suicide Cliff. It was impossible to get down that way, so we headed back up. At some point we were bound to reach level ground and a trail that ran along the top of the cliff, leading to the memorial site where the Japanese soldiers chose their own manner of death. By now we were both exhausted. The rain kept coming down.

Eventually I saw above us how the light broke through a clearing, and I dashed for the top. When Oscar caught up with me we were standing on level ground and we found the trail that leads about a half-mile through shoulder high grasses to the memorial site. I walked ahead. After a while Oscar started to say, "Paul, how come you're not tired? Paul, how come I don't hear you breathing hard?" When we found the memorial site we were able to catch a ride back down to the parking lot. Oscar told me I was the only one of many victims he had taken out on his weekend jaunts who had managed to tire him out. (I'd maintained my cross-country running all those years.)

During my two weeks on the islands, I did a lot of thinking about my father's sacrifice when he was in his mid-twenties. Key choices I made through the years were as much a reflection of the sense of duty that I had inherited from him as anything else.

Philly Courthouse Circus

It didn't help my attempts to adjust into my new role as IJ in Philly, that the courthouse sometimes seemed more like a madhouse than a hallowed judicial forum. One of the judges had serious anger management problems. He had a tendency to start shouting when he felt that his authority was being threatened. He would berate everyone in the courtroom, especially the poor quivering migrant respondent. Lawyers who observed this phenomenon over time noticed that, ironically, the more he shouted at the respondent, the more likely he was to grant the case. He seemed to be trying, in his own way, to help the migrant out, by shouting him/her into conformity with whatever it was he imagined that (s)he needed to say in order to prevail in her case.

During the first few months that I was there, I would occasionally hear an explosion of shouting coming from the courtroom next door, and then a hollering that carried all the way down the hall. Everyone in my courtroom would look at each other – oh, there he goes again – and we all kind of smiled among ourselves, like it was a big joke. At least once a week, the halls would resonate with the sounds of the judge going ballistic. But over time I realized that this was not simply a quirky aspect of that judge's personality which, like so many things in life, helps to color and enrich our appreciation of the world around us. He had a serious problem that was only getting worse. I spoke with him about it several times, encouraging therapy, but he refused to acknowledge there was a problem. At the same time it seemed that he saw more and more of the world ganging up against him. It didn't help matters that in addition to several individual complaints filed against him by private attorneys, the INS District Counsel filed an official complaint with our agency's ethics department and an investigation was launched. From what I learned, the main issue was the question of judicial impropriety of some of his remarks and outbursts in court. But he left the job for another opportunity before the investigation was completed.

Contrast that judge with another judge in Philly who was notorious for putting words in the mouths of respondents in his courtroom and then ordering them deported based on testimony that he had created for them. He told me once that he had only been reversed by the appellate court, the BIA, once or twice in his whole career. Curious, I watched for the daily mail that came in from the Board of Appeals (I was professionally curious anyway to see what decisions were coming back from the Board) and I confirmed that he was in fact often reversed, because his findings that the respondents had lied on the stand didn't withstand judicial scrutiny.

Some judges have been raked over the coals by the appellate courts for the way that they twist or even make up testimony in order to find that a respondent is lying, and then use that as a pretext to deny their application based on credibility. It is especially damning to a judge when the appellate court decides to name them in their decision, but I know several of my colleagues who have had this public indignity visited upon them. This particular judge was castigated three times by the 3rd Circuit Court of Appeals, and it was only after the third time, when on each occasion lengthy parts of the transcript were quoted in the circuit court's opinion, that the Justice Department finally yanked him from the bench and launched an investigation. It should have happened years earlier – all of the indicators, the complaints, the abusive behavior, the bad decisions, had been in plain view ever since he took the bench. (See the article by Gaiutra Bahadur, in the Philadelphia Inquirer, dated June 2, 2006, entitled, "Bullying Philadelphia Immigration Judge Absent, Replaced).

In the case *Cham v. Gonzalez*, No. 04-4251, (3rd Cir. Apr. 28, 2006) Judge Barry wrote,

> "The case now before us exemplifies the "severe wound… inflicted" when not a modicum of courtesy, of respect, or of any pretense of fairness is extended to a petitioner and the case he so valiantly attempted to present. Yet once again, under the 'bullying' nature of the immigration judge's questioning, a petitioner was ground to bits. That immigration judge's conduct has been condemned in prior opinions of this court. (citation omitted). ('intemperate and bias-laden remarks'

interjected by the immigration judge, 'none of which had any basis in the facts introduced or the arguments made, at the hearing'); (citation omitted) ('bullying' and 'brow beating' by the immigration judge; 'continuing hostility towards the obviously distraught [petitioner] and his abusive treatment of her throughout the hearing,' reducing her 'to an inability to respond'; and an oral decision, later 'sanitized,' which was 'crude (and cruel)).'

I guarantee that a poll of immigration lawyers in Philly would turn up dozens of such cases they experienced with the same judge; and that moreover, a poll of immigration lawyers nationwide would turn up dozens of such abusive judges.

The same judge was a gun nut. He considered himself a champion of the law enforcement community. The INS district office at that time shared the same building with the immigration court on Callowhill Street, and he made frequent visits to the investigating agents on a different floor, even though, according to my sources, they considered his attention to their business laughable. If, in the course of testimony, a witness would mention a gun, the judge would take over the questioning, wanting to hear all of the details about the make and model of the weapon, even though it was totally irrelevant to the issue at bar. I personally observed him do so in a hearing that I sat in on. Once, when one of the GSA guards was speaking with him during a break, he asked the guard if he could examine his service revolver. The guard handed it to him, and he reportedly remarked, "This gun's no good, the mechanism is rusty. You should complain to your union." When the court administrator learned that the two men had been examining a loaded weapon on the premises, he lodged a complaint, rightfully concerned for the safety of the court employees and the public. As a result, the guard was fired for brandishing a weapon, but the judge was untouchable. (This is only one of two cases I am aware of where an immigration judge was permanently removed from the bench for outlandish conduct.)

Liberia and Charles Taylor

I had several asylum clients from the West African country of Liberia while I was director of the George Washington law school clinic. One of them was the widow of one of the dozen government ministers whom Samuel Doe ordered to be marched out onto the beach and summarily executed when he took power through a coup in 1980. When I became an IJ in Philly I was already pretty familiar with the country conditions of Liberia. A lot of Liberians had settled in the Philadelphia area, and I presided over dozens of their asylum hearings.

Liberia was founded by freed slaves who were sent from the U.S. by the American Colonization Society in 1820. But as things go, there were already native people living there. Funny about that. The newcomers soon began to see themselves as superior (ain't that the age-old story?) and over the decades, they and their descendants became the oppressors of the native people. For one hundred and thirty years, five percent of the population dominated the political structure, until, in 1980, Sergeant Master Samuel Doe engineered a coup d'états and assumed power. Nine years of bumpy rule and fierce political repression followed. But during this time, the U.S. supported Doe, largely because of his anti-Communist façade. In 1990, Charles Taylor, a former ally of Doe, escaped from a county jail in New Jersey where he had been residing and returned to Liberia, invading from neighboring Ivory Coast with an army of rebels. Thus began thirteen years of intermittent civil war, during which several hundred thousand non-combatants were killed and roughly two million refugees fled into neighboring countries.

Under dubious conditions, Taylor was elected President in 1997 and became the *au courant* poster child of American foreign policy self-delusion. The U.S. government went in to try and support the new "democracy", throwing money around like it was going out of style. An insurgency against Taylor continued in the countryside, and Taylor proceeded to lock up and torture his opponents, while the flow of refugees fleeing Taylor's oppression continued.

The cases I heard in Philly involved asylum applicants who feared being returned to Taylor's Liberia. The INS attorneys came into court on these cases and argued, with straight faces, that conditions in Liberia weren't so bad, surely they were better than before, and now that our government had given the official seal of approval to Taylor's democracy, the poor individuals before me, with torture marks on their bodies, should be sent home. I didn't go for it. In fact, I was so outraged by that argument from such fresh-faced INS prosecutors, especially when there was ample evidence from human rights groups to the contrary, that in my decisions I began "indicting" Charles Taylor. I pointed out on the record that, according to reliable reports, he was guilty of crimes against humanity, and that his proper place should be before a UN Tribunal investigating such crimes rather than enjoying life in the Presidential palace with the unmitigated support of the U.S. My remarks were widely circulated by pro-immigrant attorneys in the community.

Guess what happened? Charles Taylor's complicity in fostering the murderous and particularly savage rebellion in neighboring Sierra Leone, where rebel groups, supported by money from his government, would hack off the limbs of women and children with machetes, became known to the world, while the situation in Liberia continued to deteriorate. Finally, in a U.S.-brokered deal, Taylor was escorted out of the country. He was later brought to trial at the International Criminal Court in the Hague, indicted in March 2003 on seventeen counts of war crimes, and was sentenced to 50 years in prison May 30th, 2012, one of the longest sentences for war crimes ever handed down by any tribunal).

From my perspective, our government's attitude as represented by the INS prosecutors in immigration court was just a replay of our earlier history regarding Central American refugees in the 80's, when our State Department reported that the human rights situation in El Salvador and Guatemala wasn't so bad. The INS lawyers came into my courtroom, citing flawed State Department reports about Liberia, which were written by ambitious State employees stationed in Liberia, who *wanted to believe* that Taylor was a good guy, because the U.S. government had thrown its weight behind him. The INS attorneys had been too lazy to conduct any other kind of independent research – had not been brave enough to doubt the State reports. They were unable to exhibit the same kind of independent thinking that I cited earlier, that Craig DeBernardis had exhibited in the Arnulfo Diaz hearing.

I would like to know how those INS attorneys, who argued before me that Taylor wasn't so bad and that I should send his political opponents back to Liberia to be at his mercy, felt after they heard about the latest developments – that Taylor was now considered a war criminal, on trial in the Hague, and later, that he was a convicted war criminal?

Playing In the Band—Part II

When I moved to Philly I brought my saxophone with me. Philly has a great tradition of jazz, being either the home or the early incubus of the careers of such greats as John Coltrane, Stan Getz, Grover Washington, Jr., Jimmy Heath, and the Klugh brothers. I was looking for a venue to play. When I moved into Ann Marie's row house in Roxborough I discovered a neighborhood bar not far away, on Ridge Avenue called Fat Edna's. It was a typical Philly neighborhood hangout. It had a long bar in the shape of a horse-shoe, offering nightly drink specials, food specials, an area to play darts, and a group of colorful patrons from the working-class neighborhood. The bar had two regular Monday-night features – a food special, all the mussels you can eat, and an open-mike jazz jam session.

For several years I was a regular on Monday nights, eating the mussels that were basted in a wonderful garlic broth, and playing jazz. The sessions were headed by the fabulous Budesa Brothers on guitar and organ, with a phenomenal black drummer, Jimmy, holding down the beat. The Budesa Brothers were a class act – I don't say it lightly when I say they were absolute masters of their instruments. Upon first impression, they looked like a couple of South Philly mobsters (I say that with affection, boys) but I was blown away every time I heard them play. Those Monday night sessions gave me my sea legs in playing straight-ahead jazz and improvising in public. I cut my teeth on such tunes as Stolen Moments, Footsteps, Impressions, Naima, and Billie's Bounce.

In order to spare Anne Marie having to listen to me rehearse at home after her long, exhausting days teaching Hispanic kids, I used to stay after work and play in my office. I would be all alone in the building, and I could just blast out. One nice thing about my office was that it had a tall, thirteen-foot wide window facing the Philly skyline, and we were only four blocks from the heart of down town. I would turn off the office lights and have the full canvas of Philly's city lights before me. It felt like I was playing in a fifties noir movie. I spent hours there after work, playing back the recordings of Miles Davis, Wayne Shorter and John Coltrane and replicating their style. Deputy Chief Counsel Geri Richardson later told me she used to hear a ghostly saxophone echoing through the building when she worked late and wondered where it was coming from.

For several years I had a dream, a fantasy really, of playing in a jazz combo for the local attorneys who I worked with every day. Like the teenage dreams of dating the most popular girl in school, I didn't think it could ever be realized. But amazingly I did have my opportunity. At the beginning of year 2001, when the announcement was made that I was leaving Philly to fill a slot with the court in San Francisco, the local chapter of AILA, the American Immigration Lawyers Association, decided to throw a party for me. The upstairs bar was reserved at a great restaurant called the Brewery on Main Street in Manayunk, a venue where I had gone to hear music many times. When I asked the AILA organizers of the event if there would be a music budget, they said they'd arrange it. They asked if I had a band in mind? You bet I did. I invited the Budesa brothers to play, featuring myself on sax, at my going away party.

The party was on a Friday night in the first week of March. When the Budesa brothers showed up to set up their instruments, they were surprised to learn from the party attendees that I was a judge. All the time that I had played with them, I'd never said a word about it, answering instead to the standard question, "What do you do?" that I was an immigration lawyer. I had never wanted the title of 'Judge' to somehow color my relationship with the musicians and other bar patrons.

The party had a good turn-out, and I was told that it was the first time in Philly history that the private immigration bar had socialized with attorneys from INS. It was a great honor for me. I really enjoyed fronting the band and playing my sax for the crowd. Life doesn't get much better.

PART THREE: IMMIGRATION JUDGE, SAN FRANCISCO

Preface: I was unhappy with my working conditions in Philly. The court was small, and although I came to appreciate the city of Philadelphia in many ways, it really isn't an international city, which is what I longed for. I had always thought it would be fun to live and work in San Francisco (I was born in San Diego), and when Phil Williams, the Assistant Chief Immigration Judge told me there was an opening there, I grabbed the opportunity to transfer.

I spent a week driving across country in my pickup truck, stopping at cities and places along the way that I had always wanted to visit: Nashville for two nights of music, then Memphis and Beale Street, and visiting the Sun studios where Elvis and Jerry Lee Lewis and Johnny Cash got their start. Then on through Oklahoma, the Texas panhandle, Albuquerque, Flagstaff, and the Grand Canyon, where I stayed in March just one week before opening season.

In comparison to the small Philly court, the San Francisco immigration court, with its sixteen judges and large support staff, was a cauldron of ethnic and cultural diversity. I felt right at home working with my colleagues of Mexican, Chinese, Japanese, and European descent, and our support staff included many Mexican-Americans and Asians. For the next four years I would work in one of the most diverse and fascinating cities that an immigration specialist could hope for.

When I first arrived in San Francisco I rented a room from an elderly lady in the Outer Sunset, on 20th Avenue at the corner of Quintara. I had found the rental on Craigslist before moving out there. Over the years I had usually gotten along very well with grandmother types and so I looked forward to the living arrangement, but there were two major problems with the circumstances in that particular location. First of all, the woman, although very nice, was very depressed, having to face the realization that she was no longer employable and looking forward to a lonely existence with no close relatives. So her state of mind was unfortunately bringing me down. The other thing was that the Outer Sunset basically exists in a fog bank much of the year. I of course had heard about the San Francisco fog, but I discovered, when I moved in there in the spring, that basically every day, after leaving work in the Financial District where the sun would be shining, I would drive home into a dark cloud. Going home to relax in such thick fog after work was a bummer.

So after a few months there I looked around and found a nice one-bedroom in the Inner Richmond district, on the other, northern side of Golden Gate Park. At Geary Boulevard and Presidio Avenue, just the short distance from my former location seemed to make a huge distance in the sunshine quotient. Of course there were still foggy days, which in fact I loved, as long as they weren't every day, but the sunny days and the weather in general were wonderful in that part of town. And I discovered what would become by favorite street and neighborhood in the city, Clement Street, which runs parallel to California and Geary.

The apartment was unique, in that it was the only residential unit in a two-story modern building, the first floor being the offices of a real estate company. The owner was a German gentleman, and he and his two grown children managed the company and also my rental. For me it was great because that meant that at night, after business, I was the only person in the building. I could come home at midnight and break out my saxophone if I had a mind to, and blast away into the night without anyone paying notice, except perhaps a wayward passer-by on the sidewalk.

The offering of restaurants was out of this world in ethnic varieties. Just a couple blocks down Geary was a huge record and music CD shop, a couple blocks in both directions were historic movie theaters, and I was just as happy as could be with my new-found neighborhood.

Two years later I moved to another great location, also in the Inner Richmond.

My Judge Day — San Francisco

I wake up at 6 o'clock, my habit since childhood. I was a military brat, and Dad rousted all of us at 6, just like the men in his company. I couldn't sleep late now if you paid me to.

I live in a great old corner apartment building in the Inner Richmond district, on the 3rd floor overlooking Lake Avenue and 7th Avenue, just a block from Mountain Lake, where the first Spanish explorer Juan Batista de Anza camped in March 1776; a couple of blocks from the Presidio golf course, and one mile from Baker Beach, with its beautiful backdrop of the Golden Gate and Marin County shoreline. All great places to go running after work or on the weekend.

By 6:30 I'm at the Starbucks in Laurel Heights on California Street, for a large regular coffee – none of that sissy stuff! – and the New York Times. Addicted to international news, I can't start the day without it, and I can't tell you how many times I've found something in the morning paper that bears directly on one of my cases that day. For example, in the morning I have a courtroom full of detained Sri Lankan cases, and the paper reports that the tentative peace agreement in Sri Lanka between the government and Tamil Tiger rebels has just been shattered by a rebel offensive. I try to be more up-to-date about country conditions of the asylum applicants in my court than either the government attorney or the applicants' own lawyers –

I consider it my responsibility to be, and one of the fun things about the practice of asylum law has always the challenge of keeping abreast of country conditions .

I'm in my office, on the 6th floor of the government building on Sansome Street, by 7:30 – a half-hour before anyone else has arrived. Court doesn't start until 8:30, but I've become compulsive about getting in early, reviewing websites that cover country conditions and legal developments in immigration law that may impact my cases, and writing up a couple of decisions that I've put on hold. I keep the backlog down.

Mei Young, my excellent clerk, arrives at 8, and she brings to my attention any developments I need to know about – last-minute motions, an attorney who called in sick or will be delayed, someone on the detention calendar who the government couldn't move from the detention facility in time to get to court this morning; or maybe the whole bus with 40 detainees is still caught in traffic a couple hours north of here.

I enter the courtroom a couple minutes before 8:30, as soon as the detention officers have managed to seat the 50 detainees for the morning's calendar. We'll get through the cases by 11:30 or 12. I'm known for my expeditiousness with these preliminary matters. Some will only be reset for a later date when attorneys can be sought or can make appearances they couldn't make today.

I've got the nicest courtroom of any immigration judge in San Francisco. An old courtroom dating from the 2nd World War, all wooden paneling, worn and funky, with a wide row of dirty industrial windows running along the wall to my right letting filtered sunlight in. This is the custody courtroom that Judge Yamaguchi and I share. Justice Department seal behind me, American flag to my right.

Two rows of five benches each that seat a potential seventy people. (This wonderful courtroom was later retired from service.)

I like to eyeball the respondents, see if there is any particular case the detention officers want to bring to my attention, maybe someone with special medical needs. These officers often get a bad rap from the private bar, but the ones I work with in San Francisco, and their deportation officer colleagues in the building, are for the most part top-notch professionals with a tough job, and I try to work with them to accommodate everyone's needs, respectful of their requests relating to difficult or delicate situations they have to contend with.

I also want to know which attorneys are present and ready to go. Many of them will have other matters before other judges in our larger building down the street. I want to get them out of here as quickly as possible so that they can appear on time before the next judge.

The contract interpreters approach the bench with their paperwork, so that I know they are present; no use calling a case if the interpreter isn't in the courtroom yet. In addition to our own excellent Spanish interpreter, the wonderful Lucretia Hug, who doubles today as docket clerk, our morning calendar calls for two Chinese interpreters in Mandarin and Fujou dialects; an Armenian, a Russian, a Tamil/Sri Lankan, a French, a Portuguese, and Mayan dialect interpreter. The regulations provide for a court interpreter in every case that the respondent requests one – to go forward on the merits of a case without one would result in an automatic reversal on appeal.

The INS lawyer, Larry Gallagher, comes into the courtroom wheeling his big briefcase, accompanied by an assistant with an armload of files. Larry is one of the finest human beings working for INS, a former military career attorney who served in Taiwan during the Vietnam war, married to a Philippine woman. I first met him when I was a judge in Philadelphia and he came out there on a detail assignment. Originally from Western Pennsylvania, he speaks with a homespun drawl. I've always had the highest regard for his ethics and the way he approaches a case and handles himself in court.

The clerk begins calling the cases. A group of five Mexican laborers, all living at the same house in Marin, were busted when an ICE investigator went to that address in search of an absconder. Their tough luck. I only need a couple of minutes on each case to advise them of their right to an attorney, get affirmation that they each want a chance to try to contact a lawyer, and set them over for next week's calendar.

Mr. Gallagher routinely requests I set a high bond such as $10,000 in each of their cases (it's what his supervisor demands). My mind always returns to the summers when my brothers and I worked in the strawberry and bean fields, the apple and cherry orchards in Oregon, alongside Mexican laborers, when I was in my early teens during the summer months. (Now forbidden by child labor laws). (The Beatles song Strawberry Fields Forever always had special resonance with me). I remember the difference between us students, who were there just for the summer months to earn some extra income, and the Mexican migrant workers, for whom the work was a life or death proposition.

Now when such field hands are brought into my courtroom detained, either because they have an immigration violation or have committed some rather minor criminal offense, I remember those migrant laborers working so hard to feed their families. I don't see any percentage in the federal government keeping them detained at taxpayers' expense, when they could be out of jail, working to sustain their families and adding to our tax base. It's always perplexing to me, how fervently the ICE attorneys will argue that I should deny such laborers bond and keep them locked up for months while their court cases are pending.

Sometimes I'll allow myself to have fun with the INS attorney: "Mr. Gallagher, have you ever picked beans or strawberries under the hot, burning sun alongside Mexican laborers?"

"No, your honor."

"Well, I have! $1,500 bond for Mr. Gutierrez."

Next we have seven Chinese women, ages 19—25, all detained over the weekend at the airport when trying to enter on fake Japanese passports. An attorney from New York has entered an appearance in all their cases. He wants to make the initial appearance by telephone. Given the nature of their arrival, and that they haven't technically "effected an entry" into the country, I can't bond them out. I can only set them down for the inevitable asylum hearing. The only issue today is whether it will be held in San Francisco or New York. It's obvious, from the law firm that is representing them (known among our staff as a firm that collaborates with Chinese 'snake heads', alien smugglers), and from the age of the women, that they have been smuggled into the States as fodder for one of New York's massage parlors, where they will exist as virtual slaves until thousands of dollars of inflated, bogus fees have been paid off to the organization. We all know the reality of the situation, but we are powerless to do anything about it. That's up to ICE , the enforcement branch of the agency, and other federal investigators. All I can do is treat them like any other respondents in my courtroom. I will have to listen, in two months time, to their asylum stories, enter a decision and let the appellate process take it from there.

I set their cases over for later in the morning, when we can connect with the lawyer by telephone, once we've cleared the courtroom of the cases which have lawyers present in court. My underlying goal on these master calendars with so many people is to whittle down the number of people in court, reduce the chaos and confusion level to a manageable amount.

There's another Chinese respondent, age 32, who wasn't caught at the airport with the others. Rather, she's been living in the States for a year as an overstay on her tourist visa. The clerk calls her name, and a local Chinese-American lawyer, a young guy who I don't know, comes forward to represent her. I review the I-213 quickly in the file, the document prepared by the arresting ICE agent that gives a background of her history in the U.S., and criminal priors, family background, and any health issues.

Because she originally entered the U.S. legally, she's eligible to be considered for bond, and the information in the document is important for me to get a handle on issues like potential danger to the community and risk of flight. The lawyer tells me that she has a witness in the courtroom, who will testify that she can stay with him if set free, that he will pay the bond, and that he plans to marry her and file a family petition for her, which would make her eligible to stay in the States. The witness is a State Department contractor, in his mid-50's; someone who retired from a career at State and is now back on a part-time consulting basis. I glance at him, sitting in the last row. Looks like a fine enough chap, in a dark blue suit, distinguished silver hair.

I review the information under the heading 'medical' on the I-213. The woman is currently being treated for syphilis. She acknowledged to the arresting agent that she has worked in the States as a prostitute. I call the attorney to the bench, and whisper, "Counsel, is he aware of the information in this report?"

"Yes, your honor, he is informed."

"And he still wants to vouch for her?"

"Yes, your honor."

"How did they meet?"

"At a Starbucks, a couple of months ago."

Now it's all clear to me. I call the case, and her lawyer calls the State contractor, who testifies as to their loving relationship, and how he realized, after meeting her, that this is the woman of his dreams.

I ask him, "Sir, have you ever been to China?"

"No, your honor."

I feel empathy for him, I want to pull him aside and counsel him. I want to tell him that in China there are literally tens of thousands of bright young women with Ph.D.s and promising careers, who would be delighted to meet someone as good looking and as wealthy (relatively) as he is. Why throw your chance away on a syphilitic prostitute who picked you up at a Starbucks? I would tell him to take the bond money and spend it on a trip to China, if that's how desperate he is to meet a Chinese wife. But of course I can't indulge that human impulse, and so instead, after he explains how he will cover the cost of her medical treatment and personally assure that she returns to court, I grant bond in the amount of $5000.

There are three female lawyers in the courtroom today, all of whom represent the very finest of the immigration bar. Alisa Thomas, Alison Dixon and Nancy Fellom. They are each bosses of their own firms. Immigration practice tends to attract a lot of female lawyers, it seems in higher percentages than many other areas of practice. And women often hold the top positions in professional associations such as American Immigration Lawyers Association, national and regional chairs and committee heads, local presidents, all pressing for improvement of the system, fighting in the trenches. This phenomenon seems especially fitting in San Francisco, where a majority of the judges are female, most of whom used to be activist lawyers.

These three are very similar in certain characteristics that I admire in a lawyer: They're all very intellectual, they know the law and can cite it back to you, and they like to advance novel legal arguments, getting obvious pleasure from exploring the more creative side of litigation. They're all tough as nails in court, they'll stick up for their client and do everything in their power, within ethical bounds, to achieve the client's goal. And they don't engage in grandstanding in court, they present themselves as moderate but firm, no histrionics or irrelevant sideshow, just good solid lawyering. It's always a pleasure to see any of them in court. They all are here today representing Central Americans who have already been bonded out, filing their clients' applications for cancellation of removal and asylum. Each case takes five minutes to find a calendar date.

Next we have six Tamils from Sri Lanka. They are short, thin, dark-skinned, all wearing paper-thin button down shirts and jeans and prison sandals. Their attorney has flown in from L.A. to meet them today and enter his initial appearance. There aren't any Tamil-speaking immigration lawyers in San Francisco. Ever since I transferred to the San Francisco court there have been at least a half-dozen Tamils on every custody calendar. They tend to be good candidates for asylum, but they'll have to remain locked up until their hearing because they were all busted at the airport with fake documents. The soonest I can squeeze them in is within sixty days – I schedule each one for an individual merits hearing within that time frame (if they weren't detained the merits hearing would be more like two years down the road.)

Next, an Indian national, a Sikh, who was already granted asylum, but his attorney in Sacramento, also an Indian, has recently been convicted of conspiracy to commit fraud in hundreds of Indian asylum cases for having fabricated his clients' claims and submitted fraudulent documents in support. The government is reviewing all of his clients' cases, and in those where the language on the forms is identical to the attorney's pattern of "cookie-cutter" fraud, the dupes are being bounced into deport hearings, charged with fraud. In this case, Gallagher requests a high bond, and I grant his request, setting it at $50,000. I don't appreciate people who come into the country and commit fraud in our asylum system. I consider the right to asylum as something sacred and not to be abused.

Next, a Brazilian female who entered across the southern border illegally. There's been a recent increase in illegal border crossings by Brazilian migrants trying to find jobs in the States. Her attorney, a female recent law graduate, tells me she will be filing for asylum based upon the woman's "lesbian orientation" – those are the words she uses. Having traveled to Brazil twice, I know that, on the one hand, Brazil has the most open society in the southern hemisphere; one the other hand, the culture and male establishment are still infused with the machismo culture. Let her file her application, we'll see – anything's possible.

Now we have a Mexican, with a green card, who was just released from the county jail serving time for a conviction of spousal abuse. He's deportable for the offense, a crime of moral turpitude and a crime of violence, but he will fight it, and so the issue now is bond. His wife and three children are in court with him to testify in favor of his release. Mr. Gallagher argues for a high bond, knowing that I won't go too high on this case because the whole family is before me, and the wife pleads that she wants him back, needs him for the children and as a wage earner. My inclination is to give the family a break, the wife's plea tugs at my heartstrings, but sociologists say that he's going to go out and do it again, get drunk, knock the wife around. There's no easy solution. What would you do?

Next up, after all of the attorneys have cleared out, and last task of the morning: a group of Salvadoran detainees, all of whom have been in court a couple of times already, and have remained detained over the course of a month because they couldn't make bond or get a lawyer. They're ready to receive deportation orders rather than continue to sit in jail. I feel sorry for them, because at least some of them might have good claims for relief from deportation, but the system is too tough for them to fight. Without money for an attorney or bond, they see no recourse. This is where a public defender, someone to advise and represent the detainees, would be a big boon to the system; for the respondents, the court, and the INS. (see later chapter on reforms).

One of them is eligible for voluntary departure, which is a remedy that avoids him having an order of removal or deportation on his record. Since he is detained ICE will still escort him to the border or even put him on a plane to El Salvador, but his future prospects of returning are better without a deport order. The deportation officer addresses the court.

"Your honor, in this individual's case we don't really have any proof that he's from El Salvador, otherwise we wouldn't object to an order of voluntary departure."

I know how to solve this question, and have a little fun at the same time. Having been to El Salvador, and having worked closely over the years with so many Salvadoran clients, I know a sure-fire test to determine Salvadoran authenticity.

"Sir, what is your favorite kind of *pupusa?*"

A *pupusa* is a traditional Salvadoran dish made of a thick, handmade corn tortilla that is usually filled with cheese, pork, or chicken, cooked on a hot griddle and served with cabbage relish or *curtido* and *salsa rojo*, red sauce. They are a perfect street food, and all Salvadorans love them, not to mention most visitors to El Salvador.

When, without hesitation, the man said, "Well, senor Juez, I like *pollo, chicharron, puerco, con queso…*"

"He's Salvadoran alright," I say, to laughter from the deportation officers of all people. Dilemma solved.

Lunch time. The court building is on the edge of Chinatown (the court was moved from Kearney Street to the corner of Montgomery and Market in 2006) so we have our pick of the very best Asian food in the nation.

There are upscale, touristy places, and other really great restaurants frequented by the local population, where the menus are only available in Chinese and the waitresses don't speak any English. There's the ornate, two-story Golden Dragon on Grant Street, where a gang of shooters with assault rifles shot five innocent diners dead, wounding eleven others, during an attempted hit on a gang member in 1977. And there's my favorite place, right on Kearney Street, where I have fallen in love with their pork/oyster hotpot. I eat there twice a week. That's where I go now. Today I have my meal alone, not at all unusual, and it's delicious as always. I can read some of the menu and order in Chinese. Another good thing, they're really fast, and today that's important, because the judges are getting together at the main court building for their monthly noontime coffee klatch. I like to make an appearance when I can, to keep up on the court gossip.

Coming out of the building, I run into Farshad Owji, one of the fine new generation of practitioners. Half Turkish and half Iranian, fluent in both languages, he's tall and handsome, very suave', went to University of Miami law school. He's made a good impression on me in court, and I chatted with him at one of the bar functions, coming to the conclusion that he's an enthusiastic advocate. He shares office space in one of the majestic, historic buildings on Pacific Avenue around the corner that survived the earthquake and fire of 1906. Today he wants to know if I'll be handling the custody calendar in December, when one of his clients is scheduled for a hearing. I answer no, that's when I'll be on personal leave, going to Cambodia for the first time to have a look around.

By 12:30 I'm up on the 12th floor of the main court building on Kearney Street to enjoy a coffee and tune into the other judge's complaints. There's Dana Marks, a brilliant lawyer and aggressive advocate , who was the attorney on the most famous asylum case in American history, *Cardoza Fonseca*. She has been for many years, on and off the president of the National Association of Immigration Judges and a single mother. I took my whole group of clinic students to the Supreme Court in 1986 to hear her argue that case. And Polly Webber, a past national president of the American Immigration Lawyers Association, a brilliant lawyer and a single mother; Laura Ramirez, former immigration clinic director at Santa Clara Law School, married to another immigration activist; Carol King, who worked for an NGO in Nicaragua during the same period that I worked for the Central American Refugee Center; Bette Stockton, a former AILA activist; Marilyn Teeter, a former EEOC judge and a single mother; Miriam Hayward, former Supervising Attorney at the International Institute of the East Bay and AILA activist; Tue Phan -Quang, a refugee from Vietnam; Mike Yamaguchi, former U.S. Attorney for San Francisco; Alberto Gonzalez, an immigrant from Juarez, Mexico, and a very compassionate judge; and Larry DiConstanza, a solid liberal on immigrant rights issues. (A couple other judges are absent). All of them are tops in their field. I am certain this is the most amazing and brightest collection of immigration judges in the nation.

Today the big topic is the new deadlines that management has imposed on the judges. The courts are faced with big backlogs, some judges have calendars extending out by two years, with some cases that were initiated five years ago. Such backlogs have always been a fact of life, a part of immigration practice. My calendar isn't so bad, because the custody calendar moves much quicker. Management has recently issued an arbitrary decree that all cases initiated by a given date must be completed by September of this year. All other cases must be reshuffled in order to accommodate. Some of the judges have hundreds of cases being reset because of this. And many of the respondents and their lawyers are receiving short notice of the reset, without any inquiry from the court about whether they are even available on those particular dates. Some lawyers with big practices have received hundreds of reset notices. Judges are being asked to work as late as it takes to complete their cases. As usual, management hasn't said anything about the quality of our adjudications in the directive – it's all about numbers, case completions.

This short-sighted policy will result in appeals being generated, on due process grounds, that take years to resolve. (After leaving the bench I wrote a brief as a consultant for a local lawyer on this very issue, where a judge on one of these September deadlines refused to grant an extension of time. We prevailed at the 9th Circuit on due process grounds). But such is the mentality of managers who've spent their whole careers in the bureaucracy and have never had a real human being for a client. One of our judges is very depressed because of the enormous backlog that she is being required to complete by the set date. Another, one of our finest, has decided to leave the bench and take a job with another agency, where the treadmill isn't so frenetic. His departure will be a big loss to the court and to the area's immigrant community. I volunteer to take a handful of each of the other judge's cases to ease their backlogs, especially fishing for Chinese cases because it gives me an opportunity to listen to the Mandarin language in court and continue to expand my vocabulary.

The only other topic of discussion is the request, by the Lawyers Committee for Civil Rights Under Law, for a guest speaker on the topic of 'asylum cases in immigration court.' I volunteer my time, because I always enjoy meeting the very fine staff of lawyers and volunteers who have been in the forefront of pro bono representation in San Francisco since the 1980's, when the NGO stepped in to help assist with the Central American refugee crisis.

(Such requests have to be run through the Washington bureaucracy of EOIR for approval. The particular manager for our court, so-called Assistant Chief Immigration Judge, had visited our court recently, and had seen, at our luncheon, me wearing a black leather baseball cap, admittedly not the usual judge attire. In his note granting my request for this particular speaking engagement, he indicated, "Grussendorf can do the event, but he can't wear that cap.")

Back to my courtroom for the one o'clock hearing. I enjoy the ten minute walk through the cheery sun, which takes me through a small stand of redwood trees in a park midway between the buildings, because the next four hours will be spent in a small, windowless courtroom upstairs. I have two cases on the afternoon calendar – a Sri Lankan asylum case, and an Afro-Colombian asylum case.

The first case, the Tamil Sri Lankan, is represented by the lawyer who was on the morning's Tamil cases at master calendar. For the INS, Paul Nishie, in my opinion the brightest ICE lawyer in San Francisco. A Japanese American, former Naval intelligence officer who had been stationed in Okinawa, he puts to shame some of the other lawyers from his office who often act like Goliaths trying to slay Davids in court. He's always well prepared, and unlike too many ICE lawyers, he can be accommodating. If he thinks a respondent has a strong case, he'll say so, and won't waste everyone's time trying to oppose a grant – in other words, he's happy when justice is served. Of course, if he thinks the case is bad or bogus, he'll fight like a true advocate to make the government's case.

This first case of the afternoon is one of those strong cases – the Tamil respondent testifies credibly that he was kidnapped by Tamil Tigers, forced to dig ditches in their camp, escaped, and then was arrested and tortured by the military as a suspected rebel. If he is believable, it's an open-and-shut case, and this guy is believable. Nishie only has a couple of questions on cross-examination, and when I indicate that I will grant the asylum application, he doesn't oppose and waives appeal.

The next case is more problematic. Carlos is one of a half-dozen Afro-Colombians who stowed away on a freighter and were arrested in Oakland harbor a month ago. I was the lucky one chosen to hear all of their cases, which are identical – but funny thing, when they were first detained and made statements to INS, the stories were radically different. Only one of the six said that he had any real fear of the authorities if he should be returned to Colombia. The others all said the obvious – they were coming to the States to work. Once they had a chance to talk it over together, in detention, their stories all miraculously became the same as the guy who was afraid to go back. If they had been truly running for their lives, as they now say, there were a lot of countries closer and easier to get to than the U.S. where they could have found safe haven, like a dozen right next door to Colombia. The only credible part of their synchronized asylum applications is that they were blacks living in a country where the majority is Hispanic. But they were all living in predominantly black neighborhoods, and there's no reason they would have come to the attention of the authorities any more than any of their neighbors, except that they all insist that they were mistaken for members of an insurgent Afro-Colombian organization. They all claim to either have been jailed because of the mistaken association, or to have fled just before the authorities could nab them.

The respondent, Carlos, is represented by the pro bono department of one of the top immigration firms in town, so the two attorneys are well prepared with country evidence. They come to court with their legal research team, including a law student who will argue the case. Paul Nishie is replaced by one of the INS attack dogs, a seemingly very unhappy person with zero social skills, who refuses to shake the hand or even acknowledge through eye contact any of the opposing side. This attorney does such a great disservice to the government, with the consistently over-the-top anti-immigrant attitude and lack of professionalism and common courtesy, that a job as a file clerk would be more appropriate. The image of the Department of Justice is tarnished by such an attitude in court, which is a public forum. The judges all have their pet stories about these kinds of over-zealous INS attorneys. It would be funny if not for the consequences of their actions involving real human beings. Of course, this particular attorney has since been promoted to an even higher level of responsibility.

In Carlos' case, although his attorneys do an excellent job and make their best argument, I have to deny the case, because all that he has credibly shown in court is perhaps a life of discrimination. If that were sufficient, than at least ten percent of our own citizens would be eligible for asylum. There are exceptions under international law to the rule that discrimination alone is not sufficient for a grant of asylum (see the UN Handbook on Procedures and Criteria for Determining Refugee Status, paragraphs 53 – 55), but Carlos hasn't met any exception by a long shot. I issue a denial, and the attorneys indicate they will appeal.

I leave the building at 4 o'clock, driving straight to Golden Gate Park for my hour of writing if the sun is out. I love driving the steep hills, like California Street, enjoying the sites from the cab of my Toyota pickup. The architecture, the trees and landscaping, the sea views that can always be glimpsed, are just breathtaking.

I change my clothes while parked in the truck. I have a favorite writing spot in front of the arboretum, just off of Fulton Street, next to the Azalea garden, where I can do some catch-up work on a couple of backlogged cases that are awaiting a decision – maybe I just want to read one or two precedent decisions before finalizing my draft for a particular case. I enjoy the sun, watching the other park guests who are out enjoying the air. It's a lovely afternoon. After an hour of research and writing, I go for a run along John F. Kennedy Drive in the park, crossing a bridge at Stow Lake, to circle Strawberry Hill on the running path, the aroma of pine needles thick in the air, past the Chinese Pavilion and up the hill to the top where I pause to catch my breath. I can see the ocean and the Golden Gate Bridge. Life is great.

Back home to shower and collect my materials for my 7 p.m. class. I teach immigration law at San Francisco University Law School, as an adjunct, once a week, 13 weeks in the semester. The baton was passed to me by Judge Dana Marks when I moved to San Francisco. She had been teaching it for eight years and reluctantly offered to hand over the honor to me because of her many other obligations including as president of the National Association of Immigration Judges. Since I taught immigration law at George Washington University for ten years, it's not that much work to prepare classes and it's something I really enjoy doing. The students are more laid back then at G.W., the difference between east coast and west coast mentalities, which fits my style fine. Teaching in San Francisco gives me the opportunity to cover in depth the notorious Chinese Exclusion Cases of the late 19th Century. The Chinese immigrants were detained at Angel Island in the bay, now a museum to the oppressive mentality of the INS. Times have changed, but not the mentality of some of the employees.

I teach in the attractive new law building on campus, right across the street from the university cathedral. I performed in the Cathedral one time with the San Francisco Bach Choir, singing bass, for their Christmas candlelight performance, quite a treat.

Every Tuesday evening, after class, I treat myself to a Sushi dinner at Sushi Boom, just two blocks down from my former apartment on Geary Boulevard. Owned by Koreans, with Korean cooks and staff. Wonderful sushi at good prices. I really like to unwind there, with the great food and ambiance and a couple of beers. They have a specialty, the Volcano Roll, which is a must.

Then it's home for the late news, and a snooze.

Cuban Detainees – History of Abuse

I have been involved with dozens of cases of detained Mariel Cubans, or so-called *marielitos*, first as an attorney at the university clinic and later as a judge.

The background: in April, 1980, approximately 120,000 Cubans departed from the port of Mariel, 45 kilometers west of Havana, with Castro's approval. Castro used the opportunity to empty his prisons and mental hospitals, and Jimmy Carter accepted the mass exodus, deploying immigration officials to process them in Miami. Those who admitted to, or were otherwise suspected of having been jailed, or having committed crimes in Cuba, were detained by INS, some to languish for years in INS detention. Because there were no formal diplomatic relations with Cuba, such unlucky individuals could not be returned, nor could other Cubans who subsequently committed crimes in the U.S. and were deemed deportable. As a consequence, they were detained and held for a fictitious eventual deportation.

In 1987, Castro actually agreed, through diplomatic negotiations, to receive a total of 2,500 returnees per year, and at that time, those who had been ordered deported but had waited years for their return were afforded an opportunity to have their cases reviewed one last time in what were called "repatriation hearings" by the INS. My clinic at George Washington University represented a dozen such individuals who were detained at St. Elizabeths hospital in southeast Washington.

After the first annual batch of 2,500 *marielitos* had been returned, Castro reneged on the agreement, out of protest to our policymakers' brilliant decision to implement TV Marti, the propaganda broadcasts from the Florida Keys to Cuba. As a result, further returns of Cuban detainees to Cuba were stopped. When it became clear to those thousands of Cubans who were languishing in INS custody that they weren't going home after all, and that they also were not going to be released from detention, they became understandably incensed; riots broke out in many of the detention facilities. The INS detention facilities at Krome, Miami, and a newly constructed facility in Oakdale, Louisiana, were burned to the ground.

After the Krome riots, the government responded by implementing the Cuban Review Panels, which supposedly provide an annual review by INS officials of those Cubans who remained detained, to determine whether they are too dangerous to release back into the community. Our clinic continued to be involved representing Cubans in those reviews.

Later, as a judge, I had the difficult duty of presiding over many deportation hearings of Cuban *marielitos*, some of whom were clearly mentally disturbed, were angry at the system after years of incarceration, were without any meaningful family ties in the U.S., and usually were without an attorney. Such a client is often very difficult to work with and most attorneys naturally shy away from the huge hassle. There were no pro bono organizations in San Francisco that came forward to represent the half-dozen *marielitos* whose cases I saw in there.

There were other more recent Cuban arrivals who also found their way into my courtroom. One such case that I handled in my last year as a judge illustrates how our government often operates at cross-purposes, one agency not knowing or caring what the other is doing.

Maria's story

A young mother in her late twenties, who I'll call Maria, was brought into my courtroom in shackles. She and her husband had fled Cuba ten years earlier, in the second wave, in July of 1994, during the so-called *balsero* crisis, or raft crisis.

Maria and her Cuban husband had picked up convictions for dealing cocaine in Texas. Both served prison time, and she was released earlier than her husband, having been sentenced to a lesser term as a co-conspirator. Her two young children were being cared for by her sister. If the mother had not been an alien, the normal course, after serving her prison sentence would have been to return her to her children. They needed her and she needed them. Makes sense?

She couldn't be returned to Cuba, even with a deport order. If I had been the ICE official in charge of such decisions, I wouldn't even have brought immigration charges against her, but would have returned her instead to her family as quickly as possible. Just the fact of issuing a charging document and putting her into proceedings meant that she would continue to languish in jail for months at tax payers' expense and continue to be separated from her children, even if she eventually prevailed in court.

Because of the nature of her conviction, she was ineligible to file for asylum, but she *could* file for protection under the Convention Against Torture, and the Bush administration had recently been waging a public campaign to emphasize to the world that Castro's government tortures its own citizens.

The facts that came out in her testimony before me were very compelling. Maria and her husband had actually made two attempts to flee Cuba. The first time, they were involved with a dozen other Cubans who crept aboard a fishing vessel and commandeered it. Once on the high seas, they were intercepted by a Cuban patrol boat, and everyone on board was arrested and charged with hijacking. They were at first imprisoned, but then released on bond to await trial. Maria and her husband didn't like the odds of getting a fair trial in Cuba, so they made secret arrangements and fled again, this time with more success. If they *were* ever returned to Cuba, there was still the outstanding charge of hijacking a boat pending against them, and a trial with guaranteed swift justice awaiting them.

Just one month before our hearing, the Cuban government had executed a dozen of its citizens on charges of hijacking a boat in order to use it to bring them to the U.S. Again, this was something that the Bush Administration had played up and trumpeted in the media. In her court hearing, Maria's testimony about the events described was credible, leaving little doubt in my mind that there was at least a very strong likelihood that the same fate awaited her in Cuba, especially now in the heightened atmosphere of diplomatic tensions between our two countries. And the ICE attorney didn't dispute her credibility. Nevertheless, the ICE attorney strenuously opposed her application to remain in the US under the protection of the Convention Against Torture (CAT), and when I granted the case, the government appealed my decision.

Maria appeared before me without an attorney, and she would be without the assistance of one for the appeal. The appeal had the automatic effect of keeping Maria locked up for at least another six months until the Board could review my decision. Thus, another minimum of half a year separated Maria from her infant children, during which she would be unable to contribute to the family livelihood in any way. And this in spite of the fact that there was an absolute diplomatic bar from actually returning her to Cuba in the foreseeable future; that our administration was emphasizing the lack of freedom and due process in Cuba as well as the recent abomination of the Cuban government's execution of hijackers.

In such cases, the kind which I saw repeated so many times it would be impossible to count, I was unable to figure out if the ICE attorney was really daft, or just mean-spirited, or a combination of both. But it was really her manager who was to blame, who could have waived the magic wand of prosecutorial discretion and let things lie. If (s)he was too timid to make such a common sense call before the deport hearing, which in my view was a no-brainer, the appeal could at least have been waived in order to get Maria back home to her children, using my decision as a rationale for not continuing with an appeal. In such cases, I never understood whether the responsible official was mean-spirited, or a moral coward, or just afraid of being perceived by her peers as being soft on criminals.

Government Lawyer Helps Prove Case

One of my most memorable cases in San Francisco was unusual, both because of the strength of the asylum application of a young Palestinian couple, and because of the way that the government counsel, in her overzealousness to deport the people, helped prove their case. The couple, who I'll call Suzanna and Tauriq, were Arab Palestinians, both born in Bethlehem, with Jordanian citizenship. They were both practicing Christians from traditionally Christian families. They had come to the U.S. in 1997 on visitor's visas and had overstayed.

The couple were represented by the law office of Sharon Duhlberg. Sharon received her law degree from University of Michigan Law School in 1994, after working in Central America for a while. She established her own firm in 2001. She's a very solid attorney and activist in the American Immigration Lawyers' Association on such issues as LGBTQ asylum cases.

Her well-meaning but relatively inexperienced associate who handled the hearing did a competent job in court, but, I believe, also learned a valuable lesson. She had clearly worked hard preparing the case and gaining the trust of her clients, but her courtroom skills were still in the developmental stage. And that's where the bungling government counsel came to her assistance.

Our hearing lasted two days, on April 5th and April 8th, 2002. Both Suzanna and Tauriq, and Susanna's father testified. Their story was that they were both born into Catholic families and baptized as infants. They both attended weekly mass at the Roman Catholic Church of Bethlehem and lived in a Christian neighborhood in Bethlehem. Suzanna's family had moved to a Moslem neighborhood when she was fifteen.

During the late eighties they received constant pressure from other high school students and neighbors to join the Intifada uprising against the Israeli occupation, which they were reluctant to do. Threats against Suzanna escalated, until her father's car was firebombed. A month later, leaflets were distributed in the neighborhood naming Susanna: *"Beware of Informer."* Her name was painted in graffiti on a fence and on building walls. In March 1990, a Molotov cocktail was hurled at their house, partly damaging it. Suzanna was staying home from school at this time, and after the Molotov cocktail incident, her father decided it was time to clear out and move back to Manger Square. They sold the house at a great loss.

Tauriq testified that, before marrying Suzanna, he and his father had been abducted by Palestinian radicals while driving home one night in his father's taxi. Four armed men forced them to drive to a remote area, where Tauriq's father was then taken and held all night and subjected to brutal torture, accompanied by allegations that he was an Israeli informant. He was hospitalized for a week afterward and suffered a series of heart attacks.

After their marriage, Suzanna and Tauriq continued to be harassed and threatened because of Suzanna's alleged informant activities. Her younger sister was also threatened. The father's car was firebombed again, and the younger sister attempted suicide several times apparently because of the stress. Suzanna and Tauriq finally decided that they had to flee, and were able to travel on their Jordanian passports to the U.S. (I have greatly simplified a very lengthy story).

After they came to the U.S., things back home heated up. Suzanna's brother was dragged from a car by Palestinian radicals and beaten with a tire iron, requiring 25 stitches. Then he was interrogated and tortured by Palestinian authorities on trumped-up charges of having marijuana in his car. He was hospitalized and then transferred to the psychiatric ward because of a breakdown due to the mistreatment.

Only days before our hearing, the Israeli army used tanks to re-occupy all of the major cities in the West Bank, searching for Palestinian gunmen. The couple's family members in Bethlehem were all living under circumstances of virtual house captivity. The events were played out in dramatic imagery on the nightly news. On April 2nd, about a hundred Palestinians, including a group of Palestinian gunmen, took refuge from Israeli forces in the central Church of the Nativity. Suzanna's uncle had been the church bell ringer there for thirty years. When the gunmen burst into the church, taking Christian worshipers they found there hostage, Suzanna's uncle was shot dead. His name was broadcast on the evening news. It was the most visceral experience I ever had, of actually seeing the events happen in real time, even as we were conducting a hearing about the same events.

In the face of such a strong case, why had the government not simply conceded that the couple should be granted asylum? One explanation is that there was a subtext of fraud to the couple's actions in America. After traveling to the U.S. as a married couple, they had foolishly taken the advice of a local Arab immigration attorney-shyster, who advised them to get divorced so that Susanna could marry a U.S. citizen that he knew. The idea was that after she got her green card through this phony relationship, she would get divorced from that guy, remarry her true husband, Tauriq, and then he would get the green card through her. This fairly common and lame-brained scheme was found out. An anonymous caller accused the couple of being terrorists, and they were placed in deportation proceedings. The government's attitude in the case was, once fraud, always fraud. Thus, the government wasn't about to accept their asylum story as credible, and therefore credibility was the big issue in their hearing.

Suzanna and her husband were good, persuasive witnesses, but it was really Suzanna's father who was a mountain of moral persuasion. He had traveled to the U.S. for the single purpose of being a witness at the hearing, and after his arrival he had learned, along with the rest of the world, that Bethlehem had been occupied by an invasion force of tanks and soldiers. As I said in my decision, "He is the type of witness whose demeanor does not well translate onto a typewritten transcript. He has the bearing of solid integrity which is the combined result of his age and the extent of the hardships that he and his family have endured. It seems to the Court that it would be impossible for this man to come into court and give false testimony, yet alone fabricate the kinds of things that he said have befallen his two daughters and even more tragically his son."

Now here's the lesson: the INS attorney made the case for the respondents. Suzanna's lawyer took her best and last witness, Suzanna's father, through only a very basic direct examination. She was well-intentioned, but didn't yet have her court "sea legs" to know how to work with this most crucial of witnesses. But then the INS trial attorney, one of the government's more aggressive attack dogs in court, proved herself to be lacking in her cross-examination skills. Not only did she repeatedly violate the most hallowed maxim about cross-examination, "Never ask a question to which you don't know the answer," but she insisted upon drawing out the man's story at length. As I wrote with irony in my decision, "He initially gave only brief testimony on direct examination, but with the assistance of government counsel on cross-examination he gave lengthy, detailed testimony that was extremely helpful to the Court in its adjudication of the case."

This was not the first or last time that I chastised an INS lawyer for doing the work of the respondent's lawyer for them. But this was the only time that the practice was so blatant, with such opposite effect from what was intended, that I put it into a written decision.

(In December 2019 I was informed that new ICE attorneys still only receive a week to ten days of initial training and indoctrination, *with no court practice*, before being thrown into court to represent the government. Mind-boggling).

Then, I had to resolve the issue of the fraud that the couple had attempted with Suzanna's sham marriage, by balancing that bad act against the compelling nature of the asylum claim. "The respondents entered into a marriage fraud scheme so that, in their own admission, at least the female respondent could gain the immigration benefit of lawful permanent residence. If this case had been heard only weeks prior to the actual date of the hearing, the Court would have been inclined to find that this nefarious scheme to defraud the United States and undermine the immigration laws did indeed qualify as egregious and could be significant enough of a factor to deny asylum in the exercise of discretion. However, given that the respondents' home town of Bethlehem is currently occupied by a foreign army, that the act of invasion by Israeli forces has been condemned by several international bodies, and that their own immediate relatives presently are cowering in their basements, cut off from food and water and uncertain of their survival from day to day (one of them was shot dead), the Court elects to forgive the respondents their trespass against the law of the United States and afford them an opportunity to remain in the United States under the protective mantel of asylum. This is the time for America to invoke its proud history of offering protection to those fleeing persecution and the catastrophe of sectarian warfare."

The associate who represented the couple went on to a brilliant career in immigration practice and now has her own firm.

I spent time relating this case simply because it dramatically underscores the astonishing lack of skills and training that so many INS/ICE attorneys exhibited in every courtroom that I worked in. Typically, only the government attorney who came from a criminal law background had any inkling how to conduct a cross examination. Otherwise the standard practice was to take the witness all the way through their story again, not only wasting everyone's time but all too often, as in this case, bolstering the story of the witness in favor of the respondent. Why didn't their managers catch it? Equal lack of trial skills. And to think how much such attorneys are paid to consistently bungle cases in court as representatives of the Department of Homeland Security – is anybody listening?

The same ICE prosecutor, in another case, again shot herself and the government in the foot. The case involved a Vietnamese national and permanent resident who had been convicted and just completed a sentence for home invasion involving violence. Given his lawful resident status, he was eligible for consideration of relief from removal under the Convention Against Torture out of fear of return to Vietnam. He was scheduled in my court for a bond hearing, and if I determined that bond should be denied, I would also conduct the merits hearing.

The ICE lawyer brought in a Chinese-American detective from Oakland, where the crime had occurred, who was the regional police expert on Chinese and Vietnamese gangs in the Bay area. This guy was out of Central Casting, with Hollywood good looks and demeanor. The ICE attorney's intention was to tarnish the Vietnamese guy by putting the detective's testimony about his knowledge of the guy's background in the record, thus making a case that he was far more dangerous than the record itself indicated. She wanted to get the detective to testify that the respondent had earlier been implicated in a murder, which, if true, would have been a reasonable argument against the granting of a bond. I had the luxury of listening to this incredible witness testifying about gang activity in Oakland for an hour. In reply to her question about the alleged murder that she was hoping to taint him with, the detective answered that this respondent had *never been a suspect* in the murder. Talk about good lawyering skills. I granted the bond.

Romantic Postscript – Not!

About a year after our hearing with the Palestinian couple, I finally worked up the nerve to invite the lawyer for the applicants in that case, R.C., to lunch. She was a lovely Asian-American and smart as a button, and I had hopes of getting to know her better. The lunch went well. I'm psyched. I asked her out to lunch again a week later. Again at that lunch things are looking good and I think sparks are flying. My heart is going pitter-patter. But I make the mistake of giving her, at the third lunch, a copy of my book, **Latex Monkey with Banana**, written under my pseudonym Jonathon Worlde. It's a satirical mystery, what I call Latino-noir, about a Puerto Rican sax player who navigates the pitfalls of trying to be a drug dealer in the Hispanic nightclubs in the Washington, D.C. area. The club scenes were all derived from the time I had played sax with Orquesta Candela in the same clubs. The book had won the prestigious Hollywood Discovery Award with a $1000 prize, and I was quite proud of it. I thought she would dig the immigration theme. I should have realized that perhaps the sex scenes, which were all satirical in nature, and tame by any comparison with other popular fare, would nevertheless spook her. Whatever it was, after receiving the book she totally ghosted me, before the term was even invented. No returned calls, refusal to even make eye contact or acknowledge my presence when passing in the street. I had thought she was hipper than that. (The book, available on Amazon Kindle, has become a cult classic with thousands of sales. I currently have an option from a studio). Her reaction was of course very disappointing, and in reflection I was an idiot for giving her the book before our relationship had advanced further, but on the other hand her reaction shows that she wasn't hip enough for me.

Gay San Francisco

I grew to love San Francisco, now my favorite city in America. (I won't expound here on how events in Silicon Valley have in many ways destroyed the city for the non-rich class of artists and bohemians and characters who used to make it so great). One of the things that lends the city notoriety and diversity is its relatively large gay community. The Castro district is a neighborhood of distinctive Victorian houses and folks with an attitude – a great place to hang out. I love the movie-going experience at the Castro Theater, one of the most beautiful, historic movie houses in the country. Before every show, an organist rises out of the floor with his Wurlitzer organ, to play show tunes, before disappearing back under the stage. The theater shows a great mix of European and independent films, and used to have an annual film noir festival.

One early experience I had kind of paints a picture of the offbeat culture in the city. One night I went to one of my favorite bars, on California Street at Filmore, which hosted live blues music every night. As I walked back to take my usual place at the corner of the bar, I saw a group of three people sitting round a small table – a guy who was dressed like a chic cowboy, with white cowboy hat, white pants and boots and finely tailored black jacket. With him were two women, who were done up like "floozies" or Old West-style hookers, in over-the top make-up and outfits. As I took my place at the bar, I chuckled to myself at how hip they looked. A few minutes later, when one of the two women came back to the bar to order drinks, I got a closer look at her, and realized she was a guy in drag. Then I took a closer look at the other two, and I was able to discern, after a couple minutes of observation, that the faux cowboy was actually a woman, and the two women were guys. You gotta love San Francisco.

It should come then as no surprise that San Francisco is also home to many gay immigrants, including a large gay Mexican population. As with any other immigrant or undocumented population, many of them end up in deportation hearings – usually as the results of ICE dragnets in Mexican restaurants or clubs. Thus, I was able to hear several asylum cases where the theory of the case was that the gay Mexican would be persecuted, in Mexico, because of his sexual orientation. I was by no means the first judge to hear such a case in San Francisco, but I had some very compelling cases early in the history of the "sexual orientation" theory of asylum law, and I joined my San Francisco IJ colleagues in accepting the theory as a legitimate ground for asylum.

At the time, the only guidance we had from the Board of Immigration Appeals was a case involving a gay Cuban man. The Board, in an interesting analysis, had ruled that it is acceptable for a country, such as Cuba, to criminalize homosexuality, but if an individual was punished in an egregious manner, or extra-judicially, because of his/her sexual orientation, than the circumstances could give rise to a claim of asylum.

But only months before I had arrived in San Francisco, the 9th Circuit Court of Appeals had entered a historic ruling, in that it was the first of any federal circuit court to acknowledge the theory of gays belonging to a 'particular social group' that merited asylum protection. The case of *Hernandez-Montial* held that "gay men with female sexual identities in Mexico constitute a 'particular social group' under the asylum statute." The federal court thus overturned the BIA's earlier decision in that case, which had found that Hernandez merely needed to change his appearance in Mexico, or to "butch up" in order to escape persecution there.

It was not unusual in my courtroom, when I was hearing the initial arraignments of a group of fifty detained aliens, to see an attractive Mexican woman sitting in the men's section of the courtroom, and upon closer examination to discover that she was a 'he' who simply chose to dress and groom herself like a she. As far as the detention officers were concerned, if she still had her male working parts then she would be seated with the men, but if she had already gone over to the other side, as in post-op transsexual, she would be placed with the women. Often, the case would lead to a claim of asylum to prevent deportation back to Mexico.

The first of several cases I heard involved a Mexican transvestite, who credibly testified about the horrors visited upon him by Mexican police since his early teenage years, simply because he was perceived as being gay. He had essentially been kidnapped and raped several times by police, the most brutal time involving rape by instrument, police baton. Because, within the macho culture that still prevails in Mexico, he was not able to find recourse in the justice system, he was forced to move to another city. Later, when he developed HIV, he was denied any meaningful access to medical treatment, again because of his sexual orientation.

He appeared without counsel in my courtroom, the casualty of a restaurant raid by INS, where he had worked as a short-order cook. I could tell by his demeanor during the hearing that he was convinced that I would act like all other officials he had encountered "in the system" up to that point. The INS attorney argued vigorously against a grant of asylum, even though the man's testimony about the horrible things he had endured in Mexico was completely credible. My clerk, the wonderful Lilian Shevchenko, who sat through the hearing, was brought to tears. I spent some time to research and write up the decision, because at that time it was still such a novel issue, and we were completely without guidance from headquarters. When I granted the case, the government appealed it, but I was upheld by the BIA in my decision.

You've Got To Know Your Client

One of the luxuries of working at a non-profit like the George Washington law school immigration clinic was that I was able to spend as much time with my clients as I thought necessary. I learned that, especially in an asylum case or a court case, where your client will be required to testify, the more times you can meet with him/her, the better off you'll both be, meaning especially you will be able to avoid any potential surprises during the heat of battle. Over the years, it never ceased to amaze me what new details would emerge if we just spent one more cession with our client prior to trial. Often my student would come to me and say, "Professor Paul, you'll never believe what Antonio just told me!" Naturally it's all about trust, and the more that your client gets to know you and to realize that you have their best interests at heart, the more open they will be with important and often intimate details of their lives.

This was especially proven to me one day when I was hearing a case in San Francisco court. The applicant was a 60-year old Mexican migrant worker. He had worked in the fields of California, Oregon and Washington for 25 years, had been arrested numerous times for DUI and alcohol-related offenses, and was just coming out of a jail term for DUI when he was brought into my courtroom. Only one person in his life, his grown daughter, was there to assist and testify on his behalf, the rest of his family having long since abandoned him. He was a lawful permanent resident (green card holder) and so, in spite of his relatively minor crimes, he was eligible to apply for cancellation of removal and ask the judge to waive the crimes and allow him to remain in the States. He had no property of any kind and practically lived the life of a vagrant. He had a young, well-meaning but inexperienced attorney who had agreed to represent him for a meager fee after being contacted by his daughter.

He had lived a sad, harsh life with nothing to show for it but this one family member who still supported his efforts to remain in the U.S. I was naturally inclined to help him out if the case merited it, but it wasn't easy – the INS attorney had taken a belligerent attitude toward him, and he wasn't a very good witness on his own behalf. He had too many alcohol-induced lapses in his memory – dates and addresses had slipped away, it was hard for him to even give a chronology of where he had lived and all the places he had worked. (Again, when he described his life as a migrant worker, my brief but impressive experience working with Mexican migrant workers in the fields in Oregon when I was a teenager resonated.)

I was listening to his attorney struggling to get his story out on the record in a coherent fashion, wondering whether I should feel more sorry for the lawyer or his client. Suddenly something the old farm laborer said piqued my interest. It had already been well-established that the man was an alcoholic, and had been in and out of many court-ordered programs to no avail. But the lawyer, trying to go back to the basics, asked him the name of his deceased wife of twenty-five years, the mother of the daughter who was in the courtroom, and he couldn't remember it. Well, of course it must be related to alcohol-induced memory loss – that was the logical assumption of everyone in the courtroom. He was asked a second time, and he just couldn't remember her name. Something didn't feel right to me. I started wondering if there might be physical trauma to the head in his background.

I interrupted the questioning. "Sir, have you ever been in a bad accident, maybe something where you were hospitalized?"

He hesitated, looked sheepishly around the courtroom, and answered, "Well there was that one time in Mexico when I was twenty-two, a car accident, when I woke up in the hospital they said I had been in a coma for three months."

Suddenly with that one detail, so much of the tragedy of this man's life was illuminated. The lawyer was able to take it from there, following up with questions about medical treatment, medications which he ultimately had been unable to afford, a long downward spiral of self-medicating with alcohol, seasonal work from one crop to the next, migrating north and south to follow the cycle of harvests, bringing his family in a broken-down old Ford to find the next temporary home of rickety migrant shelter.

I remembered the lessons I had learned years earlier at the clinic, when I would have the luxury to spend extra time with my clients. By my prompting that one question, the narrative of the man's life took on an extra shade of meaning that explained so much, awakening sympathy in such a dramatic way that when I granted his application for cancellation of removal, the previously antagonistic INS attorney waived appeal.

Fraudulent Korean Green Cards

In recent history there have been many visa scams involving large numbers of persons from particular countries. Sometimes, shamefully, U.S. diplomats or INS agents are involved. To name just a few such large-scale scams:

In 1998 a group of Americans and Philippine nationals were charged with having smuggled into the U.S. over 500 Philippine nurses by using fraudulent visas.

In March of 1999, an Iranian national, Bahram Tabatabai, and fifteen others were charged with running an immigration fraud ring that obtained fake documents for Iranians to enter the U.S., such as birth certificates, bank and employment records and school transcripts, so that once they entered the country they could apply for political asylum. Tabatabai would then fabricate asylum stories for them to submit to immigration. He pled guilty in October of that year to the charge of providing material assistance to members of the People's Mujahadeen, which is on the State Department's list of terrorist organizations. He had appeared over 300 times at the asylum office as interpreter for his clients. (As a consultant, after leaving the bench, I worked on a federal 9th Circuit Appeal for one of the individuals whom he assisted; that person, even though he had a perfectly legitimate asylum case of his own, nevertheless accepted the bad advice and fabricated story that Tabatabai had created for him, and tried to present it to the immigration court).

In 2003, two Pakistani immigrants who had offices in Sacramento, California, were charged with falsifying asylum applications for Pakistani and Indian clients. They also appeared as interpreters for their hundreds of clients at the Los Angeles and San Francisco asylum offices. (I saw several of their clients in my courtroom, who, subsequent to the unraveling of the scheme, were charged with deportability for fraud).

In December, 2004, sixteen people were arrested and charged with fraudulently assisting two thousand Indonesian nationals, by helping them to file bogus asylum applications on the East and West Coasts. The ringleader reportedly earned over a million dollars from the scam, and was gearing up to start smuggling in women for sex trafficking when he was arrested. The INS investigation into the conspiracy was dubbed "Operation Jakarta."

Cases involving fraud at U.S. embassies include:

A consular officer at the U.S. embassy in Prague accepted at least fifty thousand dollars over a period of two years in exchange for issuing 85 fraudulent visas between April 2000 and May 2002.

An investigation at the consular post in Nuevo Laredo, Mexico, actually caused the temporary closing of the office, and led to charges against three consulate employees and a Foreign Service officer.

In June 2002 a consular officer who had been assigned to the embassy in Guyana received a 21 year sentence for having sold 800 visas for between ten and fifteen thousand dollars each.

In the wake of the 9-11 tragedy, it was revealed that the U.S. embassies in Qatar and Doha had issued fraudulent visas to groups of twenty and thirty Jordanian, Bangladeshi and Pakistani nationals.

In January 2005 a consular officer based in Mexico City pled guilty and received a year and a day in prison for issuing approximately 180 fraudulent visas to Colombian nationals.

In April 2004, two U.S. citizen employees at the U.S. embassy in Colombo, Sri Lanka pled guilty to participating in a large scale visa fraud scheme, having received hundreds of thousands of dollars in exchange for issuing fake visas to foreign nationals, primarily from India and Vietnam. They were sentenced to a minimum of five years in prison and forfeiture of $750,000 in personal assets

Not too long thereafter, a State Department official was indicted on fraud and bribery charges for issuing, from the U.S. embassy in Armenia, fake visas to Armenian nationals for ten thousand dollars each.

Two brothers, attorneys who are Indian nationals, have recently been convicted in Sacramento federal court for fabricating fake Indian and Fijian asylum cases. One of the brothers used to appear regularly in my courtroom, and was one of the most erudite and well-spoken attorneys appearing before me. Investigators found bogus notary stamps from the countries of origin of the asylum applicants under the bed of one of the firm's legal assistants.

Closer to home, a Supervisory District Adjudications Officer with whom I had dealings early in my career, at the Arlington District office, Robert Schofield, was sentenced in U.S. District Court, Eastern District of Virginia, in April 2007 to 15 years in prison for the crimes of Bribery of a Senior Public Official and Naturalization Fraud. He had purportedly taken in $600,000 in bribes over a ten year period from mostly Chinese applicants.

And finally, one of my favorites, a U.S. consular officer in Ghana issued hundreds of fake visas to Chinese nationals, in cooperation with Chinese smugglers or "snakeheads." He was found out because, when he was being transferred to another post, he tried to recruit his replacement into the scheme. As foolish as this may sound, insiders say that his life was threatened by the snakeheads, and that he had no choice other than try to recruit a replacement.

During my last year on the bench, I was point man to hear the first of hundreds of cases involving a massive fraud, one involving a senior INS adjudicator in San Jose who collaborated with Korean "consultants" to issue 275 bogus green cards to Korean migrants. The cases involved the dependants of forty eight families. He was tried and convicted of conspiracy and fraud. Then all of those Koreans who had received their green cards through him were placed in deportation proceedings. Making the case especially interesting for me was the fact that the convicted INS officer appeared in my court as a witness for the government. Also, INS investigators testified about how they had investigated the case. And I became convinced that most of the family members in the cases, the dependant wives and children, probably didn't even know that their green cards had been obtained illegally – the husbands had been the ones in the family with the guilty intent, who had contracted with the consultants to bribe a government official.

A local Korean attorney, Alex C. Park, represented the family in my courtroom. He ultimately handled 141 of the 275 cases. He was not originally an immigration practitioner, but being located in

Santa Clara, he found himself close to the "scene of the crime" and many of the families went to him for assistance. He had a fascinating immigrant story in his own right.

Alex C. Park immigrated to the United States in 1972 at the age of twelve. His grandfather had been a wine tycoon in Korea, and Park describes growing up in a mansion, with servants and limo drivers. Due to political machinations of the competition, his grandfather was driven into bankruptcy, and the family came to the U.S. to start over again. Park is one of four generations of males in his family who have made the U.S. their home: his grandfather, father, himself, and his teenage son. Park's wife works in the law office with him in Santa Clara.

Park describes living in San Francisco's Tenderloin district in a small tenement flat when his family first migrated. He worked as a newspaper boy, then as a fisherman for two years, and then he became a member of a teenage Asian motorcycle gang. Later, he joined another extremely violent gang: he joined the 81st Airborne Division, and was stationed in Fort Bragg, North Carolina for two years, before returning to the Bay area and graduating from UC Hastings School of Law. He settled in Silicon Valley to handle the needs of Korean business people.

Heading up the government's team in the prosecution of the cases was Peter Vincent, a capable young attorney who impressed me, during the course of the hearing, both with his litigation skills and with his ability to recognize the underlying humanitarian aspects of the case. Peter Vincent had done undergraduate studies at USC-Berkeley in political science, and then spent two years in the Peace Corps in Guatemala. He returned to the U.S. to get a law degree at the University of Virginia School of Law, and while there he was editor of the school's Journal of International Law. Assisting him on the case was ICE attorney Jo Ellen Ardinger.

The main culprit in the case, Leland Dwayne Sustaire, had been an officer with the INS for twenty years at the time that he was busted for fraud. In court, he testified in a soft but steady voice, reluctantly complying with his commitment to the government as part of his plea agreement to testify in the first of many such hearings. His last position had been as Supervisory District Adjudications Officer, a job that included supervising five INS examiners in the San Jose office. He had the power to approve or deny an application for a visa or a green card, technically a lawful permanent resident visa, without any supervision from above.

According to his testimony, beginning in 1986 he began accepting monetary bribes to approve applications for green cards without following the proper procedures. He worked with two Korean "business partners," the two brokers who would bring him the clients for processing. He took a fifty per cent split of a usual $30,000 fee per client, sometimes more, sometimes less. He would set up dummy files and assign them "A" numbers, the INS tracking system which is assigned to every alien who makes any kind of application to the agency while in the country – and those numbers would be entered into the system. He met the clients at the houses of his partners or in hotel rooms. They would provide him with the bare-bones application form, and he would then send the green card, technically a form I-551, to their residential addresses. As anyone who has been through the process knows, a genuine application requires a lot of documentation, including medical and security checks including fingerprints. He confirmed that such checks were never done. He would then store the files in his garage at home.

Already back in 1994, Mr. Sustaire learned that he was the subject of an investigation by the Office of Inspector General. Amazingly, he somehow skated at that time, but years later he *was* indicted and convicted. But when he heard about the initial investigation in '94 he decided he'd better cover his tracks. He made a hand-written list of all of the names of people whom he had helped obtain the green cards fraudulently, along with the "A" numbers written next to the names, and then had a fire in his back yard where he burned the files. He consulted with a criminal attorney during that first investigation, and he left a copy of the list with the attorney. He never explained why he had made such a list, but it certainly became valuable to him later on when he *was* indicted, because he could use it as a bargaining chip in his plea negotiations. He eventually saved himself a lot of hard prison time by agreeing to testify against all of the people on the list, even though he had received approximately $500,000 in bribes. He was eventually sentenced to six months in a halfway house and six months in home confinement.

Sustaire and four co-conspirators were convicted of conspiracy to commit fraud, and his partners were also convicted of conspiracy to bribe a public official. Sustaire also testified against his partners in federal criminal court.

DHS Special Agent Leslie Brown took the witness stand next. She testified about how she had led an investigation into all of the people on Sustaire's list. She began her career with INS in 1991 as an immigration inspector, and was a Senior Inspector at the time of the hearing. A stocky woman with dirty blond hair, she appears like a no-nonsense type, the kind that you want to have working with DHS to protect our nation.

She explained that a task force was set up by INS in 2002, to track down everyone who was on Sustaire's list. One way that they were able to catch people was by setting up a lookout list for the airport inspectors – anyone traveling back into the U.S. after a visit home to Korea would be automatically flagged and questioned. That was what happened with the Korean family in my courtroom. Agent Brown interviewed Mr. Cho (not his real name) and his wife in April of 2003. They had been stopped at the airport while returning from Korea, had given a statement at the time to the airport inspector, and then had been scheduled for a follow-up interview with Agent Brown's team.

During that follow-up interview, Mr. Cho told her that he worked as a chef at Flames Coffee Shop, a business that was owned by his cousin. Mr. Cho explained that he had obtained his green card legitimately, based upon his job, that all of the proper paperwork had been completed and filed. He was a businessman in Korea who had substantial real estate holdings back home. Yet he had kept no copies of any of the documentation that he had supposedly submitted to Sustaire for processing of the green card.

The statement that Mr. Cho gave at the airport was significantly different from the one he gave to Agent Brown later, and when Mr. Cho testified in his own defense at our hearing he came up with a third version of reality. He had come to the country in 1991, and had only worked intermittently at several restaurants as a part-time cook or helper. He admitted that he had lied under oath while being questioned by agent Brown. He admitted that he had only been working part-time, and off the books, at the restaurant, in order to recover a loan he had made to the owner when he first came to the U.S. He had paid a total of $60,000 dollars for the green cards for himself, his wife, and two children, or $15,000 each, making an initial payment of $30,000 in cash. And yet his green card had been issued on the basis of his supposedly being an E-visa investor, or someone who invests a minimum of one million dollars to establish a new company.

In none of the three sworn statements given, either at the airport, or to Agent Brown later, or in my courtroom, could he explain how, as a part-time chef, he had qualified for a millionaire investor-visa green card. It also rang untrue that, as a supposedly astute Korean businessman, he would conduct his business with large amounts of cash and not keep any records of the transactions, and then claim that he had been duped by Sustaire's partners.

The hearing lasted a total of three days. During this time, Cho's attractive wife and two fine-looking teenage children, brother and sister, sat through the testimony, apparently convinced that their husband/father had done nothing wrong other than trust an unscrupulous countryman who had roped him into the conspiracy.

Attorney Park made the argument that his clients were innocent sheep who had been snared by corrupt wolves. It was clear that he was planning to make the same argument in another 140 cases. I sympathized with the wife and children. The kids, who had grown up in America and lived the American dream, probably had no inkling that their father was a crook. They had been infants when they arrived in the States, and by the time of the hearing they were about to enter college. But I had different thoughts about the father. He was ordered removed from the United States.

I agreed with government counsel Peter Vincent, that the wife and children appeared to be innocent of any knowledge of the husband's dirty dealings, and so, rather than ordering them to be deported, they were given the relief of voluntary departure, so that there would be no order of deportation on their records to haunt them in the future. At last report, practically all of the Koreans who were put into deportation proceedings had been found deportable based upon the charges.

Hawaiian Dream Nights

If you thought my earlier story about scaring off the female immigration attorney by giving her a copy of my book, **Latex Monkey with Banana** was pathetic, here's an even sadder story. When I was on my Guam deployment in 1999 to adjudicate the Chinese boat people cases, I met a lovely CBP (Customs and Border Protection) agent who was assigned there from her office in Hawaii to assist with the detainees. I'd never dated a woman in uniform and who was authorized to carry a gun before, and I didn't on this occasion in Guam either, but I never forgot her. Later, when I was transferred from Philadelphia to San Francisco in 2001, it occurred to me to give her a call. That led to a year-long romance including incredible Hawaiian nights, tropical breezes, palm trees and luaus with really hot coconut-clad dancers, and dreams of moving to Hawaii and getting married.

No, really, it got pretty intense. After I reached out to her, she invited me to visit in Hawaii, and since I'd never been before it was a lovely adventure. Since she was a resident of Hawaii she could get me really good deals on hotel bookings. I learned that Hawaii is only a five hour flight from San Francisco, and given the time change, you could board a flight at 9 am in San Francisco and arrive at 12 noon in Hawaii and have the whole day left to enjoy, plus the rest of the three-day weekend that you had planned. For nearly a year, I would visit her, and then a month or six weeks later she'd visit me in San Francisco. She showed me all the islands and I showed her the Bay area and the northern coast and Vegas and… How was I to know she was a nut job?

I fell in love with Hawaii, and she had a great house in the hills outside of Honolulu in Kaneohe. I was thinking marriage and moving to Hawaii or dividing time between the islands and San Francisco.

Imagine my disappointment when I discovered that she was so possessive and jealous, she had abused her law enforcement authority to obtain my cell phone records. I began to notice, in our discussions she would drop little clues about certain calls that I had made or people I had called, until I started wondering what was behind it all. When I found out that she was monitoring my calls and confronted her on it, she at first claimed that an ICE agent in San Francisco had given her the information. But then when I started pressing her for details about this alleged co-conspirator, she confessed that she had worked out the surveillance all on her own.

It hit me bad because I was really into her. But as they say in Hawaii, there's more than one fish in the sea.

Attorney General Massacres Board of Immigration Appeals

Shortly after Attorney General John Ashcroft took office during the George W. Bush administration, someone in the Department of Justice convinced him that it would be a good idea to reform the Board of Immigration Appeals by firing half of the Board members.

The Board is the appellate court for immigration deportation/removal matters and for certain types of visa applications. Any case appealed from the immigration court goes to the Board. When first established in 1940, Board members made initial decisions on deportation matters, but restructuring in 1982 gave the Board appellate review of all deportation decisions by immigration judges.

Since I began my career in immigration law, the number of Board members, which is set by regulation, had grown from nine to twenty-three. This was an attempt to address the backlog of cases, which had only continued to increase – a migrant might wait up to five years for a decision on an appeal. As the adage goes, "Justice delayed is justice denied." In many cases, the delay really was harmful to peoples' lives; but in the field of immigration law, many more people could actually benefit from delays, since for them, if they might not have a good case in court, the more time they could win before the final order to leave the country, the better.

Ironically, there were already streamlining measures in place at the Board when Ashcroft made the decision to streamline by firing judges, and the measures were already having positive results. Anderson LLP had performed an independent study of the effects of the streamlining measures in 2001 and found them to be "an unqualified success," in part because more cases were now being completed by the Board than were coming into the system. ANDERSON LLP, BOARD OF IMMIGRATION APPEALS (BIA) STREAMLINING PILOT PROJECT ASSESSMENT REPORT 12 (2001).

But that wasn't good enough for Ashcroft's advisers. Not surprisingly, most of the Board members who were fired were judges who came from the liberal spectrum in immigration issues, and in fact tended to be senior members of the Board. They were judges with huge reputations in the profession like Board Chairman Paul Schmidt, and Lory Rosenberg, whose dissenting opinions often turned out to be the majority opinions when the federal courts of appeals exercised their review. Regrettably, since the Ashcroft reforms have been in place, the Board rubber stamps government appeals, and shifts the burden to the higher federal appellate courts, so that the federal courts' case loads have increased tremendously: according to published reports, the load has increased in the 9th Circuit, by 560%, and in the 2nd Circuit, by 1,400%.

I realize that this last remark about "rubber-stamping" cases is controversial, but several studies have born out this opinion. I quote at length from a fascinating article: "Federal appellate judges in circuits around the country are expressing mounting concern that cases rushed through an administrative review process have not only flooded some circuits with appeals but have also caused lives to get lost in the shuffle of streamlining. Restive federal judges have become more pointed in their critiques of immigration judges, with phrases like, "ignored the evidence" or "riven with error" or "astounding lapse in logic" or analysis that was "woefully inadequate." The criticism has been growing in the wake of a three-year-old program to speed up resolution of a 56,000-case backlog at the time of the Sept. 11, 2001 terror attacks. The program has worked for the U.S. Department of Justice (DOJ). The process cut DOJ's backlog of pending cases to 29,000 this year, according to Gregory Gagne, spokesman for the Executive Office of Immigration Review. "The biggest problem is the administrative appeal process has been eviscerated, if not wholly eliminated," said Lucas Guttentag, director of the American Civil Liberties Union national immigration project in Oakland, California." (excerpted from Pamela A. Maclean's October 24, 2005 article in the National Law Journal).

This is only one of many such articles reporting on studies that come to the same conclusion. The tragedy is that, in typical bureaucratic fashion, people are being rewarded for producing numbers instead of quality. One of the important lessons I learned in government, was that if you can get the file off of your desk and over to somebody else's desk, then you have succeeded and will be rewarded. It's a shame when the bean counters prevail in such a way that human lives are jeopardized, and that our nation's most cherished heritage of affording refuge to the needy is sacrificed so that second-rate managers can report that they have improved the system.

(Since I wrote the above passage, the damage that the Aschcroft downsizing of the Board has caused has been recognized, and six additional Board members have been hired, but some of them through the dubious method reported below, in the chapter, Blatant Nepotism.)

Since the time my book first appeared, Judge Paul Schmidt retired from EOIR. A lion of immigration policy and profundity, he had been Chairman of the BIA up until shortly before the time of the Ashcroft purge, and he has spoken freely about the view from the inside. I liberally quote here from The Asylumnist, an excellent immigration blog managed by renowned attorney Jason Dzubow, both as to what happened at that time, and then about his views of requirements for future reform of the Board. I don't know anyone who can speak to such reforms more astutely:

"Then came the reorganization where Ashcroft cut Board Members. He removed Board Members John Guendelsberger, Cecelia Espenosa, Lory Rosenberg, Gus Villageliu, and me. Technically, Lory left before the final cut, and another Board Member who undoubtedly would have been axed, applied for a voluntary transfer to an IJ position in another city. I learned about it when Kevin Rooney (who at one point was my career hero) called me up to his top floor office. He was shaking, and he told me, "You did not make the cut." He said, "They did not like some of your opinions, particularly dissents where you joined with Lory Rosenberg." There was no application or interview process to decide who should stay and who should go. There was no interview. The reason I was cut is because they did not like my opinions—Ashcroft apparently wanted a cowed, compliant Board where nobody would speak up against Administration policies or legal positions that unfairly hurt migrants or limited their due process.

Part of the stated rationale for the reorganization was that there were too many Board Members and it was too contentious, and therefore not "efficient." In the Government immigration world, "efficiency" is often a buzzword for actions that take away or reduce the rights of migrants. But the workload clearly demanded more than the 12 Board Members that Ashcroft left. A few months after the cut, they had to start using BIA staff attorneys as "temporary" Board Members because they needed more Board Members to do the work. Some of these attorneys eventually became Board Members. So they were upgrading staff, rather than doing independent hiring. Basically, this was a cover up for Ashcroft's inappropriate and politically motivated reduction in permanent Board Members. The real reason for the reduction.

The summer of 2000 was the last time that an outsider was appointed to the Board. In my view, many of the current Members are "going along to get along," because the clear message of the Ashcroft cuts was that resisting the majority, particularly speaking up for the rights of migrants, could be career threatening. The Board has abandoned the pretense of diversity. Also, the idea that they can operate effectively with a smaller number of Members is simply a ruse. The BIA uses temporary Members to fill the gap. But they cannot vote *en banc*, so this truncates the *en banc* process. The Board ends up rubber-stamping cases. Also, since mostly three-Member panels, rather than the *en banc* Board, now issue precedent decisions, the majority of Board Members are able to escape accountability on most such cases because they don't have to take a public vote. Only the votes of the three panel members are publicly recorded. The BIA also seldom hears oral argument anymore, so it has become very distant and inaccessible to those most affected by its decisions. Moreover, quietly and gradually, the BIA has had to add additional permanent Board

Members because the Ashcroft cuts left the BIA short of the number required to do the work. But, there never has been a public acknowledgement by EOIR or the DOJ of what Ashcroft did and why it has been necessary to take corrective action.

And as to reforms?

First, and foremost, the Immigration Courts must return to the focus on due process as the one and only mission. That's unlikely to happen under the DOJ – as proved by over three decades of history, particularly recent history. It will take some type of independent court. I think that an Article I Immigration Court, which has been supported by groups such as the ABA and the FBA, would be best. Clearly, the due process focus has been lost when officials outside EOIR have forced ill-advised "prioritization" and attempts to "expedite" the cases of frightened women and children from the Northern Triangle who require lawyers to gain the protection that most of them need and deserve. Putting these cases in front of other pending cases is not only unfair to all, but has created what I call "aimless docket reshuffling" that has thrown our system into chaos. Evidently, the idea of the prioritization is to remove most of those recently crossing the border to seek protection, thereby sending a "don't come, we don't want you" message to asylum seekers. But, as a deterrent, this program has been spectacularly unsuccessful. Backlogs have continued to grow across the board, notwithstanding an actual reduction in overall case receipts.

Second, there must be structural changes so that the Immigration Courts are organized and run like a real court system, not a highly bureaucratic agency. This means that sitting Immigration Judges, like in all other court systems, must control their dockets. If there are to be nationwide policies and practices, they should be developed by an "Immigration Judicial Conference," patterned along the lines of the Federal Judicial Conference. That would be composed of sitting Immigration Judges representing a cross-section of the country, several Appellate Immigration Judges from the BIA, and probably some U.S. Circuit Judges, since the Circuits are one of the primary "consumers" of the court's "product."

Third, there must be a new administrative organization to serve the courts, much like the Administrative Office of the U.S. Courts. This office would naturally be subordinate to the Immigration Judicial Council. Currently, the glacial hiring process, inadequate courtroom space planning and acquisition, and unreliable, often-outdated technology are simply not up to the needs of a rapidly expanding court system like ours. The judicial hiring process over the past 16 years has failed to produce the necessary balance because judicial selectees from private sector backgrounds–particularly those with expertise in asylum and refugee law–have been so few and far between.

Fourth, as you know, I would repeal all of the so-called "Ashcroft reforms" and put the BIA back on track to being a real appellate court. A properly comprised and functioning BIA should transparently debate and decide important, potentially controversial, issues. The BIA must also "rein in" those Immigration Courts with asylum grant rates so incredibly low as to make it clear that the generous dictates of the Supreme Court in *Cardoza-Fonseca* and the BIA itself in *Mogharrabi* are not being followed." Judge Paul Schmidt, The Asylumnist

Special Registration – Ice Targets Muslim Men

After the tragedy of 9-11 came the repression. It was so predicable, and yet so sad, that so many of those in our proud nation who are sworn to uphold the law were so quick to trample on our flag. The witch-hunt for Muslims was on. The FBI abuses, in the context of blatant singling-out and harassment of Muslim men in our country, are embarrassingly-well documented.

In September 2002 a special regulation was promulgated, the National Security Entry-Exit Registration System (NSEERS), requiring the registration at a port of entry of nationals from certain countries, and, more onerously, the domestic registration of those citizens from the same countries who were already in the U.S. On November 6th, 2002, all male aliens from mostly Middle East and South Asia nations were required to register under hastily promulgated "special registration" regulations at the end of the year and in the course of the coming year. Anyone on the list who did not appear at the designated INS office could be arrested and deported. It was a good time to be an immigration lawyer, for many on the list were desperate for advice. Droves of people who had been existing underground since their tourist or student visas had expired took the government at its word, that if they came forward and registered everything would be all right. They were informed that they had nothing to worry about, they would not be abused or unnecessarily detained, that this was a mere formality of a security measure.

The lists of countries from which aliens should register were announced in stages:

the first group, Iran, Iraq, Syria, North Korea and Sudan. Of this group, around three thousand presented themselves. Next, Afghanistan, Algeria, Bahrain, Eritrea, Lebanon, Morocco, Oman,

Qatar, Somalia, Tunisia, the United Arab Emirates, and Yemen; from this group, more than seven thousand registered. Next, Egypt, Jordan, Kuwait, Indonesia and Bangladesh. Next, Pakistan and Saudi Arabia.

After the initial reporting and registering to be photographed, fingerprinted, and in many cases, arbitrarily detained, the individuals were expected to continue reporting in one-year increments. The types of people who were excluded from the list included lawful permanent residents, or people who had applied for asylum by a certain date, or had been granted asylum, as well as diplomats or employees of international organizations such as the World Bank.

I heard many credible reports of elderly people and the sickly being separated from their families and their medications, some to languish for months in squalid county jails that substituted for INS detention centers; many were transferred half-way across the country to detention centers. These victims were guilty of nothing worse than having let their temporary visas lapse, and, in most cases, of being Muslim.

My courtroom was suddenly flooded by men who had been detained with names like Mahmoud, Mohammed, Yosef and Yusuf. Many of them had already sat in jail for ten to fifteen days by the time they were brought into my court. They were often preyed upon by their own countrymen, immigration lawyers acting in that grand shyster tradition of charging whatever the traffic would bear. I bonded out most of them immediately with the minimal bond allowed, even though the INS attorneys vigorously implored me to set high bonds in their cases. "Your honor, we consider him a flight risk." "Counsel, he turned himself into your agents, in good faith, responding to the Attorney General's request, and now you've already had him locked up for two weeks. He's going home today on a fifteen hundred dollar bond!"

Our agency designated me as their point man, or point judge, in San Francisco to hear the case of anyone who was identified by INS as a "suspected terrorist." I was given a higher security clearance, bumped up to "top secret" after a ten minute telephone interview with a security specialist in Washington. A special GSA safe was installed in our office, in which the files of any such suspected terrorists should be stored. It was never used for anything other than to store our peanut butter and jelly sandwiches. If there was a "suspected terrorist" who should be brought into court, the individual's name could not even be listed on the court docket: everything hush-hush, you understand. In the beginning of the excitement, the INS attorneys who were entrusted with the "special terrorist" detail in San Francisco would call our clerk, indicating that in the next day a terrorist would be brought to court, and all manner of special, confidential arrangements should be made in order to process him in my court without the knowledge of the public. The INS attorneys were falling over themselves with self-importance and the belief that they were protecting San Francisco from another terror attack. Inevitably, and in every single case, after such a frantic call had been made and we had set up the procedure, the next day the INS attorney would call and tell us, "Sorry, false alarm," and the migrant in question would be processed like any other migrant.

After two years of futile, meaningless harassment of such individuals, the government suspended the program for domestic registration. It is reported that 82,581 individuals appeared to register and of those people, 13,531 were placed in deportation proceedings. More individuals had reported for registration than even expected, but the program only netted a handful of common criminals, and not a single suspected terrorist was apprehended through that particular program. In my courtroom, I heard an increased number of asylum cases from the countries on the list, from aliens who had been arrested when they complied with their civic duty to show up for the registration, but otherwise, the whole flap was befitting that quote from Hamlet: "full of sound and fury, signifying nothing."

How many terrorists, after all, would be so dumb as to turn themselves in upon the request of their sworn enemies? The terrorists apparently weren't as dumb as whichever Deputy Attorney General in John Ashcroft's stable or White House crony had dreamt up the plan. But countless lives had been destroyed, families permanently torn apart, and men forced back across the globe to regimes where torture is commonplace. And for those totalitarian countries on the receiving end, arguably the mere fact that someone had been deported from the U.S. must be a sure sign that they had done something wrong, so let's torture them and find out what it is.

The port-of-entry portion of the NSEERS program, or those migrants just arriving, continued to be enforced until April of 2011, under much criticism and opposition from human rights groups.

A year after leaving the bench, in 2005, I collaborated with the indefatigable Banafsheh Ahklaghi, a dedicated spirit, Iranian-American attorney, who stepped in to try to fill the breach and represent many of the Muslim aliens who were being singled-out and mistreated by DOJ. I'm proud to say that I was advisor on some cases for her organization the National Legal Sanctuary for Community Advancement, located in Portrero Hill, San Francisco. She founded the non-profit to represent the many Muslim respondents who were being pulled into immigration court on trumped-up charges, and she now generates impact litigation and class-action suits on behalf of the South-Asian and Middle Eastern respondents. She was a tremendous inspiration to me when I stepped back into the role of attorney after my years as a judge.

You Can't Win 'Em All

There were a couple of times in my career as a judge when I realized later that I had failed and made the wrong call. I'm human.

One case comes to mind, my last year as an IJ in San Francisco. A young Iranian man, I'll call him Reza, a permanent resident, was in deportation proceedings for a couple of criminal convictions. He was a classic screwball – kept getting himself into trouble for the most ridiculous things. There were a couple of charges of spousal abuse, and he had been convicted of one charge and served six months in jail. That was what brought him into my courtroom. Perhaps the most bizarre conviction was for stealing a UPS van for a joyride.

Before his most recent conviction for spousal abuse, he and his wife had been living in the Lake Tahoe area, one of those dream landscapes. He'd had odd jobs and no jobs. One might ask, why let this clown stay in America? Why not ship him home if he's such a trouble maker? Good question. The answer is that his lovely and hardworking wife, an Iranian-American who was a naturalized U.S. citizen, came to court twice, traveling long distances to support him, taking the stand to testify about some of the more embarrassing aspects of their relationship. My heart went out to her, and I basically thought, if she wants him so bad, she can have him.

His application for relief was cancellation of removal, which would essentially allow me to waive his minor convictions, in my discretion, balancing the positive factors, his relationship with his wife, against the negative factors, his bad attitude. It was the type of case that I had relished sinking my teeth into as a defense attorney. He had a good, conscientious lawyer making the arguments for him.

Reza had never gotten a serious grip on life. He had an explanation for every arrest and conviction, always ending with either, 'I didn't do it' or 'It wasn't my fault.' He claimed it was his friend who'd stolen the UPS truck and then picked him up for the ride. I didn't like the man, but he had two things going for him in my courtroom: I didn't want to ship him back to Iran, and his wife pleaded for mercy on his behalf. I couldn't help recalling during the hearing how many times I had advocated for Iranians in court when I was a defense attorney and how many times I had managed to keep petty criminals like Reza in the country so they could stay with their family and have another chance.

After hearing all the evidence and testimony, I was hopeful that his recent jail experience and the realization of how close he'd come to deportation would finally wise him up. I told him, "I'm not doing this so much for you as for this fine lady, who has come to court and allowed herself to be subjected to cross examination about the most intimate details of your relationship so that she can keep you here and start a family with you. It is only because she has so persuasively begged for you to be given a second chance that I have decided to do so. You are a very lucky man, and hopefully you will realize that now and make a commitment to lead a productive life with her."

It was a close case, but the female ICE attorney agreed with my decision and waived appeal. I felt good about the decision, I felt wise about my choice of words, I was happy that this good woman, so deserving of a good husband, was going to get her wish to resume a life with Reza, start a family and live happily ever after in Lake Tahoe, California.

A year later I saw Reza's lawyer at a conference and asked him how the couple was doing. "Judge, that was a really tough case for you, I know it, and I really respected how you grappled with your decision."

"That's fine, but how are they doing?"

"I'm afraid not so good, judge. They had a fight and he broke her jaw. He's back in prison."

The Most Dangerous Alien In America

April 1, 2003 marked one of the worst blows to justice that I had the misfortune of experiencing in my legal career. The United States Supreme Court reversed the 9th Circuit Court of Appeals decision in the case of *Denmore v. Kim,* 538 U.S. 510 (2003).

Some background: I was one of three judges in San Francisco assigned to the custody calendar, which meant that every migrant who arrived at the airport and was detained came into my courtroom. Also, those who were released from jail after serving time and were picked up by INS, and those unlucky ones who were caught in INS workplace raids and neighborhood sweeps, ended up before us. Judge Michael Yamaguchi, former U.S. Attorney for San Francisco, and one of the finest immigration judges employed by DOJ, was the other judge on the custody calendar. (Judge Anthony Murry joined the last year I was there).

The morning of April 1st, I had just taken the bench for my custody arraignment calendar, when one of the most over-zealous, mad-dog INS prosecutors came waltzing into the courtroom with her stack of files for the morning session. Although she often represented outrageously extreme positions against the respondents in our court hearings, I had never allowed her to get to me – I simply considered her excesses and frequent outbursts as entertainment value to help break up the daily routine.

"Judge Grussendorf, did you hear the good news?" were the first words out of her mouth.

"What, you resigned?" I allowed myself that little joke because I knew it would be like water off a duck's back to her.

"No, the Supreme Court overturned Kim."

The *Kim* decision of the 9th Circuit had monumentally affected the way that we conducted our custody hearings. *Denmore v. Kim* had held that the government could not deny a migrant in deportation proceedings who had a green card (lawful permanent residence) a bond hearing, in spite of criminal convictions. That decision had allowed Judge Yamaguchi and myself to hold bond hearings for many people who came before us, who otherwise would not have been eligible to be released during their deportation hearings and appeals (which could often drag on for years). Many people who otherwise had strong cases to fight the charges of deportation would elect to take a deport order, simply in order to get out of INS custody, but with the 9th Circuit decision, we could alleviate their harsh circumstances by bonding them out if their background merited such leniency. Not any longer.

More background: Mr. Kim, a young man from Korea who had received his green card when his family immigrated, had been detained by INS pending his deportation to Korea, because of several shoplifting convictions and one burglary conviction he had picked up over the years. He had challenged in federal court the right of the agency to detain him indefinitely pending his removal hearing. The general rule was that INS could hold anyone convicted of certain types of crimes as long as the agency wanted. He had argued that, as a permanent resident he had a greater liberty interest than undocumented migrants who had been convicted of the same crimes. The 9th Circuit, in its landmark decision, had agreed with him, finding that the immigration judge should have the discretion to set a reasonable bond in such a case.

That meant that at our custody bond hearings, rather than being required to issue blanket denials of bond to green card holders with such convictions, we could hear the evidence in a case and weigh the circumstances of the crime against the other factors in the alien's life. Important factors to consider included: length of time in the US, work history, family circumstances (such as marriage, children, and number of pets). Mike Yamaguchi and I had been able to release hundreds of people from custody, in spite of the harsh language of the statute, because of that court decision – people like housewives and laborers, old ladies convicted of welfare fraud, and fieldworkers with minor convictions who otherwise couldn't have gotten out.

Generally I didn't like the idea of anyone spending a single day longer in jail than necessary, and certainly not in INS custody, after they had served their prison sentence. My attitude was that it was much better to get them reunited with their families, get parents back with their children, get wage-earners back on the street earning those wages and paying taxes, rather than have our tax dollars pay for their stay behind bars – especially when the State had already extracted its pound of flesh in the criminal setting and determined that they had paid their debt to society and did not represent a danger to the community.

The INS attorney didn't agree. The Supreme Court decision to overturn the 9th Circuit in *Kim* followed a long and disturbing line of precedent decisions holding that the INS can virtually do anything it wants with migrants in our country. So as of April 1st, after the Supremes overturned the *Kim* decision, Judge Yamaguchi and I no longer had any discretion to cut such people as young Mr. Kim loose. They had to remain detained while their deportation hearings were proceeding, which would usually take months, and with an appeal thrown in, years.

As a lawful permanent resident, Mr. Kim became eligible for cancellation of removal, to have his possible removal "cancelled", which meant that he could bring family members and other witnesses to court to demonstrate why he deserved another chance. But now he would have to remain locked up during the court proceedings.

Given the extremely minor nature of Mr. Kim's convictions, and his exemplary record of rehabilitation and work history, combined with his strong family support network, this should have been a slam-dunk case. In fact, the case was so strong for Mr. Kim that ordinarily the government, on a case such as this, might have signaled their non-opposition to the case, and would have been satisfied with an abbreviated hearing – perhaps only requiring that Mr. Kim take the stand, assert that he had seen the wrong of his ways and had reformed, and promise to go straight from now on. I personally had been involved with many cases, both as an attorney and a judge, where the underlying crimes were much more egregious, but because of other factors the case had been granted.

Not this case. As I said in the courtroom during his subsequent hearing, the government was acting like an old blind dog that had hold of a rotten bone and was afraid to let go (I copped that quote from celebrated attorney Gerry Spence, the colorful frontier lawyer in buckskins from Wyoming). From the beginning, I could see that this case was being treated differently – in addition to the government trial attorney assigned to the case (not the one referred to above) who in her own right was very competent and more than able to handle such a routine case, the government had assigned a second chair trial attorney, and the Chief Counsel and his deputy sat in the courtroom behind their attorneys, basically acting like high school kids – passing little notes up to their attorneys from the peanut gallery during the whole hearing.

Kim was represented by Zachary Nightingale, a partner in the firm of Van Der Hout, Brigagliano & Nightingale. Marc van der Hout, the founding partner, is an activist attorney in the field of immigration law, always advancing cutting-edge arguments in court and on appeal. Zach had appeared many times in my courtroom, and I considered him an excellent lawyer. He had decided to go to law school only after studying mathematics at the graduate level at Stanford. In the course of his studies, he decided that math was a little too theoretical and that he would prefer to work with real people and their real problems. He took some time off from school, interned with the ACLU in New York while thinking about his options, and decided to go to law school. He went to Stanford law, and began as in intern in the Van der Hout firm in 1996, where he has worked ever since. He is now a partner in the firm.

In the course of the hearing, it was proved that Mr. Kim had acted as an impulsive teenager – a "rebel without a cause" was the way that I put it in my decision – who liked to steal video games, which he could have otherwise afforded to purchase, for the thrill of it. Not unlike certain Hollywood celebrities. (When I was a teenager, I shoplifted some paperback Tarzan books from the local Piggly Wiggly, and so I had a hard time seeing such teenage shoplifting activity as anything other than pranksterism). He and his pals had evolved to stealing some guns one night from an unoccupied shed in a neighbor's back yard. He had never used the guns, or any weapon, in the commission of a crime. After this conviction for burglary, it was determined that a bit of hard time in the State pen would teach him a lesson – it did. He worked hard in prison, and when he got out he enrolled in college. By the time of his hearing in my courtroom, he had a solid work history (working part time as a highly-paid computer geek) and he had completed several semesters of college classes after his release. In such a hearing, the case law is clear that he need not even show rehabilitation in order to be granted permission to remain in the country – it was just one of many factors to be considered – but he clearly had a good record of reform.

What did the government have to counter this unusually strong showing? They argued that he was a kleptomaniac, and thus a danger to the community. I could see that someone had stayed up all night scouring the record to deliver that little mouse turd. The government referred to a report in Kim's prison record by a social worker, who had speculated that Kim might be a klepto. When they dropped that little item in court, Kim's attorney's properly objected that the author of the report was not made available for cross examination, and thus the report should be given little weight.

During a continuance in the case, Kim's lawyers arranged to have him examined by a highly-credentialed prison psychologist, whose subsequent report contained two conclusions: first, kleptomania is actually a fairly rare disorder; and second, Kim definitely did not suffer from it. In fact, according to standardized tests, in comparison with the general prison population his tendency to steal was below-average. Kim's lawyer presented the shrink as a witness who was very convincing, while the government never did produce the author of the prison report as a witness.

As far as I was concerned, that was the clincher for the case. If this case had been rated on a scale of 1-10 for similar cancellation cases, I would have given it an 11. I granted the case. Shamelessly, the government appealed, keeping poor Kim detained. But the Ashcroft Board of Immigration Appeals disagreed with me, and in a very unusual move overturned my grant of Kim's case, finding that I had not given sufficient weight to the gravity of Kim's offenses. I could only speculate to a high degree of certainty that politics was involved in the unusual decision to overturn my discretionary finding in a case that was so strong for Mr. Kim.

Mr. Kim had been detained during all of this, since April when the Supreme Court decision was announced. It was now months later, during which time the government had callously kept this young man in jail. I did not have the power to release him – the Supreme Court had said so – but as the prosecutors, the INS could have released him, so that he could have rejoined his family, continued his schooling, and continued to work while the appeal was pending. But no, this poor schmuck was too dangerous to let out on the streets; you never know, he might slink into another video store and steal another video game! He continued to remain detained for nine months after our hearing, while his attorneys took the matter into federal district court on a habeus corpus proceeding. Finally he was released on bond while his appeal proceeded.

On January 26, 2014 the excellent Judge Ramirez, in a rehearing of the case, ruled that the burglary conviction, which was the reason he had been detained in the first place, didn't even qualify as a Crime of Moral Turpitude, in light of a recent federal circuit court decision, and found that therefore Mr. Kim was not even deportable as charged! She terminated the case, the government waived appeal, and that's the end of the saga of Mr. Kim. Ten years to reach that point, and how much of this productive individual's life thrown away behind ICE bars?

There is no reasonable doubt in my mind that Kim's case was mishandled in that fashion because he had had the nerve to take his underlying bond issue to the 9th Circuit and his victory there had eventually landed in Supreme Court. Thus someone in the agency had an ax to grind against him. Meanwhile, from the time after the Supreme Court overturned *Denmore* in April 2003, Mr. Kim was taken back into ICE custody and forced to remain detained at the Yuba County jail for a year until attorney Nightingale could manage his release through a *habeas corpus* petition.

Postscript: In August 2016, Acting Solicitor General Ian Gershengom filed a letter with the Supreme Court in a similar pending case, asserting that the information that had been provided by the government in Mr. Kim's case as to average length of time of imprisonment of aliens pending deportation proceedings was grossly understated, and that in fact average detention times were more realistically a year, or four times the four-month average that the government had argued in Mr. Kim's case. Reporting on this issue and the circumstances of the bombshell *mia culpa* letter that the government submitted indicated that the misreporting, including faulty statistics that were submitted, was done intentionally. Either way, another example of how a gross miscarriage of justice was committed in Mr. Kim's case.

Mr. Kim is now head of sales at a leading medical research software company in the Bay area. His clients include Stanford and Harvard universities, U.S. Department of Agriculture and Department of Defense. It would be nice to say to those bungling, dull-witted and abusive ICE managers who appealed my decision in his case, forcing him to remain detained and for his case to drag out all that time, that "I told you so!"

Blatant Nepotism In Immigration Judge Selections

It has now been widely reported that under both the Aschcroft and the Gonzalez Attorney Generalships, their own political cronies were put into immigration judge positions, often in place of career DOJ employees with vast experience in immigration law (see both Washington Post and New York Times reportage). One repercussion of the Gonzalez scandal, when it was revealed that U.S. Attorneys had been fired from their posts for political reasons, was the revelation that at least one such U.S. Attorney was offered a position as an immigration judge as a mitigation prize, and that even some very experienced Republican ICE attorneys were passed over in favor of White House cronies. For example, top Justice flunky Monica Goodling testified before the House that she had used political cronyism as a factor in hiring immigration judges. (see, Immigration Judges Often Picked Based on Political Ties, Washington Post, June 11, 2007, article by Amy Goldstein and Dan Eggen; and, Meltdown at DOJ: the Story of the Immigration Judge Scam, Harpers Magazine, May 30, 2007, by Scott Horton; and reporting by the Legal Times). It is now estimated that as many as 40 judges were appointed, some without even submitting an application or being interviewed, because they were political favorites of the White House, during the years 2004 – 2006. *See*, Playing Politics at the Bench: A White Paper on the Justice Department's Investigation into the Hiring Practices of Immigration Judges, Penn State Law's Center for Immigrants Rights, 2009. And *see* OIG, An Investigation of Allegations of Politicized Hiring by Monica Goodling and other Staff in the Office of Attorney General, July 20, 2008.

I have many other concerns about the hiring practices of EOIR, one that appoints individuals to such positions of power over the lives of so many people. In the year 2004, the agency entered into a settlement of a class action lawsuit, in which it paid eleven and a half million dollars to a class of individuals who claimed they had *not* been hired for the position of immigration judge because the agency had instead intentionally selected either women or candidates of non-Caucasian ethnicity, over members of the class who demonstrably had better experience and credentials for the job – a classic "angry white guy" or reverse discrimination lawsuit. When discussing this particular lawsuit, a female IJ colleague of mine, who is Asian and had interviewed for the job in 1995, admitted that at the time of the interview she had only practiced immigration law a couple of years and had only been to immigration court about five times; while at the same time a good friend of mine, who was also interviewed but not selected in 1995, had been practicing immigration law for ten years, was a professor in the field of immigration law with a national reputation, and had been appearing in immigration court approximately 3-5 times a week for the past ten years. You go figure.

Postscript: In May of 2018 a group of eight Democratic lawmakers filed a letter with the Department of Justice's Inspector General's office alleging that they had insider whistleblower information that immigration judges and judges on the Board of Immigration Appeals were being hired based upon political affiliation. At the same time it became known that the White House bureaucrat who was in charge of coordinating recommendations for immigration judge positions was under the false impression that immigration judges are political appointments, and for the past year had been forwarding selections based upon cronyism (a replay of the Monica Goodling scandal). And this when there are so many talented attorneys who have dedicated their lives to toiling in the fields of immigration law and procedure and who would make such good candidates for the immigration judge position.

Time to Leave the Bench

I resigned from the bench in 2004 because I wanted to pursue my interest in overseas refugee protection, which is a logical extension of my interest and expertise in asylum law. My international career had been on hold long enough. Naturally most immigration judges stay in their positions until retirement age or beyond, either out of dedication to the duties of the position or in some cases because they just don't want to abandon the federal gravy train. But tropical climates and urgent humanitarian mobilizations were beckoning me. My first contract with UN High Commissioner for Refugees was in 2005 as Legal Protection Officer in South Korea. That experience could be the subject of another book in itself. And that is where I met my lovely wife, a Korean artist, photographer and teacher for special needs children.

Since then I have worked in UN refugee camps and other resettlement offices in northern Kenya, Tanzania, Ethiopia, Rwanda, Malaysia, Thailand, Vietnam, Nepal, Jordan, Lebanon, Syria, Egypt, Tunisia, Turkey, Vienna and Havana. And the beat goes on.

I think I had a good run as a judge. I met and worked with a lot of wonderful people and tried to make a difference where I could. At times I still dream about it at night, and my dreams are never negative, more like impressionist memories of attorneys and staff with an occasional courtroom drama mixed in. I will always have affection for my IJ colleagues, the court staff and the attorneys who came before me in court.

But it's true what they say – it's lonely at the top. I was spoiled from my years as an advocate for migrants at the non-profits, the Central American Refugee Center and the university legal clinic. In such a job you have close, meaningful relationships with people in need from all walks of life and regions of the world. You learn so much from your clients, and you celebrate with them and their families when you pull off a victory for them either in court or at the agency. Being a judge is a strange, artificial role, in which one has to put on a stoic face, pretend indifference, remain neutral to the best of your ability. It's like the black robe is an invisibility cloak around your heart. And when you can do a good deed and grant a case, it's more often an empty feeling in the end, because the migrant and her family happily go off to celebrate and you're left sitting there in the sterile courtroom, only to call the next case. I'd had enough of that. I needed to get out and work again with real people.

My Approach to Lawyering

My approach to the legal profession, and my identity as a lawyer, was tempered by my personal experiences as a political activist in the early seventies, and, later, by my work with the Public Defenders Office in Washington, and with the Federal Defenders of San Diego.

On three separate occasions during the seventies, a decade before I went to law school – twice in Baltimore and once in D.C., I was arrested and jailed for the night, simply because I had been exercising my 1st Amendment rights of free speech; that is, I was arrested at political demonstrations by overzealous cops. All three cases ended in dismissals or acquittals. I saw the kind of mentality that leads to abuse of the system by police forces, or what has come to be termed 'malicious prosecution." Thankfully in my case they were only minor brushes with the law.

At the point in my life in the early eighties when I was thinking of a career change, I thought of the law in terms of defense of the Constitution, and of myself as a criminal defense attorney. I attended law school with plans to practice criminal law. My exposure to criminal law, prior to the launching of a career in immigration law, included the criminal law clinic at Howard; internship with two highly-regarded defender organizations, the D.C. Public Defenders, and the Federal Defenders of San Diego; and an internship with the U.S. Attorney's Office in D.C. Superior Court. Later, as Director of the Immigration Law Clinic at George Washington University, I continued to handle criminal matters occasionally, when, for example, one of our immigration clients would cross paths with the criminal justice system – that is, get arrested.

I accepted the role of defense attorney as a sacred calling. Your commitment to representing the best interests of your clients is like a religious oath – even if your client might have been acting like a little devil. That doesn't mean, of course, that you have to agree with your client's actions, or even have to like your client, and you are always free to decline the invitation to accept a case; but once you do accept it, it is your honor on the line. That means that you work the case hard, you do your homework and be as prepared as possible when appearing in court, and – you always show up on time.

That is the concept I tried to drill into the heads of my students, and, when I was on the bench, I didn't lightly accept the attitude of certain attorneys who were just showing up to collect a paycheck by going through the motions and providing shoddy representation for their clients. It was amazing to me how many lawyers made it a habit of showing up late – not only an act of disrespect to their clients and the court, but something that could even hurt their client's case.

Of course I understand that the world needs good, and competent, prosecutors, and there are far too few of that breed of lawyer as well. The career prosecutors who dedicate themselves to getting convictions for the violent offenders who *should* be locked up are truly heroes. Unfortunately, too many prosecutions are motivated by political considerations, as I have seen both on the criminal and the immigration side. Even the pressure for high volumes of convictions, or in immigration court for deportation orders, is a political expedient, and is inexcusable when it becomes the motivating factor driving prosecutors or ICE attorneys in their decisions.

The ICE lawyers have a really tough job, and, especially in immigration court, where they are usually considered the bad guy, not an easy reputation to live with. But I noticed a crucial difference in the approach to people (the client, or defendant) between prosecutors and defense attorneys. A prosecutor has to think in terms of black and white. They usually can't allow such thoughts as "well maybe he really didn't do it" or "he's not such a bad guy after all" or "am I sure I'm doing the right thing here?" get in the way of their job. If their boss brings the case (either District Attorney or U.S. Attorney, or, in immigration court, ICE, Immigration and Customs Enforcement), they have to go with it. (Although not always – see chapter below on Prosecutorial Discretion). Whereas the defense attorney has to be more of a humanitarian, accustomed to seeing things in shades of grey instead of black and white. Maybe your client didn't do it, there are so many other potential bad guys who could have done it; or even if he did do it, did he do everything that he's accused of doing? (Police and prosecutors love to 'pile on' charges). And even if he did, is there an explanation why, a mitigating factor? And even if he did do it and there are no real mitigating factors, is the law just, and applied in a just way to both upper class and poor defendants?

I guess it comes down to the bottom line: if you are an attorney, would you rather have the job of putting people in jail or getting them out of it? Or in the case of immigration law, would you rather be the one arguing for their deportation, or arguing that they be allowed to remain in the country with their families?

A defense attorney will have an irreverent, rebellious streak, and a healthy skepticism (or perhaps overriding cynicism) about authority, especially about the kind of power that is put in the hands of prosecutors and so easily abused. The defense attorney will have experienced many incidents where such power has been misapplied, or even maliciously applied, upon defendants during the government's supposed pursuit of justice. The defense attorney has a secret knowledge – anyone from the unsuspecting public could be picked up and falsely charged, at any time, and in fact it happens frequently.

The Innocence Project in Boston and other such projects around the country have proven all too well how even capital murder cases can be brought against completely innocent people. Such high profile legal programs are too few in number and only have resources to handle the most egregious of cases involving serious felonies. Imagine how many thousands of cases are brought against innocent people, or people who are less guilty than accused, but never get exposed, due to lack of resources or because of defense counsel who are not diligent enough in their defense.

The prosecuting attorney, on the other hand, will have a reverential respect for authority – if for no other reason, because his supervisor is that authority. But also, in order to perform his job, to work hard and diligently, to believe in his cause, he must believe that the person before him is guilty, or, if in the immigration field, deserving of deportation. Otherwise, how could they even function day in and day out and live with themselves? Of course, I am speaking here in generalities, and I have known many fine prosecutors who didn't take every case all that seriously. But unfortunately, the stereotype is all too common and true, to the ultimate detriment of the system in general.

I highly recommend the book by former Manhattan prosecutor David Heilbroner, Rough Justice, Pantheon Books. He speaks of prosecutors who think that every defendant is scum deserving of the maximum penalty, rather than being able to see that almost every case has ambiguities and that most defendants are themselves social victims coming from broken families and abusive childhoods.

Any trial attorney knows that witnesses will take the stand in court and lie, for many reasons. These include police and other government officials, and – if you are a defense attorney – some of your clients.

A footnote to add about government lawyers, and I'm speaking from experience about lawyers working for the Department of Homeland Security, in the sub-agencies of Citizenship and Immigration Services (CIS) and Immigration and Customs Enforcement (ICE) – (prior to 2003 both sub-agencies were under the umbrella of INS.) Again, this is a generalization about many people, but the numbers of exceptions are so statistically minor as to be insignificant. A government lawyer typically has never worked in the private sector, hasn't had the experience of representing a real life-and-blood human being. From what I have seen over many years of experience, a government lawyer will usually join the government right after law school, or, after a short, unhappy stint in private practice, flee to the protection of a government job.

Why do I think this is so important? Because a government lawyer will usually not be accustomed to reading and interpreting a statute in a critical way, to question the language, to challenge the government agency's interpretation of the wording of the statute or regulation. Most statutes (or sections thereof) are subject to ambiguity or differing interpretations, differences of opinion, if for no other reason, because Congressional aides who write them are not always paragons of lucid writing. Part of a defense/immigration lawyer's bread and butter comes from interpreting and arguing over the meaning of the particular wording of a statute. If the official at the agency intake window doesn't agree with your interpretation, you go to the supervisor, and if she doesn't agree, it goes to court, and if the judge doesn't agree, it goes on appeal, and then a subsequent appeal to the federal circuit court. And you know what? Many times in the end the court agrees with you that the government was incorrect in the way they interpreted the law, so your client wins.

However, a government bureaucrat typically has no interest in trying to understand the subtleties of a statute's wording, or making the argument that something in the statute is wrong or ambiguous. They have too much work to do already. But that's the job of a defense/immigration attorney, to challenge the statute, at times to even argue that it is unconstitutional, or that the way the agency is applying it is unconstitutional. Government attorneys take it the way it is shoveled out in their training and pass it down the line. Often, they don't even work from the statute itself, but from their training materials. How often have I heard a government attorney say, "Wait a minute, I have to consult my training materials"? That lawyer has just flunked the test of an independent thinker, but I hear it *all the time* from government bureaucrats who are either denying applicants benefits to which they are entitled, or are trying to deport them. What if the guy who wrote the training materials was wrong? Or, as frequently happens, the interpretation that is offered of a particular issue is overly narrow? Then the whole system, all those lawyers who sit in cubicles all day long, spending more time surfing the web than actually working because they are on taxpayer payroll, are infected with the wrong interpretation of the statute/regulation, and it goes all the way down the chain until it hits your client and she is denied a benefit to which she is entitled by law, or she is told she should be deported because someone wrote up the training materials wrong.

And such a lawyer, who refers to his pretty white training materials binder rather than the actual statute when making a decision that affects your client, is going to have no interest in raising an argument with his supervisor about the interpretation or issue at hand, if for no other reason than because they don't want to cause trouble, don't want to appear like they are not a team player, when they are all anxious about twice-annual reviews from the same supervisors, reviews which are used to determine bonuses and promotions. One of the points of a typical evaluation is whether or not they are a team player!

So don't expect to find a brilliant immigration lawyer, the likes of Denise Sabagh or Ira Kurzban or Michael Maggio or Marc van der Hout working for the government.

There are several books that I highly recommend for anyone who wants to see more behind the scenes of the life of either a defense attorney or a prosecutor. They are all excellent and give a stark picture of the challenges that both sides face in their daily lives. The Prosecutors, by Gary Delsohn, Plume, 2004; Defending the Damned, by Kevin Davis, Atria Books, 2007; and Indefensible: One Lawyer's Journey Into the Inferno of American Justice, by David Feige.

PART FOUR: REFORMS

Having labored in the fields, or trenches, of immigration law for over thirty years, I can allow myself the luxury of making some suggestions for our policy makers. The system is badly in need of reform, and here are a few ideas.

Gang of Eight Immigration Reform Bill

In March 2013 I was invited by Chairman of the U.S. Senate Judiciary Committee Senator Patrick Leahy to provide testimony in support of comprehensive immigration reform. As I was a former immigration judge the committee specifically wanted to hear from me any proposals to better the functioning of the immigration courts. The so-called Gang of Eight was a bipartisan group of eight U.S. Senators who wrote the first draft of what became the Border Security, Economic Opportunity, and Immigration Modernization Act of 2013, which was ultimately passed by the Senate in a vote of 68-32, with 14 Republicans joining all Democrats, but was subsequently blocked by the House of Representatives of ever receiving consideration.

My name was forwarded to the Judiciary Committee by contacts at ACLU and AILA, and I worked with their legislative teams to draft my remarks. Greg Chen, an excellent attorney whom I had known from my courtroom in San Francisco and who was currently with AILA's legislative team was especially involved. Primarily my input was to call for an expansion of immigration judge's discretion in granting of bonds, and for adjustments to some sections of the present immigration statute, and to include my call for mandatory representation by counsel for any migrant detained during removal proceedings.

Although not perfect, there were substantial gains on finding solutions for the immigration crisis as it stood at that time, including a way to shift most of the approximately 11 million or so undocumented migrants in the country into the roles of the documented with eventual path to U.S. citizenship. I toured the halls of Congress, meeting with staffers of many Senators and House Representatives with AILA legislative organizers, including with the Cuban-American legal assistant for Marco Rubio, who assured us that the Senator was onboard all the way for the proposed legislation. Rubio later lied during the 2016 presidential campaign, claiming he had never been in favor of comprehensive immigration reform.

I was probably more nervous than on any other occasion in my life when I made that appearance before the Senate Judiciary Committee (except maybe when I took the bar exam.) Talk about having to pee! And the key points of my recommendations were enshrined in the draft bill.

The world would be in a much different place if that sensible bill had been taken up by the House and reached the floor of Congress. A starting point for sensible reform would be to take it out, dust if off and re-examine its provisions. I have reproduced my testimony in the Appendix.

Our Mexican Problem – the Bold Policy Statement

Of course I've always realized that America has a lot of undocumented Mexicans within its borders – who doesn't? – and that the borders are virtually unenforceable, in spite of what clowns like TV evangelist Lou Dobbs and President Trump's white nativist buddies who are currently setting policy think. I have had hundreds of Mexican clients over the years, and as a judge I saw thousands of Mexican cases, and I have traveled extensively throughout much of Mexico trying to understand our great neighbor to the South. But I never thought of America's immigration enforcement dilemma in the particular terms of "Our Mexican Problem" until I had the privilege to take part in a conference in the Philippines about immigration to Australia, New Zealand, the U.K., Canada, and the U.S. In conversations with me, immigration specialists from the other countries consistently referred to America's immigration problem as "Your Mexican Problem." And come to think of it, if we didn't have all of the undocumented Mexicans to worry about, our immigration situation would be much more manageable. In fact, it wouldn't be that big a deal at all. So I have a solution. Why not legalize them?

There is no rational reason that our Mexican neighbors should receive any less favorable treatment than that of our Canadian neighbors, and there are plenty of arguments in favor of granting them more favorable status. You don't see American farmers and corporations inducing hundreds of thousands of Canadians to enter the U.S. in order to take laboring jobs, do you? I propose a type of "most-favored nation" visa for Mexicans to either attend school or work in the U.S., with additional measures to fast-track transition to lawful permanent residence.

The Mexican migrants who pick our strawberries and clean our hotel rooms are not only our 'hearts of gold,' and for the most part just really wonderful, decent people, but they are good for the economy, and good for Mexico's economy as well. As far as border enforcement, it would be far easier to let them in, and monitor for OTM's (other than Mexicans) who are trying to pass themselves off as Mexicans, such as from neighboring Central American countries, than it is to try to keep them out. Think of all of the resources we could save if we didn't have to deploy vast armies of enforcement agents in the southwest desert in order to stem the influx of mostly Mexican migrant laborers. The cost of enforcement of immigration laws, laws which are otherwise primarily designed to keep out criminals and terrorists, would be much cheaper, and the problem more realistically manageable. Scant resources could be used in the hunt for the terrorists who also try to penetrate our country through the Southwest border. There is not a single instance of a Mexican committing a terrorist act in the United States (at least not since Pancho Villa conducted border raids into Texas and Arizona over a hundred years ago). Anti-terror legislators should embrace this proposal, rather than squandering buckets of money in futile, anti-Mexican enforcement measures while frankly increasing the possibility of terror attacks on our soil by the real bad guys who can more easily hide among the hordes of migrant laborers forced to cross the Rio Grande and the desert.

As a nation, as a people, we have neglected our neighbor to the south, almost with a contempt that can only be explained as some kind of guilty attempt to purge the demons of our history with Mexico – namely that the U.S. manufactured a war 170 years ago, in order to rip off half of Mexico's territory and declare that land to be rightfully ours by way of some kind of mystical Manifest Destiny. Mexico is one of the richest nations south of the U.S. and should be our closest ally and trading partner. Instead we have dealt with Mexico, on a policy basis, like some kind of embarrassing relative that we don't want to acknowledge, and our denial has allowed the immigration crisis to proliferate.

We should embrace Mexico, economically, culturally and politically. Every American child should be taught Spanish in school. We should join in a partnership to assist with education, the creation of jobs, eradication of drug and other criminal elements. With some assistance, Mexico could fully stem the tide of migrants coming from points further south, and Mexico, in an alliance with the U.S., could lead the way for further economic development of the troubled Central American countries. In the long run, the only solution to massive illegal immigration in this country is the economic development of the other nations in our hemisphere. If there are jobs at home, people will stay home. I repeat: there is no long-term solution to illegal migration from the south other than the development of the southern economies. Rather than romping around the world invading countries that never posed a threat to us, we should collaborate with Mexican economists and engineers to move into a new age of Marshal Plan-type development – maybe call it the Juarez Plan – with the word *collaboration* being key. The emergence of the more recent drug cartels only underscores this urgent and single alternative to lasting chaos and dissolution of the great nation on our border.

Afterword: Beginning in 2012 but building to a crescendo in 2014, a flood of upwards of 100,000 unaccompanied minors reached our southern border and were detained by ICE. Most of these children, sometimes in the company of their mothers, came from the so-called Northern Triangle countries of El Salvador, Guatemala and Honduras. The new arrivals in fact begged to be detained in order to be processed for credible fear interviews and then be allowed to present their asylum claim in immigration court. Since that initial wave, the numbers have gone up and down, and of this writing in June 2018 all arrivals are now estimated at 50,000 a month in recent months.

I traveled to El Salvador in October 2016 with a team of adjudicators from the Refugee Affairs Division of USCIS. We spent two months processing such children for advanced parole for travel to the U.S., after conducting interviews to determine the *bona fides* of their asylum applications. We met with officials from the Salvadoran government and with the FBI agent who serves as liaison in San Salvador between that government's and our own law enforcement community. The threats are real. Criminal gangs which exert control over broad swathes of the country are ruthless in their demands for extortion and relentless in their resistance to law enforcement. Most of the families arriving at the border are not economic migrants, as the current administration would have us believe, but rather genuine refugees who flee one step ahead of the assassin.

Attempts to stop the flow of refugees through merciless policies such as ripping children from their mothers' arms and detaining them *en masse* on military bases, a policy which is described as a deterrent, represent the lowest that any civilized government can stoop to, and a wholesale rejection of America's values and any pretense at adherence to the Rule of Law. America, we are better than this.

Immigration Court Reform

Our immigration courts are a mess – poorly-run deportation factories where the emphasis is upon numbers rather than justice. My hero Judge Dana Marks analogizes that given the lack in resources and adequate time to adjudicate cases, when hearing asylum cases conditions are "like adjudicating death penalty cases in traffic court." The American Bar Association, after an exhaustive review conducted in 2010, had called for a doubling of available immigration judges and other resources.

Unfortunately the money is simply not there for a doubling of the immigration judge corps. Even with additional hires in 2016-2017, the backlog continues to rise. In that case, the only solution to the numbers problem (just one of many immigration court problems I address below) is to reduce the number of respondents in court. A couple of proposals would reduce the number by half, thus solving other urgent economic and resources considerations.

As far as specific changes to the way that **deportation hearings** are conducted, I propose the following:

1. Let all the Mexicans in. Wait a minute, you just said that in the previous section. But as a matter of fact, by adopting the sweeping reforms mentioned above, the backlog of immigration cases in court would easily be reduced by nearly half and the more important priorities of deporting criminals and potential terrorists could be more easily tackled. EOIR statistics for 2010 show that 43% of all cases in deportation hearings are Mexican. As mentioned above, there is no good reason to be deporting non-criminal Mexicans, and plenty of good reasons to be encouraging them to stay. Of course, some of those of the 43% are criminal aliens and should rightfully be in proceedings if they have been involved in violent or dangerous crimes, but the vast majority are either overstays or individuals who crossed the border illegally to find work.

2. Adopt the asylum reforms outlined below, which include pulling asylum applications out of the immigration courts. Fully 30% of all deportation hearings are asylum/withholding of removal related. Simply by adopting measures 1 and 2 the court numbers would be reduced by 50% and all fiscal and understaffing issues would be solved.

3. Create an even playing field in the way that immigration judges are hired – that is, draw equally from the ranks of government attorneys and private bar or NGO attorneys. The ranks of judges have traditionally been filled by government INS/ICE prosecutors, or others who have spent their entire

careers in the system. These lawyers can, of course, be very knowledgeable of the law and be very able attorneys, but there is a natural inclination on the part of such attorneys not to challenge the government's interpretation of the law. Or as President Obama adequately put it awhile ago, we should be choosing judges who, as attorneys, have a background of representing the downtrodden and oppressed, who have a high empathy quotient. This isn't happening. For example, in the year 2009 16 new immigration judges were hired. Reading their posted biographies on line, it was apparent that only two of the sixteen had ever had a real human being for a client – the rest were drawn from lifelong careers with government agencies. (Similar statistics have prevailed up through 2020).

4. Congress should repeal the one year bar on asylum seekers. It is a violation of international law and it doesn't work. Congress added the one-year provision in 1996, understandably as an attempt to curb frivolous claims. Anyone who has been in the U.S. for more than a year and then applies for asylum with the asylum office will automatically have his claim rejected and forwarded to the immigration court, where the applicant can still argue that (s)he should fit into one of the allowed exceptions about why she didn't apply within one year. In fact, statistics show that the measure has not reduced the number of asylum applications in the least, but has merely shifted the burden over to the courts, and precious time is then wasted in each hearing by the respondent making the argument why the tardy application should be eligible for an exception to the

one-year deadline. Instead, a late filing should just be one element to add in the mix when an adjudicator is assessing credibility. In fact, while I was working as a legal consultant with the UN High Commissioner for Refugees in Korea, the Republic of Korea proposed eliminating the one-year bar in Korea's asylum law, with support from the UN because it *is* a violation of international law.

5. Congress should review and shorten the list of Aggravated Felony convictions for which an alien can be deported – for example, remove the possibility of misdemeanor convictions qualifying as Ag. Fel.s. The list was greatly expanded in 1996, to include, among other petty grounds, any misdemeanor theft conviction where a sentence of more than a year is possible. Senator Trent Lott, who was head of the Judiciary Committee at the time he supported the legislation, later confessed in the pages of the Washington Post that he was not himself aware of the freakish consequences (not his words) of the law, which could, for example, penalize with deportability a mother who was shoplifting baby diapers if it was her second offense, leaving her no possibility of remaining in the U.S.

6. ICE attorneys should be *strongly discouraged* by management from appealing an immigration judge's decision (equivalent to the Constitutional ban on double jeopardy in criminal proceedings), except in carefully carved-out exceptions that affect broad policy or especially egregious circumstances. This would cut down by more than one third the number of appeals to the overburdened Board of Immigration Appeals

and federal courts. In spite of misguided Supreme Court decisions which have pronounced that a deportation is not punishment and therefore that a person being deported is not entitled to fundamental 6th Amendment rights, including right to counsel at government expense and right against double jeopardy, immigration advocates will all agree that quite often the consequences of deportation are far more onerous than that of jail time. In criminal law, a prosecutor is barred from appealing a jury's Not Guilty verdict. If a judge pronounces in a deportation hearing that an alien should not be deported, or that a certain kind of relief, such as asylum should be granted, the government attorney should be satisfied to take his marbles and go home to play another time, rather than appealing. First of all, the number of decisions to deport already far outweigh the decisions to grant relief. Secondly, even if a judge makes an "error" on the side of the migrant, the big, powerful U.S. government should accept the decision and go after other fish to fry, unless, for example, the judge's decision appears 1) so egregious that it should not possibly be allowed to stand, and 2) it can be shown that an extreme and imminent possibility of harm may occur if the decision is allowed to stand. The decision should not be made by a local supervisor, but rather by headquarters.

7. Public defenders for detained aliens is an absolute bottom-line requirement. Many advocates argue for public defenders regardless of whether the respondent is detained, but I am convinced that multitude and manifest injustices are committed on a daily basis in the context of detained migrants who can't get legal advice. 45% to 50% of all cases

heard in immigration court involve detained aliens. Federal judge Robert A. Katzmann stated at a symposium on May 3rd, 2011 that "a substantial threat to the fair and effective administration of justice" is posed by lack of representation. Supreme Court Justice John Paul Stevens, at the same event, said that "The need for legal representation for immigrants is really acute, the consequences are just so drastic."

The government would save money by establishing a public defenders corps of attorneys to represent detained migrants for a number of reasons; most importantly, often an informed attorney can save everyone the length and expense of a trial by simply explaining to an incarcerated individual that he doesn't have any chance of defeating the charges of deportation, and that the judge will have to keep him locked up during the whole process, including appeal. I've seen this principle in action a thousand times, including when, as an attorney, I used to counsel detained migrants who had no representation. A public defender would have no interest in misdirecting a migrant into fighting the case when there is no hope. But when the migrant *does* have a case, the assistance of counsel is crucial to someone who is incarcerated, in order to assure that documents, evidence and witnesses can all be marshaled in support of the claim. And judges should be able to draw from a pool of recognized attorneys to appoint them to particularly compelling cases.

8. Selection of Immigration Judges must be transparent merit selection system. An advisory council to assist the Attorney General in the selection of Immigration Judges should be

established, such as an Immigration Judicial Conference patterned along the lnes of the Federal Judicial Conference, to be composed of sitting Immigration Judges representing a cross-section of the country, and several Appellate Immigration Judges from the BIA. (thanks to Judge Paul Schmidt). The decision should include input from the American Immigration Lawyers Association, in much the same way that the appointment of federal judges receives input from the American Bar Association. A lot of grief and damage to our system of justice could be spared, if lawyers who have a reputation for professionalism and integrity in their communities could have a chance to comment on the merits of particular candidates or bring forth instances of unprofessional conduct they are aware of.

The current EOIR management, under guidance of Attorney General William Barr, has been promoting manifestly unqualified "hanging judges" to the Board of Immigration Appeals, such as judges whose asylum denial rate exceeds 92%. Such judges and their brethren, newly selected Immigration Judges who believe their job is to stop the "invading barbarian hordes", are nothing but deportation hacks in allegiance with the administration's nativist policies. A new administration, with new EOIR management, must reverse such grotesque hiring decisions.

9. Department of Justice oversight of Immigration Judges who have a pattern of culturally/racially insensitive remarks or outrageous decisions is paramount. In today's world, there is absolutely no reason or basis to tolerate such behavior on

the bench, yet I know a handful of judges who continue to abuse aliens in our courtrooms, treating them like illiterate children or criminals at every opportunity. Such judges should be transferred out of such positions of sensitivity and responsibility to corner offices without windows and with big stacks of files where they can't hurt anyone. The agency seems incapable of policing itself, because in spite of calls for reform, and EOIR's insistence that matters have improved recently, such incompetent and sometimes barbaric judges as those I have referred to in these pages continue to torment respondents in their courtrooms. A neutral panel of attorneys who are experienced professionals in the area of deportation practice should have be invited to provide input on particular cases and their findings be made public if EOIR does not respond to well-founded complaints.

In the current system, it is virtually impossible to have a judge censured or removed. The following incident is a rare exception, and the only such suspension of an IJ that occurred during my seven years on the bench. Judge Thomas Ragno, sitting in Boston, was suspended (only temporarily) in August, 2003, when he said to an African asylum seeker in his courtroom, whose name was Jane, "Jane, come here. Me Tarzan." He then laughed and talked about how funny the Tarzan cartoons were. The woman, a native of Uganda, had been a victim of political imprisonment and rape in her home country.

"After more than three decades in the Justice Department, the Immigration Courts have not developed in a way that fulfills their essential role in insuring fairness and guaranteeing due process in the removal hearing process. Waiting for the Justice Department to appropriately reform the system is like 'Waiting for Godot.' It's time for bipartisan action in Congress to remove the Immigration Courts from the Department of Justice and create an independent, well-functioning Article I Immigration Court. Only then with the Immigration Courts be able to achieve their "noble vision" of "through teamwork and innovation be the world's best tribunals guaranteeing fairness and due process for all." Judge Paul Schmidt.

Such an Article I Immigration Court is supported by the American Bar Association, the Federal Bar Association, the American Immigration Lawyers Association and the National Association of Immigration Judges.

Immigration Judges should receive one month of specialized training, with emphasis on the part of the immigration law relating to deportation defense, and with special emphasis on asylum and torture cases. If a selected candidate is not already an immigration specialist, the learning curve is just too great to set them loose in a courtroom where life-and-death decisions are being made daily. Training should include extensive moot court exercises in the conduct of a hearing. The agency should craft a special upper-class course on asylum law specially tailored for judges, with specialists drawn from EOIR, USCIS, and the private bar.

In addition, and more of a wish than a realistic demand, I recommend that each future judge be required to spend a night in jail. No one should have the power to consign people to custody without knowing what it is like themselves. (This is actually a recommendation for any judge who has the power to put someone behind bars).

10. The definition of "refugee" at section 101(a)(42) of the Immigration Act should be amended, removing the language that refers to those who oppose a "coercive population control" program. The inclusion of this language in 1996 was a bad idea promoted by the conservative, anti-planned-parenthood lobby in Congress; I know exactly who drafted the measure. Such a fundamental document as the refugee definition should never be amended in order to appease special interest groups. The result has been a catastrophe: an incitement to millions of Chinese to fabricate stories about forced abortions and unwanted sterilizations in order to be granted asylum in the U.S. Rather than tampering with the time-honored definition of a refugee, which in U.S. law comes almost verbatim from the 1951 Convention on the Status of Refugees, the BIA could simply issue a precedent decision that clarifies how such practices as forcible abortion and sterilization "may" give rise to a colorable claim to asylum. Anyone who has really been subject to a coercive abortion would be covered under such a ruling.

Also, language should be included in the statute that all forms of gender/sexual identity-based persecution, including LGBTQ persecution fall under the category Particular Social Group. This would codify what is now in effect in practice but still not uniformly enforced across the different circuit courts. (The Trump nativist administration is attempting to reverse decades of jurisprudence and practice by eliminating gender-based asylum and protection of asylum based upon LGBTQ identity.)

11. We've got to get back to conducting real reviews of immigration judge decisions. The Ashcroft streamlining rules that make a mockery of the Board of Immigration Appeals must be rescinded. I support Congressman Howard Berman's proposal, under the Civil Liberties Restoration Act, to set up an independent agency of three-judge panels to review the appeals. The appeals board must be able to give such cases the serious attention that they deserve, for deportation hearings are surely among the gravest and compelling of adjudications in any of our courts across the land, with outcomes that result in life-and-death determinations.

    One personal example to illustrate the point. Twenty years ago, one of my clients at the immigration clinic, a convicted drug user, was denied an application for a 212(c) waiver by an immigration judge who had quite a reputation for making outrageous decisions. One of the reasons that he cited for denying my client, who was from Lebanon, the relief requested, was that the client's mother had appeared in the courtroom but had not testified. He had held it against my client. There could be many innocuous reasons why we might have elected not to put her on; in this case, she was just too terrified to testify.

The Board granted our appeal, citing in particular the judge's error holding it against our client because his mother hadn't testified. Rather than remanding, the Board granted 212(c) relief based on the record. Now, exactly twenty years later, the same judge has been chastised by the 7th Circuit Federal Court of Appeals, for having made exactly the same ruling in a recent case. (See *Castilho de Oliveira v. Holder,* No. 07-3307, 7th Cir. 2009). Quoting from the decision, the appellate court said, "The IJ repeatedly interrupted the testimony to ask irrelevant and sometimes inflammatory questions, refused to consider important evidence, and decided the case without seriously engaging with the evidence in the record. Indeed, so troubling are some of these lapses that we are left with the impression that the IJ cared little about the evidence and instead applied whatever rationale he could muster to justify a predetermined outcome." *The court specifically stated that the IJ was wrong in basing his decision in part upon the fact that the respondent didn't have his mother testify.*

The behavior cited by the appellate court is exactly how the same IJ handled himself on several of my cases twenty years ago, which I won on appeal. Now twenty years later?

In spite of self-serving declarations by EOIR management that the system has been improved and that judges are under greater scrutiny today, I can assure you that a poll of AILA attorneys would turn up dozens of cases of sitting veteran judges who, just like the case cited above, continue to act with contempt for the people who come before them, utter disregard for the Rule of Law, and with complete impunity. I hear about such cases every day from practicing attorneys.

12. And finally, and this recommendation would make irrelevant some of the foregoing proposals, the immigration courts should be elevated to Article I status, as most informed immigration practitioners and academics call for.

Drastic Reform of America's Asylum System

I have enjoyed a wonderful career specializing in asylum law; at first representing asylum applicants in immigration court and later, as a judge, adjudicating asylum applications in court. That's why I'm qualified to say that the courtroom is not the proper place to hear an asylum application.

I loved the excitement and drama of the courtroom, the adversarial challenge of doing my best to get my client's case before the judge, fighting to get all relevant evidence on the record; parrying the often outrageous arguments and cross-examination of the INS opponents, and preparing and then making "brilliant" oral arguments to the judge. But all of these dramatic trappings do not produce a conducive climate for testimony by an asylum applicant who has truly been persecuted and traumatized, or who genuinely fears persecution upon being sent back to her country.

A simple comparative analysis shows that the U.S. has more opportunities for an asylum applicant to make their case to the government and for judicial review of an adverse decision than any other country in the world. An asylum applicant can apply to a USCIS asylum office to have her case heard. If unsuccessful, typically her case will be "referred" to immigration court where the judge can hear the case all over again, complete with testimony of supporting witnesses and cross-examination by an ICE attorney and submission of evidence and arguments from both sides. From there the case can be appealed to the Board of Immigration Appeals, and finally if the case is denied by the Board the applicant can appeal to the federal circuit court for further review. Occasionally an asylum case will even be appealed from there to the Supreme Court. I respectfully suggest that this is a bit excessive.

I propose that asylum cases be removed from the jurisdiction of immigration courts. We've all seen occasions where our client is too timid or terrified or even traumatized to testify effectively in court. A less formal and less public forum is more appropriate for a genuine victim of torture or persecution. This proposal includes asylum-related matters such as applications for withholding of removal and for relief under the Convention Against Torture.

I propose that the position of Asylum Officer be elevated to Special Hearing Officer, that it be an attorney position at the GS-13 to GS-14 level, and that an appeal from a denial should go directly to a specialized panel of 3 judges at the Board of Immigration Appeals, that is a panel of asylum experts. The advantages are manifold:

1. More expeditious completion of cases.

2. More appropriate, confidential setting.

3. Hearing officers who are experts in the field.

4. Tremendous savings to the immigration court system in terms of time and money.

As far as the immigration courts, which now are so notoriously backlogged that many respondents have to wait as long as five years for a final hearing, this proposed scheme would eliminate half of the caseload of the courts. There is still plenty of work to go around, so those sitting judges needn't feel threatened that they will suddenly be out of work.

Cases could be heard much more expeditiously before the special hearing officers. Attorneys could be present, but only for the applicant. Their function could be limited to that of a mostly silent representative, facilitating the applicant in the production of testimony and evidence, and if desired, providing a brief opening or closing statement to help the hearing officer understand and summarize the evidence (this is pretty much the way it works in the present system at the asylum officer level.) By eliminating the adversarial element, the applicant would be much more comfortable in testifying, and attorney egos would be left outside the door. The job that an ICE attorney fulfills in sometimes putting adverse or conflicting evidence from government files in the record could be achieved by the hearing officer herself, she would have access to all government security systems that an ICE attorney normally has, and that asylum officers in today's system have.

If the applicant has already been issued a Notice to Appear in immigration court and wishes to apply for asylum, then the judge would refer the matter to the special hearing officer, in effect putting the court matter on administrative hold, until a decision has been made at the first level, and if the outcome is negative, giving the case time for appeal before the special panel at the Board. This could all transpire in the course of a year. If the Board also shoots down the case it would be returned to the Immigration Judge to handle issues of deportability and relief, except for the relief of asylum and related applications which would already have been heard. Then, if the applicant is ordered removed/deported by the judge, there would still remain the right to appeal all issues to the federal circuit court as is now the case.

The Special Hearing Officer *should* be an attorney for several reasons: often documentary evidence is introduced and reviewed that only a trained attorney can make sense of, especially such things as conviction records and police reports. Additionally, if it is an attorney position, qualified experts in the private sector would be more motivated to compete for the positions. Heck, it even sounds like a job that I might like.

To summarize, such a system would remove all of the time-consuming pomp and circumstances of immigration court, allow the cases to move more quickly but in fact still afford an applicant a better climate and allow more time in which to present a story before a neutral and highly-qualified official, the Special Hearing Officer; would provide better conditions of confidentiality for a genuine applicant to reveal intimate and embarrassing facts about a case, and especially to facilitate testimony from someone who has been traumatized and is possibly suffering from Post Traumatic Stress Disorder; and would not sacrifice any of the due process protections that are currently in the system. A specialized panel at the Board would review a denial, and a denial from that panel could still be appealed to a federal circuit court.

I'm sure that many of my attorney colleagues may be incensed at this proposal, because they can make a good income through representation of clients in immigration court, but again, based upon my experience on both sides of the fence, I am convinced that this system would advance the best interest of the applicants and promote true justice. I repeat, a courtroom with black-clad judge behind a big bench, with court interpreter and court clerk listening, and with sometimes a multitude of other witnesses all present at once, and with an ICE attorney cross-examining and often badgering the applicant, is not the most conducive environment to get at the truth in an asylum application.

Legal Education Reform

Perhaps this is a good juncture to talk briefly about my theory of legal education and the state of the system in the U.S. In two words, it sucks. I agree with the many critics of the legal education system in our nation who insist that the system demands fundamental reform, that the law schools for the most part are graduating students who don't know how to practice law, and that they are in effect committing consumer fraud upon those students, because in fact most students still have to learn how to practice law through on-the-job training in their first job after school. There *are* schools that pride themselves on being teaching colleges, where most of the professors are professionals in their field who are drawn to teaching because they want to pass on the skills that they have spent years acquiring – but those schools are definitely in the minority, and certainly not the law schools that one thinks of when any discussion of the "big" law schools is held.

Typical law schools emphasize, in their faculty hiring practices, Ivy League credentials and publication in irrelevant journals over any real legal experience or ability to teach. When filling a faculty position, most schools are more likely to hire a recent graduate from Harvard who worked on that school's law review but has never set foot in a courtroom, over someone with years of experience in the practice of law but who never saw any reason to squander their time writing law review articles. For those who don't know, such articles are suitable for starting campfires, but are rarely read by any serious practitioners in the field – and this is especially true for those disciplines, such as criminal law, civil rights litigation, and torts, where courtroom experience is of the highest priority. I saw this very principle played out many times in the faculty meetings at George Washington Law School, when the faculty was debating and voting on candidates for positions at the school. (By the way, one interrogation technique that might be useful to use on terror suspects would be to force them to sit through just one such faculty meeting – they would be begging for mercy and willing to share their deepest secrets after being exposed to that form of mental torture). Once hired, such faculty members are expected to continue in the production of erudite scholarly articles, at the expense of time that could be spent with their students. A student could care less how many law review articles the professor has published. The student wants information delivered in an exciting, meaningful way, but how can a professor who doesn't even practice law make the world of law meaningful to a critical student?

Ninety percent of the texts in use in law schools are merely collections of appellate court decisions. Certainly it is useful for a lawyer to be able to read and interpret such a decision, but it only takes one semester, not three years of law school, to learn how. Upon graduation, the only students who will continue to use the skill of working with those appellate decisions are the tiny minority of students who get jobs as judicial clerks or law professors. The expensive, time-costly three year education should be reduced to two years, and most of those mind-dulling law books should be trashed.

I would recommend a law school organized in the manner of former Antioch School of Law, where the emphasis from the students' first semester is upon clinical work. The law schools can be an incredible force of empowerment and betterment in the community, providing representation for the most needy of our nation's citizens and residents. The student will be motivated from the very beginning by the experience, under proper supervision, of working on real cases that affect real individuals' lives. The exciting thing about the practice of law is the human drama involved, and the courtroom is a crucible of dramatic events where human conflict is at its peak. Get the students into the courtroom in the first year, and their appreciation of procedure and evidence will skyrocket. They will see how they've touched the lives of others and made a difference. There is no greater method of teaching or form of empowerment.

Over the course of ten years at GW, many of the students I worked with in the clinic expressed their loathing of the law school experience, except for their time spent in the clinics where they worked with real people from the community who needed and appreciated their talent. In other classes, students were encouraged to thrive in a cut-throat atmosphere of competition for grades. All too many of the students selected to attend GW were there so that they could become rich business people after graduation, rather than so that they could somehow contribute to the community through the use of their legal skills.

Nevertheless, in their teaching evaluations, students routinely gave the clinical faculty very high evaluations, in contrast to the more scholarly, prestigious faculty who often got dissed in the evaluations. Ironically, at the same time the dean was trying to fire me as part of the dispute over termination of the immigration clinic, I received a letter from the Assistant Dean for Academic Affairs lauding me for the unusually high student evaluations I had received. This is not surprising, for the clinical faculty member's job is to work closely with the students and actually take some interest in the students' education and progress, whereas many of the most prestigious of the faculty couldn't care less about the quality of education they are delivering. Students often find it nearly impossible to even obtain a meeting with such a professor to discuss their concerns. I experienced resentment from certain faculty members who were tenured professors but were notoriously loathed by their students, whereas excitement about my clinic and the kinds of cases we worked on was communicated openly in the halls of the law school. One of my students, who is now a high-level State Department diplomat, told me that except for the clinical experience, her time spent at GW law was the worst experience of her life, and that she would never donate a penny to the school.

It seemed that at the end of every school year, inevitably one of my students would come to me and confide that she had been distraught about her legal education and had been ready to drop out of school before taking the clinic; that it was only through her experience in the clinic that she had located any value and meaning in her law school education. Although I was naturally gratified to hear such sentiments, I didn't take such remarks as personal complements, but rather as affirmation that what we were accomplishing in the clinics was what law school should be all about. The students in the end gain as much from the experience in their understanding of life and society as they learn about the actual practice of the law.

In summary, the clinical offerings at law schools should be more than an adjunct to the major curriculum of mind-numbing texts consisting of appellate cases. Law schools should more properly be clinics where the courtroom and advocacy skills of the students are forged on a daily basis from the time of the first semester, liberating students from the yoke of exhaustive memorization of dead academic facts by coupling them with real people from the real community whose lives will be affected by the students' efforts. Two-year courses of study that elevate the students' skills and creativity, rather than three-year dead-zones that elevate the prestige of professors at the expense of their students and the community.

Appendix

"Building an Immigration System
Worthy of American Values"

U.S. Senate
Committee on the Judiciary
Wednesday, March 20, 2013
Statement of Paul Grussendorf

Thank you Chairman Coons, Ranking Member Grassley, and distinguished members of this Committee. It is my honor to appear before you today.

I've spent a total of twenty eight years working in the area of immigration law. I've been the director of a law school immigration clinic, an immigration judge appointed by the Attorney General to make the tough calls involving deportation and immigration benefits, and a DHS adjudicator of refugee applications with U.S. Citizenship and Immigration Services (USCIS).

For four years I was the sole immigration judge responsible in Philadelphia for the Institutional Hearing Program, in which immigrants who are convicted of federal offenses receive accelerated removal hearings while serving their sentences. I conducted hearings in the Allenwood Federal Correctional Institute in Allenwood,

Pennsylvania. Later I was responsible, in San Francisco immigration court, along with my excellent colleague Judge Michael Yamaguchi, for the detention docket, presiding over the cases of all migrants who were detained by Immigration and Customs Enforcement (ICE) in northern California and placed in removal proceedings. These included those who were detained on the street by ICE, those who were taken into custody by ICE after completing prison sentences and being released from state and county jails, and those who were detained at San Francisco International Airport due to document irregularities and other issues of suspected fraud. These also included the tragic cases of unaccompanied minors who were detained pending a resolution of their cases. These experiences have tempered my remarks today relative to the state of immigration detention and the issue of judicial discretion.

As a judge I presided over scores of cases involving immigrants detained by ICE, who were deported after months or even years of unnecessary detention. Typically migrant workers, construction laborers, hotel and restaurant employees would be detained during an ICE sweep of an immigrant community or factory raid. They would usually already have spent several weeks in jail before making it to court. I would inform such "respondents" (responding to charges of removability from the U.S.) at their initial court hearing, of their right to counsel, though not at the expense of the government, and whether or not, given their individual circumstances, they had the right to a bond determination. Many respondents would finally accept deportation rather than seeking relief from removal in court because of the frustration of having been detained for so long –either because they were deemed ineligible for bond under the law, or they could not afford to pay a bond even though they were eligible for release. Some of them would have qualified for refugee status, and others would have had other legal means to remain in the country. The vast majority of such detained migrants posed no danger to the community or public safety, and often had no criminal convictions that would mandate their detention. Nevertheless, they would ask me to sign a deportation order rather than enduring additional time in detention while fighting their case. Sound policy would have encouraged their release to their families so that they could continue as wage earners, sustaining their families (often consisting of U.S. citizens), and so they could continue contributing to the U.S. economy.

Restoring Judicial Discretion
Restore due process and judicial review over immigration cases.
Over the past two decades, Congress has severely curtailed the discretion of immigration judges to evaluate cases on an individual basis and grant relief to deserving immigrants and their families. Moreover, under current law, the federal courts have also been stripped of their jurisdiction to review most deportation and agency decisions. It is the great frustration of the immigration bar as well as my former colleagues on the bench that the immigration judges' discretion has been so whittled away. Congress should restore judicial review and ensure due process to all people who are facing deportation

Our system, amended in 1996 by harsh provisions of the Illegal Immigration Reform and Immigrant Responsibility Act (IIRAIRA), often blocks individuals subject to removal from presenting evidence of their equities to an immigration judge. Instead, low-level immigration officials are empowered to act as judge and jury, and federal courts have been denied the power to review most agency decisions.

Congress should restore fairness and flexibility to our system by expanding the authority of immigration judges to consider the circumstances of each case. Judges are drawn from the ranks of immigration professionals, those who have spent their careers working in government as well as those who have advocated on the side of immigrants. They should be trusted to make the correct calls. The numbers bear out their approval ratings. In fiscal year 2012, immigration judges completed 382,675 cases. Of those decisions, only a total of 26,099 were appealed to the Board of Immigration Appeals. It appears that most parties to the proceedings come away satisfied with the judges' decisions.

Cancellation of Removal

One of the few remaining opportunities for an immigration judge to grant relief from deportation based on a person's specific circumstances is called "Cancellation of Removal." Cancellation relief is available for noncitizens who have been in the U.S. for a long time, a minimum of seven years for lawful permanent residents, and ten years for non-LPRs. But Cancellation has very stiff requirements that often bar people – including long-time LPRs – from relief despite significant equities. The hardship bar, that one must show "exceptional and extremely unusual hardship" to a qualifying relative, that is a U.S. citizen spouse, child or parent, is set too high. Congress, when enacting this provision, did not inform the adjudicators how to interpret that language. Nowadays, a successful Cancellation case largely comes down to showing that the respondent's children suffer from some grave disease for which they could not receive medical care in the prospective country of removal. A very senior judge with whom I spoke last week lamented that Cancellation has become the "sick kid" provision. These requirements restrict a judge's ability to look at the totality of circumstances in a case and grant appropriate relief.

A case that illustrates the point about judges needing more discretion and how the hardship bar is too high for Cancellation: a 35 year old woman from the Philippines had a Cancellation hearing. She is the mother of three U.S. citizen children. She was convicted seventeen years ago, at the age of nineteen, for petty theft. She is the sole caregiver of her aging parents, who are not U.S. citizens, both of whom have multiple health problems, including the father suffering several heart attacks and the mother battling both diabetes and cancer. The immigration judge felt compelled to deny the Cancellation application, finding that the hardship presented did not rise to the level of "exceptional and extremely unusual." The Board of Immigration Appeals initially upheld the judge's decision and the case was appealed to the 9th Circuit Court of Appeals, but during this time the parents' health has continued to deteriorate and the children have been suffering emotionally at school. ICE opposed requests for Prosecutorial Discretion, but the BIA recently granted a motion to reopen and remand to the judge based upon the new evidence of hardship in the family. The case is now pending further deliberations. This long journey of several years litigation and appeals could have all been avoided if the judge had initially had the discretion to grant the case based upon a lower hardship bar, one of "extreme hardship."

Among the bigger challenges for LPRs is that any "aggravated felony" conviction automatically bars relief, despite the fact that this category now includes many misdemeanor offenses and crimes involving no violence. Additionally, the barriers to cancellation relief are retroactive, meaning that someone who pled guilty to a disqualifying offense *before the criteria were even enacted* is still penalized. Furthermore, the cancellation rules require an applicant to have been present in the U.S. continuously for a minimum period of years.

But this "continuous presence" period runs out when DHS (not the applicant) decides to act, meaning that people can be barred from cancellation relief based solely on agency decisions and not through any fault of their own (this is called the "stop-time rule").

Legislation should fix these problems and return to those who have deep roots in our communities and have not committed a serious offense the right to apply for Cancellation of Removal. Immigration judges should have discretion to grant relief in deserving cases by looking at the hardship to the respondent in proceedings, as well as the hardship to family members, and judges should also be encouraged to evaluate the contributions to society that an individual has made over the years.

Discretionary Waiver of General Applicability

Currently, immigration law provides only narrow and specific waivers for some noncitizens in some circumstances. Each waiver has a different (often complex) standard, and each applies to only *one segment* of immigration adjudications – either when one is technically seeking "admission" to the U.S. or when one is about to be deported from the U.S. A universally-applicable, simple and generous waiver could be proposed to provide judges the authority to grant relief. For those with prior criminal offenses, there is a waiver in the "admission" context, but it is far too narrow, does not apply to any minor convictions, and ironically punishes some long-time lawful permanent residents (LPR) more harshly than other noncitizens. In the deportation context, many minor, old convictions categorically bar even long-time LPRs from relief.

In most cases it makes no sense to place individuals into removal proceedings because of criminal violations that are remote in time.

Sometimes incarceration **does** work, either as a rehabilitative or preventive measure. As a judge I saw over the years scores of individuals who, many years earlier, had been convicted of an offense, had served their time, and had gone on to form families, create small businesses, buy houses and pay mortgages, even become "model citizens" of their communities. I personally felt in many such cases that a couple of years in the slammer had brought home to such offenders the serious consequences, including deportation and banishment from our great nation and destruction of their families, of their actions. Yet, years and even decades later, ICE would come knocking, and often, because of the categorization of "aggravated felony" of their offense, they were left with no legal means to remain in the U.S. Current immigration law provides only limited waivers for those with convictions. The lack of more generous waivers has resulted in deportations of people with extremely compelling life circumstances.

Expand Time Frame of Voluntary Departure

Often, when a migrant is apprehended and placed in removal proceedings, all that is desired is a reasonable amount of time to put affairs in order, perhaps sell a house or a business, before voluntarily returning to the home country. Voluntary Departure is a statutory remedy by which an individual can avoid an order of removal, as long as one is capable and willing to pay for the means of departure. Unfortunately, the period of voluntary departure has been reduced to a mere 120 days, thus again impinging upon the discretion of the judge to evaluate the circumstances and act according to the best interests of the community. Perhaps in many cases all an individual needs is a maximum of 120 days to depart. But several circumstances come to mind: a family is facing removal and would opt for voluntary departure, but the teenage child needs six more months to finish high school. Or, a wife is facing a serious operation which will, including period of convalescence, necessitate several months of bed stay beyond the period of 120 days. Under today's law, the respondent facing such a dilemma might opt for a costly and lengthy battle in court, rather than accepting the first opportunity for a grant of Voluntary Departure, because the stakes for the family member are so high. Judges should be afforded the discretion to use their judgment and grant lengthier periods of Voluntary Departure.

The above proposals would allow our immigration judges to more effectively do their job. Permitting judges to consider the facts presented by both parties and then to grant relief based on merit will give the American people a legal immigration system that is efficient and just, one that will serve our nation well in the 21st century.

Reform of Immigration Detention System

The use of detention for immigration enforcement has grown dramatically in recent years. In fiscal year (FY) 2011, the Department of Homeland Security's Immigration and Customs Enforcement (ICE) **detained an all-time high number of 429,000 individuals** at a cost of about **$166 per person per day**. For context, in FY 1994 the federal government detained fewer than 82,000 migrants. Immigration detention is a civil authority, despite the use of penal institutions. The sole purpose of immigration detention is to ensure compliance with immigration court proceedings and judicial orders.

For many migrants in ICE custody, detention is not legally required. In these cases, ICE has the discretion to decide whether a person should be detained, released, or placed into an alternative to detention (ATD) program. Historically, ICE has not always exercised this discretion, resulting in the needless detention of hundreds of thousands of people, and costing taxpayers billions of dollars. Recently, ICE developed and deployed a risk assessment tool to make informed detention decisions based on individual circumstances. However, because current appropriations language requires ICE to maintain 34,000 daily detention beds, individualized detention decisions may be overridden by the requirement to meet a detention quota.

At a time of unprecedented pressure to cut government spending, we should be reducing detention costs and should not be detaining people who pose no significant risk of flight or danger to the community. The total price tag to the American taxpayer is $2 billion annually. Effective alternatives to detention have proven overwhelmingly successful at a cost of a few dollars a day per person.

End mandatory spending on a fixed number of detention beds.
Homeland Security appropriations language has been interpreted as mandating a daily detention level of 34,000 people, an approach that does not exist in any other law enforcement context. The bed "mandate" distorts agency priorities and results in the unnecessary use of jail detention on people who do not need to be detained, and it makes any meaningful discretion and prioritization in immigration enforcement impossible. The bed mandate should be eliminated from future appropriations bills. Eliminating the bed mandate would enable DHS to increase the use of alternatives to detention and reduce spending on detention and custody.

Detention is a costly way for the government to ensure appearances at immigration proceedings and protect public safety. Legislation should permit judges to consider alternatives to detention for individuals who are vulnerable or pose little risk to communities, and to consider in each case whether continued detention is necessary and lawful. Legislation should also specify a clear timeframe within which ICE must make its decision whether to formally charge a noncitizen after arrest. Detainees often languish in detention with no hearings scheduled in their cases because charging documents have not been served on them or filed with the immigration court.

I propose that in the routine case of a migrant laborer or mother of U.S. citizen children who is detained at a traffic stop or community sweep, the migrant should be processed, issued charging documents, given a court date and sent home. Let them continue to provide for the family and continue to strengthen the community and the economy.

Eliminate mandatory detention except for serious offenders.
Each year mandatory detention results in the jailing of tens of thousands of people who pose no danger to their communities and are not a flight risk. Feeding this detention system is the mandatory detention provision of Illegal Immigration Reform and Immigrant Responsibility Act of 1996 (IIRAIRA), requiring that most people in deportation proceedings, based on their past offenses, no matter how remote in time, are held in custody, even if they are non-violent and the criminal system has determined they are not a risk to the community. Such a system cannot differentiate between a terrorist and a single mother of U.S. children or a green card holder who's lived here his whole life. The respondent remains in custody until completion of the immigration court case, and pending any appeals to the Board of Immigration Appeals and federal circuit courts, which can easily amount to years of detention.

Section 236(c) of the Immigration and Nationality Act provides a laundry list of types of crimes that make an individual subject to mandatory detention, most of them non-violent in nature. A term of imprisonment of one year makes one subject to mandatory detention. In many cases the sentence will be suspended, meaning the person does not even serve the time. For example, a college student who steals a candy bar from a convenience store and receives a one year suspended sentence will remain in ICE custody pending the outcome of his removal case. A case I presided over in San Francisco illustrates the problem:

> A mother from El Salvador who had received a suspended sentence for shoplifting baby diapers for her U.S. citizen child came before me on the custody docket, and I had to inform her that I could not even consider bond in her case. She chose deportation so as not to be separated from her infant, although she had compelling equities in her case.

Another case I heard in San Francisco comes to mind:

> An Iranian woman, lawful permanent resident who was married to a U.S. citizen and had two U.S. citizen children, was diagnosed with schizophrenia. She had picked up a couple of shoplifting convictions. She had already been granted asylum from Iran, and we heard her asylum application again. ICE insisted she remain detained during a protracted hearing which, including appeal lasted over a year. A female Iranian psychiatric expert testified to the horrible fate awaiting someone in the respondent's condition in Iran, and yet ICE kept her detained until the Board of Immigration Appeals finally upheld my grant of asylum. During this time she was separated from her very supportive family and medical professionals whose assistance she desperately needed.

I recently advised on the case of a Salvadoran migrant worker whose appeal was pending in the 9th Circuit Court of Appeals. He was subject to mandatory detention due to a couple of petty offenses: one DUI, and another DUI on a bicycle! He had filed for asylum in immigration court. He actually remained in custody for two whole years after his case was completed in immigration court and he pursued further appeals. He was thus removed from his family and his U.S. citizen teenager daughter, who became depressed during the separation from her father and who attempted suicide at a time that her father could not be there to comfort her. Do we really want to be paying for "three hots and a cot" for such an individual when he could be out working and helping to sustain his family and the economy?

According to 2009 ICE data, 66 percent of detained immigrants were subject to mandatory detention but only 11 percent had committed violent crimes (for which they had already served their time). Mandatory detention also sweeps up primary caretakers, leading to complications with family structure and child custody. Mandatory detention laws should be repealed for all but violent offenders. In addition, Congress should establish criteria to ensure that DHS uses detention only as a last resort.

Alternatives to Detention (ATD):

ATDs are a proven and highly cost-effective approach for ensuring that individuals appear at immigration proceedings. There are a range of options that ICE can utilize to encourage compliance. Some options, like release on recognizance or bond, carry little to no cost. More intense forms of supervision and monitoring, such as enrollment in an ATD program, cost around **$22 per person per day**. Compared to the billions spent each year on detention operations,

ATDs represent a smarter, cheaper, and more humane way to ensure compliance with U.S. immigration laws. ATDs may also be more appropriate for detainees with certain vulnerabilities. Of particular concern are asylum seekers, torture survivors, the elderly, individuals with medical and mental health needs, and other vulnerable groups.

Policy Recommendations

Congress should require any restriction of liberty to be the least restrictive form of custody necessary and proportionate to meet government interests. All individuals in detention, including those subject to mandatory custody, should be screened for eligibility for alternatives to detention and placed in such programs unless they pose a flight risk or threat to public safety. Congress should also direct additional funding for ICE to contract with non-profit organizations to create a broader spectrum of ATD programs. Community-based non-profits are best suited to build trust with migrant participants, identify the needs of individuals, address those needs with available resources, and build resilience in the individuals to face the range of potential outcomes in their legal cases. Non-governmental organizations are mission-driven and generate more community resources because of their ability to attract volunteers and donations of goods and services.

Access to Counsel

Respondents in immigration proceedings, especially those who are unrepresented, face one of the most complex legal systems, yet they are not guaranteed representation if they are unable to afford one. Having immigration counsel directly correlates to successful outcomes for noncitizens pursuing claims to relief ranging from persecution abroad or family separation from U.S. citizen relatives.

The immigration court system is struggling to meet the demands of rapidly increasing caseloads, including record-breaking backlogs of about 1.5 years. The high numbers of respondents appearing in proceedings without counsel is a major contributing factor to this large backlog.

When the immigration system fairly and accurately processes cases, it reduces court delays and obviates the need for costly appeals, helping overburdened immigration courts and federal courts. Adequate process aided by competent counsel is more efficient for the system as a whole.

EOIR has stated that "[n]on-represented cases are more difficult to conduct. They require far more effort on the part of the judge."[1] If noncitizens lack lawyers, immigration judges must guide them through the proceedings, often through an interpreter. Judges frequently continue cases to give noncitizens time to try to find counsel. The Administrative Conference of the United States recently advised that "funding legal representation for . . . non-citizens in removal proceedings, especially those in detention, will produce efficiencies and net cost savings."[2] The American Bar Association also concluded that in immigration courts "[t]he lack of adequate representation diminishes the prospects of fair adjudication for the noncitizen, delays and raises the costs of proceedings, calls into question the fairness of a convoluted and complicated process, and exposes noncitizens to

---

1   Charles H. Kuck, Legal Assistance for Asylum Seekers in Expedited Removal: A Survey of Alternative Practices (Dec. 2004), 8, available at http://www.uscirf.gov/images/stories/pdf/asylum_seekers/legalAssist.pdf

2   Administrative Conference Recommendation 2012-3: Immigration Removal Adjudication (adopted June 15, 2012), 3, available at http://www.acus.gov/wp-content/uploads/downloads/2012/06/Recommendation-2012-3-Immigration-Removal-Adjudication.pdf

the risk of abuse and exploitation by 'immigration consultants' and 'notarios.'"[3]

Every individual in immigration removal should have the right to counsel, and if that person cannot afford counsel, the government should provide counsel – especially if the person is detained. **It is un-American to detain someone, send them to a remote facility where they have no contact with family, place them in legal proceedings they are often unable to comprehend, and not to provide counsel for them.**

In Conclusion

Congress does not have an easy task before it given the present heated debate and emotional demands for immigration reform. But from the perspective of the bench, I am confidant that if some of the foregoing proposals are considered and enacted, we will have a more fair, more rational, and more economic immigration system that ensures due process and is worthy of American values.

---

3   American Bar Association Commission on Immigration, Reforming the Immigration System: Proposals to Promote Independence, Fairness, Efficiency, and Professionalism in the Adjudication of Removal Cases. (2010), 5-8.

Acknowledgments

Among the many incredible individuals who have influenced my legal career, I wish to thank the following: Professors Warner Lawson and Jerome Shuman, from Howard Law school days. Jan Pederson, who taught me how to write an asylum affidavit, and much about the intricacies of immigration law practice. The staff at Central American Refugee Center (CARECEN), my first legal job in the trenches. Professor Eric Sirulnik, and my colleagues at the legal clinics at George Washington University Law School, Susan Jones, Carol Izumi and Joan Strand. All of the fine judges I have worked with over the years, including Judges Joan Arrowsmith, John Gossart, Paul Nejelski, my friend and colleague Judge Craig DeBernardis, and my friend and colleague William van Wyke. Judge Dana Marks, gotta love her for the amazing decision in *Cardoza-Fonseca*, and her unflagging activism in the National Association of Immigration Judges. Mike Yamaguchi, and Polly Webber, and all the other excellent judges in San Francisco. Elliot Edwards, court administrator in Philadelphia and Steve Perkins, court administrator in San Francisco. Former Chief Immigration Judge Michael Creppy, and Judge Phil Williams. All of the fine INS/ICE attorneys I worked with, either on opposite sides of the aisle or from the bench, who worked tirelessly to represent the government and preserve the rule of law. All of the fine attorneys in private practice who at times supported and inspired me, and especially hats off to those who worked for the non-profits that provide the first/only line of defense for detained migrants; and the folks at American Immigration Lawyers Association who put their hearts into uplifting the standards of the practice. Michael Maggio, RIP. Richard Boswell and Karen Musalo at Hastings Law. Jane Kochman, formally of UNHCR, currently with asylum division of USCIS (now retired, back to consulting with UNHCR). Good friend and indefatigable union activist Michael Knowles. The many fine law students I worked with over the years who continue to inspire me through their dedication to the practice of law. And finally, all of the amazing immigrant clients I worked with over the years, the real reason I joined the profession and am still inspired by it.

www.ingramcontent.com/pod-product-compliance
Lightning Source LLC
Chambersburg PA
CBHW071804080526
44589CB00012B/676